THE LIFE OF FORM

What if anthropology's fundamental assumptions about cultural and social context were shaped by a philosopher many anthropologists have never engaged with? This book explores how, from the early twentieth century to the present day, anthropological ideas about context have been shaped by Ludwig Wittgenstein's evolving philosophy, often without anthropologists fully realizing it. It shows how Wittgenstein's philosophical journey mirrors anthropology's own theoretical transformations.

Through careful analysis of key figures from Malinowski and Radcliffe-Brown to Geertz and contemporary theorists, Paolo Heywood reveals unexpected connections between philosophical developments and anthropological practice. The result is a surprising genealogy of how we came to think about culture, society, and everyday life the way we do. This intellectual history illuminates the hidden philosophical assumptions that continue to shape anthropological work today. It reveals how disciplines are shaped by ideas they've forgotten they borrowed, and the surprising ways such ideas evolve in new contexts.

PAOLO HEYWOOD is Associate Professor of Anthropology at Durham University, UK. He is the author of two monographs (*After Difference*, 2018; *Burying Mussolini*, 2024) and the editor or co-editor of three edited volumes (*Beyond Description*, 2023; *New Anthropologies of Italy*, 2024; *Freedoms of Speech*, 2024).

NEW DEPARTURES IN ANTHROPOLOGY

New Departures in Anthropology is a book series that focuses on emerging themes in social and cultural anthropology. With original perspectives and syntheses, authors introduce new areas of inquiry in anthropology, explore developments that cross disciplinary boundaries, and weigh in on current debates. Every book illustrates theoretical issues with ethnographic material drawn from current research or classic studies, as well as from literature, memoirs, and other genres of reportage. The aim of the series is to produce books that are accessible enough to be used by college students and instructors, but will also stimulate, provoke, and inform anthropologists at all stages of their careers. Written clearly and concisely, books in the series are designed equally for advanced students and a broader range of readers, inside and outside academic anthropology, who want to be brought up to date on the most exciting developments in the discipline.

Series Editorial Board

Michael Lambek, University of Toronto
Laura Bear, London School of Economics and Political Science
Naveeda Khan, Johns Hopkins University

The Life of Form

Anthropology, Wittgenstein, and the Problem of Context

PAOLO HEYWOOD
Durham University

Shaftesbury Road, Cambridge CB2 8EA, United Kingdom

One Liberty Plaza, 20th Floor, New York, NY 10006, USA

477 Williamstown Road, Port Melbourne, VIC 3207, Australia

314–321, 3rd Floor, Plot 3, Splendor Forum, Jasola District Centre, New Delhi – 110025, India

103 Penang Road, #05–06/07, Visioncrest Commercial, Singapore 238467

Cambridge University Press is part of Cambridge University Press & Assessment, a department of the University of Cambridge.

We share the University's mission to contribute to society through the pursuit of education, learning and research at the highest international levels of excellence.

www.cambridge.org
Information on this title: www.cambridge.org/9781009356596
DOI: 10.1017/9781009356626

© Paolo Heywood 2026

This publication is in copyright. Subject to statutory exception and to the provisions of relevant collective licensing agreements, no reproduction of any part may take place without the written permission of Cambridge University Press & Assessment.

When citing this work, please include a reference to the DOI 10.1017/9781009356626

First published 2026

A catalogue record for this publication is available from the British Library

A Cataloging-in-Publication data record for this book is available from the Library of Congress

ISBN 978-1-009-35659-6 Hardback
ISBN 978-1-009-35664-0 Paperback

Cambridge University Press & Assessment has no responsibility for the persistence or accuracy of URLs for external or third-party internet websites referred to in this publication and does not guarantee that any content on such websites is, or will remain, accurate or appropriate.

For EU product safety concerns, contact us at Calle de José Abascal, 56, 1°, 28003 Madrid, Spain, or email eugpsr@cambridge.org

To my father.
For everything said and shown.

Like members of other tribes, anthropologists are socialized by means of legends. These legends of course need not be false: indeed the one I am about to describe has much truth in it... Once upon a time, the anthropological world was inhabited by a proto-population who were *ethnocentric* ... one day the Age of Darkness came to an end. Modern anthropology begins with good, genuine, real modern fieldwork. The essence of such fieldwork is that it does see institutions, practices, beliefs etc. *in context.*

Ernest Gellner, 'Concepts and Society', 1962: 28; italics in original

'I admit that this is a wild fancy,' the Grasshopper was saying, 'and I hesitate to tell you my thoughts. Still, I am used to being thought foolish, so I shall proceed, inviting you to make of my words what you will. Then let me tell you that I have always had a recurring dream, in which it is revealed to me – though how it is revealed I cannot say – that everyone alive is in fact engaged in playing elaborate games, while at the same time believing themselves to be going about their ordinary affairs. Carpenters, believing themselves to be merely pursuing their trade, are really playing a game, and similarly with politicians, philosophers, lovers, murderers, thieves, and saints. Whatever occupation or activity you can think of, it is in reality a game. This revelation is, of course, astonishing. The sequel is terrifying. For in the dream I then go about persuading everyone I find of the great truth which has been revealed to me. How I am able to persuade them I do not know, though persuade them I do. But precisely at the point when each is persuaded – and this is the ghastly part – each ceases to exist. It is not just that my auditor vanishes on the spot, though indeed he does. It is that I also know with absolute certainty that he no longer exists anywhere. It is as though he had never been. Appalled as I am by the results of my teaching, I cannot stop, but quickly move on to the next creature with my news, until I have preached the truth throughout the universe and have converted everyone to oblivion. Finally I stand alone beneath the summer stars in absolute despair. Then I awaken to the joyful knowledge that the world is still teeming with sentient beings after all, and that it was only a dream. I see the carpenter and philosopher going about their work as before... But is it, I ask myself, just as before? Is the carpenter on his roof-top simply hammering nails, or is he making some move in an ancient game whose rules he has forgotten! But now the chill creeps up my legs. I grow drowsy. Dear friends, farewell.'

Bernard Suits, *The Grasshopper*, 1978: 10

Contents

Acknowledgements	*page* ix
List of Abbreviations of Cited Works	xi
Chronology	xiii
Introduction: Forms of Progress	1

Part I Logic: A Culture of Context

1	In the Background	33
2	The Gods of Context	63

Part II Language: Contexts in Question

3	A Gesture to Anthropology	95
4	A Metaphysics of Magic	130

Part III Life: Contextual Aporetics

5	Life without Form	169
6	Anthropology after Wittgenstein	208

Contents

Conclusion: The Unanalysable Facts of Life 244

Notes 262
References 274
Index 295

Acknowledgements

I am extremely grateful for the commentary, advice, and friendship of those who read versions of parts or all of this book and discussed the ideas in it with me over the last few years. A great many colleagues have listened patiently as I worked through the key arguments, and conversations with several contributed to specific parts of the book.

In particular, I'm thankful to Rupert Stasch for suffering my endless questions about the history of linguistic anthropology, Tim Jenkins and David Gellner for their perspectives on the history of anthropology at Oxford, Isaak Niehaus for a fascinating discussion of Radcliffe-Brown's intellectual biography, and Andrew Beatty for the same on Clifford Geertz. Beyond these specific parts of the book many colleagues helped immensely over the years by allowing me to talk through a range of the issues at hand, including Catherine Alexander, Naor Ben-Yehoyada, Hannah Brown, Liana Chua, Morgan Clarke, Jim Faubion, Sarah Green, Michael Herzfeld, Leo Hopkinson, Caroline Humphrey, Iza Kavedžija, Webb Keane, Nicholas Long, Jonathan Mair, Perveez Mody, Tuija Pulkkinen, Joel Robbins, Andrew Sanchez, Felix Stein, Hans Steinmuller, Alice Stefanelli, Soumhya Venkatesan, Harry Walker, Marta Magalhães Wallace, and Tom Widger.

I owe a very particular debt to those who read and commented on parts or all of the manuscript. I feel very fortunate in this regard to have benefitted from the thoughts of a number of people whose advice, ideas, and in many cases friendship and companionship I very much treasure. Hallvard Lillehammer and Tanya Luhrmann very kindly read individual chapter drafts, and their feedback was extremely helpful. I'm very

Acknowledgements

grateful to Marilyn Strathern for her comments on the introductory parts of the book, which owe a great deal to her own work. Ross Harrison and Michael Potter were both extremely generous in reading the Wittgenstein chapters in particular, and I hugely enjoyed learning from my discussions with them. Mike Degani, Harri Englund, Adam Reed, and Tom Yarrow all read multiple parts of the book at different stages, and their comments were formative in shaping the final result. Matei Candea, Joanna Cook, and James Laidlaw read every single chapter, sometimes more than once over; I am very lucky to have their unfailing generosity and support, perspicacious advice and counsel, and friendship and companionship. This book would certainly not exist were it not for them. Extra thanks go to Matei for designing the chronology pages, and also to Nicholas Long for help with cover art.

The final manuscript was completed thanks to the award of a year-long period of research leave from my department at Durham, to which I also owe thanks for giving me a stimulating and productive intellectual home for the last four years. Trinity College, Cambridge, was an academic host for me for my sabbatical year, providing generous access to its library, archives, and intellectual community. Michael Lambek has been an incredibly supportive editor from the very beginning of this project and provided enormously helpful feedback on a first draft. I'm also grateful to David Repetto, Anna Hubbard, and the wider Cambridge University Press team; and I thank Broadview Press for kind permission to reproduce excerpts from *The Grasshopper* as epigraphs.

Spending a year of sabbatical doing nothing but writing a book about Wittgenstein and the history of anthropological theory may not be everybody's idea of a great time, but I was very happy indeed whilst doing so, not least because it meant spending more time with the people to whom I and this book owe the most: my wife, Jo; my daughter, Beatrice; my stepmother, Jennifer; and most of all my father, Peter. He trained as a philosopher before shifting – in a manner of which Wittgenstein would no doubt have approved – to medicine, and from him I learnt a range of ways in which it is and isn't possible to argue fruitfully with a Wittgensteinian. I also learnt from him a lot of the things that I am most grateful for about myself. Illness means that I will never hear him tell me what he thinks of the ideas in this book. But despite that silence, it was written with his voice in my mind throughout.

Abbreviations of Cited Works

BB   Blue and Brown Books
BT   *The Big Typescript* (TS 213)
CE   'Cause and Effect'
CV   *Culture and Value* (original 1980 edition)
OC   *On Certainty*
PG   *Philosophical Grammar*
PI   *Philosophical Investigations* (Part II referred to as PI II)
RFGB   'Remarks on Frazer's Golden Bough'
RPP I   *Remarks on the Philosophy of Psychology*, Vol. 1
TLP   *Tractatus Logico-Philosophicus*

References to other manuscripts are by MS number in the G. H. von Wright catalogue in *Wittgenstein* (Oxford: Blackwell, 1982).

Notes Taken by Others

AWL   Wittgenstein's Lectures, Cambridge, 1932–1933, from the *Notes of Alice Ambrose and Margaret Macdonald*, ed. Alice Ambrose. Oxford: Blackwell, 1979.

LFM   *Wittgenstein's Lectures on the Foundations of Mathematics*, Cambridge 1939, ed. Cora Diamond. Hassocks: Harvester, 1976.

LWL   Wittgenstein's Lectures, Cambridge, from the *Notes of John King and Desmond Lee*, ed. Desmond Lee. Oxford: Blackwell, 1980.

Abbreviations of Cited Works

WVC *Wittgenstein and the Vienna Circle: Conversations Recorded by Friedrich Waismann*, ed. Brian McGuinness. Oxford: Blackwell, 1979.

Chronology

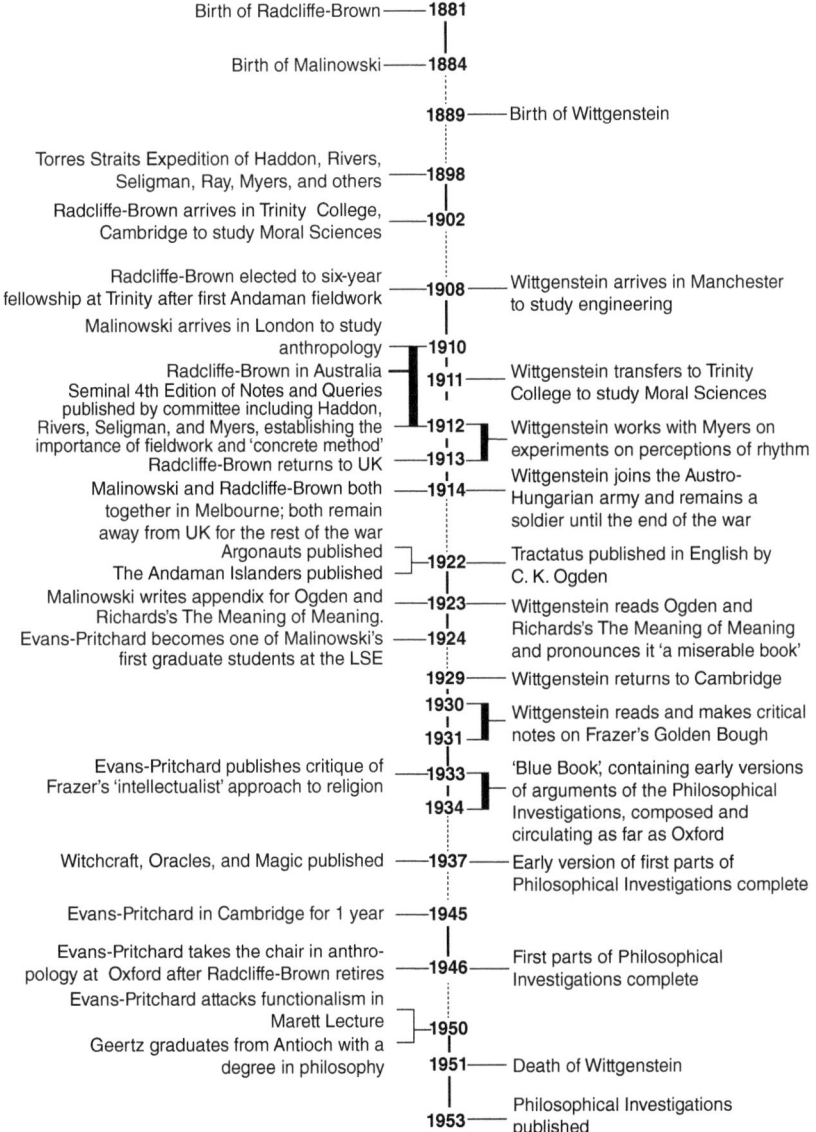

Figure 0.1.

Introduction: Forms of Progress

It was the collective ('social') dimension of life that [anthropologists] took as their subject matter. So if there is a particular loss that lies in wait for anthropology, it will not be for the idea of societies and cultures themselves, for their holism is apprehended as an artificial (constructed) tool of analysis. It will be *nostalgia for a relational view* of the world.
– Strathern (1992: 189); italics in original

Anyway, the thing about progress is that it always seems greater than it really is.
– Epigraph to the *Philosophical Investigations*

Pictures

Conjuring one of the most enduring images of twentieth-century philosophy, Ludwig Wittgenstein wrote,

A *picture* held us captive. And we couldn't get outside it, for it lay in our language, and language seemed only to repeat it to us inexorably. (PI 115; italics in original)

Though he was most likely referring to what he saw as his own past mistakes, the passage has echoed through the decades since as the epitaph for bygone millennia of misguided philosophy.

Forms of Progress

It could also, so this book suggests, stand as the epitaph for a long dead age of anthropology: an age in which we knew our models of context, our pictures of relations. Perhaps our model was logic, in its singular univocity, and we imagined ourselves mapping out the terrain of roles in a given social structure as if they were mathematical variables. Perhaps our model was the multiplicity of language, and we found constancy in the structural morphology of relations between systems as transformations of one another. Perhaps it was something else entirely – an organism, a mechanical contraption, or a text.

And then we saw that all these models and all these pictures were really prisons of form, whether explicit or hidden in the shape of anthropological thinking and for that reason constricting and constraining us. Like Wittgenstein – with Wittgenstein, in fact, as I'll try to show – anthropology freed itself from the captivity of form, of the need to give a special shape or pattern to its visions of context, and so we were prisoners no more.

What, though, if we have traded the conscious austerity of a monastic cell for the mirage of a gilded cage? What if a picture of a different sort holds us captive, still repeating itself inexorably through our language?

That, roughly speaking, is the question this book aims to pose. It asks whether, if we stand back at the right angle, or put the right parts of the story together in the right order, we can in fact make Wittgenstein's claim again, for the past half-century or so of anthropology's disciplinary history: that a picture held us captive (as one picture or another always will).

This new picture is in many ways harder to see both than the one to which Wittgenstein refers and to the latter's anthropological equivalents. All those earlier pictures had a certain clarity (and corrigibility) to them, and that clarity is in part exactly why we have learnt from Wittgenstein, among others, to be suspicious of them. Those older pictures have fairly well-defined edges; their component parts are all visible, and their relation to one another is on display. In anthropology, we might call such a picture 'social structure', or just 'structure', 'culture', or 'society'. We know the forms such a picture can take because we often teach them to our students as the history of our discipline, a history littered with the ruins of mistakes our ancestors made (Navaro 2009). The new picture, by contrast, is blurred, vague, and indistinct. It is so by design though, as I will try to illustrate.

This book tries to give form to this blurred picture by narrating the story of Wittgenstein's philosophy and the history of anthropology in a very specific arc: as one of a journey from form to formlessness, as one in which the coherence and structure of successive models for context in Wittgenstein's work and in anthropology progressively collapse until we are left with the formlessness of 'form of life', or 'ordinary life', or indeed just 'life'.[1]

To an anthropology allergic to coherence and structure, and to metaphysical commitments, as Wittgenstein always was to some extent and gradually became more so, it is hard not to hear such a story as one of whiggish progress.

But what if this formlessness is just another picture? What if it is just as possible to be held captive by blurriness and indistinction as it is by coherence and structure of one version or another? What if, for some time now, what has been repeated inexorably is that it is *only through* such blurriness and indistinction, such formlessness, that we will find truth? Wouldn't that be as much of a prison as the one from which Wittgenstein supposedly set us free?

Cultures of Context

This book is about the concept of context. It aims to describe the parallel arcs of contextualism in anthropology and in Wittgenstein's philosophy, and to show the connections and relations between the two, insofar as both arcs involve the gradual loosening and eventual collapse of formalist and systematic conceptions of context. As such, it is worth saying early on that the intent is neither to bury Wittgenstein nor to praise him, but to interrogate his effect on anthropology and anthropology's effect on him and to ask what we can learn from this interrogation.

A reflexive concern for context is at the heart of a range of twentieth-century disciplines, as I'll describe in a moment, but the history of anthropology in particular is a history of arguments about context (Dilley 1999). Although anthropologists often narrate that history as a succession of struggles between competing theoretical paradigms, a very large amount of the struggles in question were over questions of context – how much there should be of it, what it should look like, what it should be called, what your opponent had taken out of it, what you were going to put back in, who had the power to delineate it, who was misusing it, etc., etc. Most such arguments, then, were virulent disagreements about the right form or model of context, coupled with almost total and complete univocity on the importance of context itself. Still today, arguments about, for example, decolonizing anthropology (Venkatesan 2025) and the 'ontological turn' (Holbraad and Pedersen 2018) revolve in different ways around questions of context. To call such univocity 'agreement' would be to imply it was self-consciously entered into, whereas, despite its foundational status in the discipline, context has rarely emerged as an explicit object of attention or contention, presumably, one imagines, exactly because it is so foundational.

That is not entirely true. Contributions to Roy Dilley's *The Problem of Context* (1999) take up that problem in a number of perceptive ways, and Dilley devotes a brief section of his introduction to Wittgenstein's contribution to it (cf. also Salgues 2008). Writing a few years earlier than Dilley, Alessandro Duranti and Charles Goodwin set out their own vision of the kind of context with which anthropologists, linguistic anthropologists especially, should be concerned, also devoting space to Wittgenstein as a key interlocutor (1992); and in a number of publications spanning the same period, Marilyn Strathern diagnosed a number of the shifts that I try to document here (e.g. 1987a, 1991, 1992, 1995). We'll return to her diagnoses shortly.

Cultures of Context

For now, my point is to highlight the fact that anthropologists have argued often and at length about whether they should, say, think of relevant anthropological context as structural (in one or another sense), symbolic, ecological, or even ontological, but that these are in some manner or another imagined as equivalents – different ways of talking about context in the sense of relevant and meaningful environment – is plain from the nature of those arguments. Whereas anthropologists don't usually – indeed almost never – find themselves arguing with contextualism per se: with the idea that in order to understand the things they set out to understand, they have to set them within the right frame, or the right background, or the right set of relations. As Strathern puts it, 'It is an anthropological axiom that however discrete they appear to be, entities are the product of relations; nothing is not embedded in some context or worldview that gives it its special shape' (1992: 12).

All of this is to say that contextualism is and always has been a ground against which other debates in anthropology can take place. Contextualism is itself part of the context of anthropology, in the sense that if you don't understand the basic contextualizing spirit of the discipline, then further arguments within it – between, as it were, its subspecies – will have little sense or significance to you.

A part of the aim of this book is to try to point to the contingency and fragility of that contextualism. As with a basic (or 'hinge', as Wittgenstein might say) concept in any society, for an anthropologist, it may be quite hard to think of contextualism as an optional perspective, a matter of choice. Because it's the background against which many of our most important debates take place, questioning it seems to throw the whole history of the discipline itself into question, not to mention whole dimensions of the intellectual history of the wider twentieth century:

Contexts seemed real (they provide the rationale for the properties of the things) where analogies once made conscious seemed artificial or incidental, 'metaphorical'. Indeed, contexts were real insofar as they provided a perspective, even though they could always be displaced. In short, contexts have been 'natural' to the twentieth-century viewing of the world. We were organisers of the spectacle but it was in human nature to so create the contexts (perspectives) for understanding, and thus humankind created for itself its grounding for (self) knowledge. This was modernity. (Strathern 1992: 197)

The contingency and particularity of such a view was visible for 'moderns' too and below we'll come to 'postmodern' contextualism. In 'Pierre Menard, Author of the *Quixote*', Jorge Luis Borges imagines a man who rewrites – 'word for word and line for line' – several chapters of *Don Quixote* but whose rendition of the text is treated, by virtue of the contextual differences between the seventeenth and twentieth centuries, as something entirely original. The same words written by Cervantes, when written anew against the background of Nietzsche, Bertrand Russell, and William James (who are among the names cited in the text), become something else.

The conceit is a useful reminder of the fact that contextualism is not an absolute good, and nor has it always been treated as such. Indeed, historian Peter Burke makes brilliantly clear that the context in which contextualism emerged as a broadly powerful force is a fairly recent one: whilst of course variants of contextualist arguments have a long pedigree, from Renaissance and Reformation debates about the interpretation of classical and biblical texts through to Vico and Marx, it is the early twentieth century that gives birth to what he calls a 'contextual turn' (2002). To give some prosaic but fitting exempla of this turn, the word 'contextualize' was coined only in 1934, in linguistics; the word 'contextualization' in 1951, in anthropology; and – hard as it seems to believe – 'decontextualize' only appears from 1971, thanks to sociologists (Burke 2002: 164).

So whilst it might be difficult for an anthropologist to think themselves into what we might call a 'non-contextualist context', there are and have always been people like 'believers in eternal wisdom, formalist art historians, enthusiasts for generalization in social science, and so on', as Burke notes, and until relatively recently such people held significant sway in a number of relevant areas of thought (Burke 2002: 152). Anthropologists will already perhaps be thinking of Sir James Frazer and his *Golden Bough*, and both of them have, as we'll see, roles to play in this book. Philosophers may be thinking of the logical atomism of Russell, and, indeed, possibly of the younger Wittgenstein. We'll come to these too.

My point for now is a reminder that anthropology's disciplinary certainties around context have a particular and contingent history to them, and that that history is tied up with – of course – a wider context. Moreover, what emerges from this historical perspective is not just the rise of contextualism as a method but the development of distinct cultures of context – different intellectual traditions with their own characteristic ways of conceptualizing and deploying context. These cultures of context shaped how different disciplines understood what it meant to put something 'in context'.

So it would be a mistake to take anthropology 'out of context' here. In the same period in which anthropological contextualism emerged, in sociology Karl Mannheim began writing about the social 'location' or 'position' of individuals in classes or age groups, and the word 'situation' took on analytical significance in the discipline. Marxist and non-Marxist literary critics alike began writing about the relationship between literature and the social context in which it was produced, and art historians developed ideas about the 'social history of art'. Psychologists at the turn of the century wrote of the '"lifespace" or environment of an individual or group' and historians and philosophers of history like Marc Bloch and R. G. Collingwood began to stress the ways in which what might appear unintelligibly different beliefs and ideas from other historical epochs could be shown to make sense when interpreted against the proper set of background assumptions (Burke 2002: 161).

Burke's all too brief but brilliant survey of this 'context of context' masterfully connects such developments to later disciplinary contextualisms, from the legal contextualism of scholars like Ronald Dworkin, through sociolinguistics, Donna Haraway's 'situated knowledge', E. P. Thompson's moral economies, the 'New Historicism' of critics like Stephen Greenblatt, Quentin Skinner's 'Cambridge School' of intellectual history, the philosophy of science journal *Science in Context*, and 'post-processual' archaeology. The twentieth century, in other words, was a century of contextualism far beyond just one discipline, as Strathern's accounts also make clear.

Yet anthropology is at the heart of that wider context of contextualism, in lots of ways, with a special and distinctive role to play in this story. Already in the late nineteenth century, Franz Boas, as Burke notes,

> caused a sensation in museum circles in the United States by arguing that exhibits should not be arranged according to the type of artifact or the stage that the objects represented in an evolutionary sequence. They should be arranged by 'culture area'. The point of the change in arrangement was that, according to Boas, an object could not be understood 'outside of its surroundings', physical and cultural. (2002: 160)

And in Chapters 1 and 2, we'll see some of the crucial role contextualism played in the work of modernist British anthropologists such as Bronislaw Malinowksi and A. R. Radcliffe-Brown (and see Strathern 1987a, 1992). Perhaps more so than for any other cognate field, context became an integral and intrinsic part of anthropology's epistemology, and almost all of the developments listed above from other subjects drew on anthropology for authority in making their contextualist claims (see also Foks 2024; North 1999). Yet as we'll see, putting anthropological contextualism in historical perspective means moving through several distinct 'cultures of context': from context as logical structure, to context as language, to context as formless 'life'. Understanding these shifts also requires placing them within the broader 'cultures of context' from which they emerge.

That is because anthropology was not alone in its centrality to contextualism, and nor was it alone in shifting its cultures of context through time. Though Burke doesn't give philosophy quite as much credit for the 'contextual turn' as he gives anthropology, it is hard to imagine the century of contextualism going the way it did without the work of Ludwig Wittgenstein – or at least one imagines he would have needed inventing had he not in fact existed. Clearly, Wittgenstein was far from alone in his philosophical contextualism, but he is certainly exemplary of it and highly significant for it. Other obvious stand-in figures such as J. L. Austin came somewhat later, and indeed there is now persuasive historical evidence that Austin at least was significantly influenced by Wittgenstein in some of his most crucial work (Harris and Unnsteinsson 2017), an influence that was obvious to some at least – Wittgenstein's student and Austin's colleague, Elizabeth Anscombe, for instance – at the time of his writing.

So this book traces the cultures of context and contextual forms that shaped Wittgenstein and anthropology together, and the ways in which they shaped those cultures and those forms themselves, as well as one another. But putting Wittgenstein and anthropology together like this, as twin leading lights of the 'contextual turn', prompts questions of relation and perhaps of causality. To put them in the same context, as anthropologists know well, is to raise the issue of how exactly they connect to one another, and perhaps also for some to pose the question of which came first, or which was more an influence on the other.

I am an anthropologist and not a historian, and so my interest in putting anthropology and Wittgenstein in the same context arises because of an interest in their connections and relations, rather than primarily in questions of causality. Perhaps this will disappoint some who would like to see, in Wittgenstein's descriptions of his own later philosophy as adopting an 'anthropological perspective', evidence of anthropology's long reach, deep impact, and sensible instincts. Or perhaps they might like to see such reach and impact in the fact that

One might say that Malinowski formulated the key idea of *Philosophical Investigations*, almost in Wittgenstein's own words, at a time [1922] when the latter was still sunk in the darkness of the *Tractatus*! (Gellner 1998: 149; and see Heywood 2023b)

We will explore ideas like this in the early parts of this book. On the other hand, those committed to a view of Wittgenstein as a solitary and more or less sui generis genius may find in some of the discussions of the later chapters of this book confirmation of views on the extent and significance of his influence on anthropology.

We'll see versions of both these cases for influence and others in this book, but anthropologists don't generally put things in context solely or even primarily in order to establish causal influence, and indeed neither did Wittgenstein in his own version of contextualism. The point rather is usually to 'see the connections', as he liked to put it: Relations themselves are revealing from a contextualist standpoint insofar as they fill in and thicken the picture of context itself, and provide one with alternative perspectives on it.[2] Such contextual connections also usually reveal relations of causality to be multi-directional.

There is though still something odd about this particular set of connections in that they put a single man and the arc of his life and thought in juxtaposition against an entire discipline (or at least a necessarily partial view of the history of an entire discipline). There is something unbalanced, improperly scaled, or out of proportion about the comparison, as if Wittgenstein were a Melanesian Big Man and also a metonym for the clan of anthropology (Strathern 1991: xix).

That lack of balance is part of the point of this book. Throughout it, we will see the surprising ways in which transformations in anthropological thinking about context mirror transformations in Wittgenstein's thinking about context; we will see the ways in which the different models for context developed in the discipline look like the kinds of models for context Wittgenstein employed in his philosophy. That set of resemblances may seem another reiteration of the narrative of Wittgenstein's extraordinary genius, at least insofar as it leads one to imagine anthropology following meekly behind in his footsteps; but in fact the point is about Wittgenstein's exceptional status only insofar as he condenses in the figure of a single man, a single life, and a single philosophical career something important about a vast century of conceptual transformation. This may have been because he was as brilliant as he undoubtedly was, but his brilliance is beside the point. The point is that in him we can see much of the history of our disciplinary development mirrored in miniature. And seeing it that way, writ small in some ways and large in others, should tell us something important.

How can it be, we might ask, that such a condensation is possible? How could we reduce – however partially and selectively – the conceptual history of a whole discipline's most fundamental intellectual tool – context – such that it resembles the brief intellectual biography of one man?

One answer to these questions is that it isn't in fact possible. I will not convince all readers of the evidence for the connections I draw here. Also, given that the history of anthropological contextualism is essentially the history of the discipline itself, it is impossible to capture the history of contextualism in anthropology fully in a single monograph, let alone one with the specific historical perspective this one has. And yet that this is so – that the history of a single concept can in some sense be thought to epitomize the whole conceptual history of our discipline – is at least evidence that understanding how we have thought about context will show us much about how we have understood our enterprise more broadly.

The second answer is equally simple and is implied at least by much of what is written about Wittgenstein in anthropology today. It is, put

Forms of Progress

baldly and to repeat myself, that Wittgenstein was a genius, a prophet. That if the history of anthropological thinking about context so resembles the biography of his thought, still to this day, that is because anthropologists are late to the party of which he is the host. Where our thought has changed and developed over the course of this history it is because we (or at least some lucky few of us) have more properly understood what it was he was trying to tell us, an exegetical endeavour that should continue to this day and probably never end. To those in the know, anthropology is only ever 'after Wittgenstein' in this way: the best of us will carry on the enterprise (even if we don't know we're doing it), whilst the rest of us will be left one day on the wrong side of historical intellectual progress. I am sure there are many readers who will have assumed that a book about anthropology and Wittgenstein must take some version of this point of view.

My position is a third one. It is that comparing the trajectory of our views on context with those of Wittgenstein offers us a different vantage point to the one anthropologists usually adopt on the subject. I hope it has a defamiliarizing effect, like that of ethnographic comparison (Candea 2018).

In some ways, that effect should be fairly straightforward. For example, one classic contextualizing manoeuvre is to show that 'what we might take as ... a product of some continuous and taken-for-granted identity may well be revealed as equally the product of specific historical times and thus of change' (Strathern 1992: 5). There are versions of this kind of manoeuvre in this book – for instance, that of Burke's (historical) 'context of context', already deployed. One initial step in the argument is thus to see the 'context of context' itself, and to see both anthropology and Wittgenstein as shaped by and shaping of that context, together, and in partial relation to one another.

In this regard, I am influenced by other attempts to contextualize anthropology's attitude to context and contextual form, in particular, by Joel Robbins's discussions of the rise of 'suffering slot' anthropology

(2013; see also 2024; Candea 2025). These complex and multifaceted arguments have generated much commentary over the last decade, and I'll engage with different parts of them in the later sections of the book. For now, my interest is in flagging the clarity with which Robbins narrates the story of anthropology's turn to pain, violence, and suffering as its primary objects as involving a loss of interest in, amongst other things, difference, and the contextual forms with which we might make sense of difference. In Robbins's story, we lose our ability to speak sensibly about 'cultural context' as part of a wider move in Western thinking, one diagnosed by historian Samuel Moyn (2010), away from a concern for decolonization and national or ethnic self-determination and towards a globalized and undifferentiated interest in human rights (2024: 52).

Writing presciently in the very midst of the shift Robbins diagnoses in retrospect, Strathern carries out a somewhat similar diagnostic operation across several texts (e.g. 1987a, 1991, 1992, 1995). In *After Nature* and *Partial Connections* in particular, she shows, as I'll try also to show here, how questions of form were wrapped up both with the emergence and collapse of classic forms of contextualism. 'Significant', she writes, 'for the subsequent perception of system and structure [in thinking about society] was that turn of the [twentieth] century discovery of form', before going on to cite critic and theorist Clive Bell as an exemplar, a key presence in the Bloomsbury Group with which Wittgenstein was connected (1992: 119). Meanwhile, at the other end of this historical context, she points to the ways in which 'postmodern' ethnography self-consciously eschewed considerations of form in favour of an idea of writing as 'therapy', 'healing the alienating breach between self and other, subject and object, language and the world' (1991: 14) in a manner that conjures up some contemporary readings of Wittgenstein's philosophy as 'therapeutic' above all else, as we'll see.

Like Robbins, though without aiming at a strictly historical argument, Strathern also describes the context in which she is writing (the 1990s)

Forms of Progress

as a particular context, a period with specific concerns and interests. In particular, she documents,

> the 'vanishing' of three concepts, Society, Individual, Nature. They were crucial to the construction of merographic [contextualist] connections, not just because they provided the substance of the domains that clearly overlapped, but because they provided between themselves a conceptual scheme for apprehending connection or relationship as such.
> The first is publicly announced, the second is to be found in the writings of cultural critics, the third I infer, and it is the disappearance of the third that brings about the possibility of merographic collapse. (1992: 136)

Conjoining Thatcherist dismissals of society with postmodern 'cocacolarization' and environmentalist fears/hopes about the consumption of the 'natural' (and see 1995), it is hard to do justice to the complexity of Strathern's contextualization of the collapse of context. On the one hand, in a manner echoed by later arguments of this book, she points to the ways in which calls for 'multidimensional analyses' that focus on 'the unity of everyday and actual experience' of real peoples' lives are stirring but somehow insubstantial: 'the notion of a definitive unique and single life-course as embodied in the individual *has no dimension*' (1992: 167; my italics):

> Instead of composing 'a life' merographically conceived as belonging to many different external systems (health, education and so forth), life is reconceived as décor, as a whole with diversity and multiplicity contained within. Yet if in this plasti-class rendering diversity and multiplicity have no external analogue, what preserves the differences between being [in the example in question] a lecturer, a male, a sociologist? We do not really get an answer. (Strathern 1992).[3]

As she puts it in rounding off *After Nature*,

> ...[P]ostmodern aesthetics and Thatcherism alike most interestingly pull out from under our feet the grounding or reason for these constructs

[society and the individual], and thus an anterior assumption about the conditions on which we so freely play. They take from each its former context in the other. *The sense is that context itself has gone.* (1992: 195; my italics)

In a certain sense then this book is a straightforward complement to the different stories that Robbins and Strathern tell, stories that are themselves in some ways sequels to the history narrated in Burke's portrayal of the 'context of context' at the turn of the twentieth century: like them, I aim to situate the collapse of contextualism, or at least of contextual formalism, within a wider context, or rather a series of different such wider contexts: Thatcherism and postmodern aesthetics may feel to some contemporary readers as if they belong solely to the past; worries about 'cosmopolitans as consumers of world society' on the other hand are very much the order of the day.

On the other hand, though, this sort of manoeuvre is itself a taken-for-granted contextualist claim, as Strathern points out (1992: 5), and thus itself too another part of the contextualist background under investigation. As a manoeuvre, it also won't quite work in this case, or at least not as such manoeuvres normally do, as we've seen: Wittgenstein and the discipline of anthropology overlap contextually in a range of ways, but they do not – cannot sensibly be thought to – overlap entirely. Or, if they do, then must we take Wittgenstein to be 'larger' than a single man? and/or anthropology as 'smaller' than a whole discipline? Is Wittgenstein 'big' enough to stretch out into the 1990s, nearly a half century after his death? Or is anthropology 'little' enough that it constitutes only the tiniest of blips in a contextualist arc that encompasses so much more?

So, whilst there is much that is classically contextualist in my account, there is also a degree of 'postcontextualist', as it were, 'play with context' at work (Strathern 1987a). Worse, perhaps than 'play', there is a degree of deliberate decontextualization. That is, I suggest that to the extent

Forms of Progress

that the manoeuvre of putting Wittgenstein and anthropology into relation works, it must surely imply that one or other of its subjects are somehow 'out of context': for those content to take Wittgenstein as a prophet ahead of his time this poses no problems – he is for them, by his nature, out of context, and therefore already decontextualized. For anybody less inclined to take such an acontextualist approach to a single man, the implication may be that anthropology is somehow, at least in some respects, itself stuck out of context – if our arguments continue to so resemble those of a more-than-slightly eccentric Austrian man who died in 1951, and who rarely set foot outside of Europe, then what of disciplinary 'progress'?

Lest it sound otherwise, I ask that latter question not as a believer in the destiny of disciplinary progress, but as a sceptic of its implication. And progress is often implied in the commonsensical versions of the story this book tells – of a journey from the darkness of formalism to the light of open-ended freedom, from a picture that held us captive to liberation from any and all such pictures. But, as the man said, 'Anyway, the thing about progress is that it always seems greater than it really is.'

Speaking of progress, the shape of this book traces the arcs of the twin trajectories of its subjects. In Part I, we meet logic as a dominant model or form of context in the young Wittgenstein and the work he considered at the time to be his final word in philosophy, the *Tractatus Logico-Philosophicus*. Rarely discussed by anthropologists, this work is nevertheless crucial context for an understanding of Wittgenstein's later contextualism despite the fact that logic is usually taken to be inherently acontextual, a reading exemplified in one prominent anthropological take on the *Tractatus* as a sort of anti-culturalist manifesto (Gellner 1998). In fact, its logical contextualism, as we'll see, bears considerable resemblances to the conception of contextual form operative in the contemporaneous work of anthropologists such as A. R. Radcliffe-Brown, who overlaps with the young Wittgenstein in a number of interesting ways. Meanwhile anthropology's other great contextualizer of the period, Bronislaw Malinowski, also overlaps with his fellow Austro-Hungarian (as Ernest Gellner among others has described), but has a rather different take on contextual form.

In Part II, the singularity of logic as a contextual form dissolves in both Wittgenstein and anthropology, and language, in all its plurality, emerges as a key analogy in logic's place. We see this happen first in a period of Wittgenstein's work that is often described as 'transitional' in the sense that it is conceptually intermediate in many ways between the *Tractatus* and the work of his later life. A part of its intermediate nature is precisely the way in which contextual form loosens up – a multiplicity of different kinds of 'logical spaces', each governed by its own kinds of grammatical rules, replaces the apparent univocity of Tractarian logic. Yet in metaphysically weighted notions such as 'rules of grammar', and in the idea that logical spaces share a certain form or morphology, a sense of structure and system is retained. In parallel conceptually though not historically, Wittgenstein first enters the anthropological lexicon after his death through two more or less contemporaneous developments in anthropological theory, namely the so-called 'rationality debates' and British structuralism. In the ways in which they draw on Wittgenstein, they exhibit strong traces of the influence of this transitional period, and the models of contextual form they develop are similarly linguistic in nature.

Finally, if in Parts I and II we saw a process of 'deformalization', in which models of context become gradually looser, Part III traces the collapse of contextual form altogether. It does so first in Wittgenstein's later work, through an examination of the idea of 'form of life' as it appears in the *Philosophical Investigations*, and then in anthropology 'after Wittgenstein'. The latter is a loose label for a succession of increasingly antiformalist trends in anthropological theory of the past half-century that, the chapter argues, are often both directly connected to interpretations of later Wittgenstein and resemble him in their antiformalism. Yet paradoxically, as we'll see, anthropology would

Forms of Progress

ultimately go further than Wittgenstein himself in rejecting form – transforming his qualified suggestion that blurred concepts are 'often' what we need into an absolute principle that they are always the only legitimate approach. I suggest that anthropological versions of the formlessness of 'form of life' have become increasingly dominant models of context in the discipline, except that in their formlessness and their vitalism they are often less models and more claims to immediate and experiential access to the 'truth' of life.

So while this book traces anthropology's progressive journey away from formal models of context, it also reveals a certain irony in this trajectory. Where Wittgenstein took a characteristically pragmatic view of form that left room for different approaches in different circumstances, anthropology has increasingly treated formlessness as the only legitimate approach to context, a 'picture' it has been repeating to itself for some time.

The Unpleasantness of Cults

Writing about Wittgenstein is a fraught enterprise. Even as far back as the 1960s, one of Wittgenstein's most fervent philosophical admirers, Stanley Cavell, recalls a moment

> in a discussion ... in which a brilliant, successful, exasperated member of the philosophical profession said, 'You know, it's possible that Wittgenstein was wrong about *something!*'; Recalling the unpleasantness of cults, one must not ignore the sorts of behavior that can, in the most patient, justifiably produce such exclamations. (1979: xxi)

In Wittgenstein's own lifetime, he was more than capable of producing such feelings. Julian Bell, the son of Vanessa and Clive Bell and nephew of Virginia Woolf, wrote the following lines in a Cambridge student magazine in 1930, inspired by irritation at the *Tractatus*'s dismissal of aesthetics, under the title 'An Epistle On the Subject of the Ethical and Aesthetic Beliefs of Herr Ludwig Wittgenstein':

> For he talks nonsense, numerous statements makes,
> Forever his own vow of silence breaks:
> Ethics, aesthetics, talks of day and night,
> And calls things good or bad, and wrong or right.
> ... who, on any issue, ever saw
> Ludwig refrain from laying down the law?
> In every company he shouts us down,
> And stops our sentence stuttering his own;
> Unceasing argues, harsh, irate and loud,
> Sure that he's right, and of his rightness proud,
> Such faults are common, shared by all in part,
> But Wittgenstein pontificates on Art.'

Wittgenstein was not, of course, alone in inspiring this sort of irritation. Indeed, it's easy to imagine how writing about a thinker with an extraordinarily distinctive style might lead one to take up a distinctive style of one's own, perhaps even a somewhat derivative one. The philosopher Mary Warnock recounts how her friend Elizabeth Anscombe, one of Wittgenstein's most favoured and most talented students who would go on to act as one of his executors, would sometimes begin speaking with an Austrian accent when especially carried away by her teacher's thoughts (Warnock 2000: 60).

Another and related reason to worry about writing about Wittgenstein is the concern that if one does not write in a manner at least somewhat akin to his own, then one may be accused of having failed to understand him. Simply 'translating' him, as it were, into something resembling straightforward and clear argument would often completely violate the spirit of what he's trying to say (or show) (Palmié 2018). Even one of the most persuasive critics of Wittgenstein, Canadian philosopher Bernard Suits, garbed his critique in a charming if esoteric retelling of the parable of the grasshopper (1978). He may have had in mind the fate of one of the first monographs on Wittgenstein's later philosophy (Pole 1958), which Cavell made notorious early in his career by excoriating it in a review on the basis of its prosaic and pedestrian interpretations (1962). Meanwhile, on the other side of the spectrum to Suits's gentle and indirect critique is Ernest Gellner's *Words and Things*, which we'll meet later in this book (1959). So bad-tempered and controversial was Gellner's attack on Wittgenstein and his Oxford cognates that it resulted in letters to *The Times*, and in the *New Yorker* sending over a journalist to discover what was so dramatic in British philosophy that it was getting coverage in the national newspapers (Mehta 1962).

Perhaps the same fate as Pole's text may await this book, for it attempts the task of surveying a range of Wittgenstein's thought with neither celebratory nor damning intention, and therefore with neither Suits's or Gellner's rhetorical elan, and nor with the particular vocabulary of discipleship. It attempts this partly because – perhaps due to some of the difficulties I've just been describing – there are no comprehensive historical accounts of the relationship between Wittgenstein and anthropology. Brief surveys exist (see e.g. Salgues 2008), many discussions of specific texts (especially the 'Remarks' on Frazer, as we'll see), and many larger collections on the relation between Wittgenstein and the social sciences in general (see e.g. Danford 1978; Pitkin 1972; Robinson 2009; Temelini 2015; Vinten 2020), but nothing that specifically accounts for how Wittgenstein could have developed an 'anthropological perspective' in relation to the discipline itself, and what 'doing anthropology after Wittgenstein', as the subtitle of a recent book puts it, has actually meant historically (Das 2020).

Attempting some account of this relationship obviously must involve trying to interpret and present a range of relevant facets of Wittgenstein's philosophy. The result will undoubtedly fail to satisfy many of those familiar with his work, both because of the partial remit of this book and because, as I've been describing, Wittgenstein often writes in such a way as to guarantee exegetical and interpretive controversy. Where such controversies are clearly documented, I have tried to make that fact explicit in my account, so that readers may judge for themselves. Otherwise, I have done my best to present his ideas in the manner in which they have been presented by those who know his work better than I do, so that anthropologists unfamiliar with him will have a place to come to read about those ideas and how they relate to anthropology without having them either buried or praised.

All that said, even within a book of this size, I have, of course, been unable to survey all of the ways in which Wittgenstein could be said to have affected anthropology. Most notably, I have largely confined my narrative to Britain in the early parts of the book, and to the United States in the later parts. I've chosen to do that for a range of narrative and structural reasons. Part I juxtaposes Wittgenstein and British-based anthropologists who were writing about context at the same time, partly in order to make the point that they were doing so from very similar contexts themselves: Radcliffe-Brown and Wittgenstein were at Trinity College, Cambridge, at the same time; Malinowski was, like Wittgenstein, an émigré from the Austro-Hungarian Empire, and was publishing alongside Wittgenstein's collaborators. In Part II, I treat the first explicit entry of Wittgenstein into anthropology, which took place in the UK, with the so-called 'rationality debates'. And in Part III, I trace a later genealogy of Wittgenstein-inspired American anthropology that has had an overwhelming impact on the discipline overall. That said, all this means that I have not had space to discuss Wittgenstein's substantial influence on the continental discipline, including on anthropologists and anthropology-adjacent theorists such as Pierre Bourdieu and Michel de Certeau (see Bouveresse 1977; Sheringham 2006; and especially Salgues 2008 for a survey). I think their inclusion would strengthen the major case of the book, but readers will need to decide for themselves. Neither, to my regret, have I had the space to engage with some specific European anthropologists who have charted their own particular course in engaging with Wittgenstein, most notably Knut Myhre (2006, 2007, 2018a, 2018b), whose work is orthogonal to the thesis of this book but stands in many ways as a testament to the productive potential of Wittgenstein for anthropology.

As also gestured to above, whilst this is a book about Wittgenstein, it is also a book about the kind of philosophy that Wittgenstein represents. The most obvious parallels are with Oxford ordinary language philosophy, the connections and affinities of which to Wittgenstein are numerous and well-documented. In the early parts of the book too we'll see some of the connections between Wittgenstein and pragmatism, for which some philosophers have built clear cases (Misak 2016), and a different, longer book might have encompassed Wittgenstein's connection to the 'anthropological philosophy' of phenomenology too (see Chamberlain 2021: 178; Kuusela, Ometita, and Uçan 2018). This net of ideas wide enough to contain Wittgenstein, James, Austin, and even Heidegger doesn't really have a name and perhaps doesn't deserve a singular one given how internally varied it is, but I want to make the point here that while much of my discussion is about the specifics of Wittgenstein's philosophy, there are many aspects of that philosophy which could be said to epitomize a wider conceptual context.

Looking and Seeing

If it's about any one thing, doing social anthropology is surely about changing your mind; about leaving yourself open to the possibility that the things you'll find about other lives will lead you to reassess and readdress some of the assumptions about human life you'll have come with to those other lives. One knows as a teacher that this ever-present possibility of having to rethink cherished assumptions is what draws many to the discipline whilst also putting plenty of others off it. The idea that one can never rest easy in a given assumption can, of course, be immensely frustrating and also joyous and invigorating simultaneously, and living between both of those feelings is what it means to be an anthropologist. This is precisely the impetus behind the 'contextualizing spirit' I described earlier – a (modernist) practice of what Strathern (1992: 5) calls 'literalization': 'a mode of laying out the coordinates or conventional points of reference of what is otherwise taken for granted.'

This book, however, is about a particular area in which anthropologists have seemed reluctant to change their minds in recent decades about some assumptions that are core and fundamental to the contemporary discipline. No doubt there are also other such areas, but that of context, and contextual form, is a particularly important one for what anthropologists do, as I've been trying to outline and will continue to do throughout this book. For much of its existence, anthropology has taken as its basic task the job of putting things in context – so exactly how 'context' is understood matters quite a lot.

A basic concomitant of the value placed on the ability to change our minds in anthropology – and of course, relatedly, on the notion of context – is an allergy to metaphysics. That is, anthropologists usually, though not always, like to think of ourselves as reluctant to die on any given theoretical or philosophical hill if our ethnography suggests a revision of views is in order. That is not to claim that anthropology never in fact makes metaphysical commitments, or that anthropologists never hold them tightly in the face of countervailing evidence – indeed, some of this book is about the ongoing presence of such commitments despite our self-image as pragmatists *par excellence*. It is to suggest only that that is part of our self-image, and as such it has significant effects on what we do and how we think.

No matter any gaps between theory and practice, as it were, it's important to establish the disciplinary allergy to metaphysical commitments in its self-conception from the beginning of this book because it is an important component of the argument. However things work out in the reality of any given monograph or article or movement, it is written deeply into anthropology's disciplinary heart that if we make such commitments, we may prove unable to do what all anthropologists, good or bad, should be able to do: to change our minds. I frame this virtue, incidentally, as the ability to change one's mind but, of course, for many, if not most the commitment to it runs far more deeply than any shallow empiricism that formulation may suggest. It is not, or not only at least, a debt to facts that leads us to it, but to people, for reasons I hope it's unnecessary to rehearse in detail.

That allergy to metaphysical commitments has led anthropology to all sorts of interesting conceptual places. A suspicion of such commitments is quite rightly at the heart of our ability to try to understand worlds other than ones we ourselves have come from, wherever they may be.

The later parts of this book though are about some ways in which that allergy may lead anthropology into difficulty, particularly as regards context, in many ways its primary operating analytic. Not because what the allergy protects anthropologists against is, in reality, good for them – tightly held metaphysical commitments are indeed hard to square with a commitment to the concreteness of what anthropologists encounter in their fieldwork. But because sometimes the reaction is worse than the allergen itself. Being stung by a bee is unpleasant for anybody. But if your body sends you into anaphylactic shock because of the sting, then things get considerably more serious. In such a situation, your own defences are more pathological than what it is they are supposed to defend against.

Lest that all sound too colourful, one might make the same sort of point in regard to a significant difference between Wittgenstein and anthropology. Most of this book will be about similarities between the two. There are many. Not only did Wittgenstein – at least in his later philosophy – share anthropology's penchant for contextualism, he also shared this allergy to metaphysical commitments, along with a belief in the importance of the particular and the specific (indeed, all these things are connected together in fairly obvious ways). In one of the more famous passages of his *Philosophical Investigations*, he urges readers to 'look and see' at individual cases (of games, in this case), rather than assume that a generic category or a transcendent characteristic is what unites such cases, and it is this attitude, as we'll see, that he had in mind in describing his later work as adopting an 'anthropological perspective'.

And yet, as Bernard Suits noted in *The Grasshopper*,

This is unexceptionable advice. Unfortunately, Wittgenstein himself did not follow it. He looked, to be sure, but because he had decided beforehand that games are indefinable, his look was fleeting, and he saw very little. (1978: x)

Suits's aim in his own book is to investigate a series of actual, real sorts of games in an attempt to arrive at a definition of what a game is, the success or failure of which is irrelevant to our purposes. The point of raising his example is to highlight the difference in the enterprise he is engaged in and the one he takes Wittgenstein to be occupied with:

The following inquiry is not, and should not be taken to be, a kind of anti-anti-definitional manifesto, nor should it be seen as depending for its cogency upon a commitment to the universal fruitfulness of definition construction. It seems altogether more reasonable to begin with the hypothesis that some things are definable and some are not, and that the only way to find out which are which is to follow Wittgenstein's excellent advice and *look and see*. (Suits 1987: x; italics in original)

Wittgenstein, at least in Suits's reading of him, in other words, is not really interested in 'games' or any other such actually existing phenomena. In Wittgenstein, such phenomena are instead illustrations of philosophical – or grammatical, in his terms – problems about how we think and talk about things (Heywood 2023a), the central aim of which is often – always, according to some readings of him – to dispel some aura of mystery or illusion around such talking and thinking afforded by traditional (metaphysical) philosophy.

The point, in other words, is not usually – or again, not ever, according to some – to advance an 'argument', about, say, games, colour, mathematics, psychology, pain, or any of the other various topics invoked in Wittgenstein's writing, but to effect a sort of therapeutic alteration in the mind of the reader, away from metaphysical explanations. It's worth saying that not everybody thinks like this, and that Wittgenstein's views on the substance of such subjects have had a wide and significant influence. But he is not primarily known, even amongst philosophers, for any one of these topics. And for some of his readers at least, none of them are really the point: for some readers Wittgenstein *is*, as it were, the allergic reaction to metaphysics. He is what stops you from going near beehives, or dairy, or sesame; or Plato, or Descartes, or Kant.

Whilst as unexceptionable as the 'look and see' prescription is in many ways, the prescription itself turns out not to be quite the same thing as the practice; exhorting people to 'look and see' is not quite the same thing as looking and seeing; it is not the same as an enterprise like anthropology, that is, or at least often has been in the past, generally more interested in actual phenomena than in their philosophically therapeutic potential.

To give another illustration of the difference: Wittgenstein once wrote about Frazer's ethnographic descriptions that 'one could very well invent primitive practices oneself, and it would only be by chance if they were not actually found somewhere.' That is an excellent description of what he proceeded to do in his later philosophy, habitually invoking and inventing imaginary 'primitive tribes' in thought-experimental voice (in a manner quite different to, say, Austin's assiduous investigations of 'what we might say' in a given case, or his call for 'fieldwork in philosophy' 1961: 131).

Long after Wittgenstein wrote those words about Frazer, one of his most fervent anthropological admirers, Rodney Needham, developed the habit of trying to persuade philosopher colleagues at Oxford to pay attention to anthropology by saying that there was no need to go about inventing imaginary tribes, since 'practically anything that could be imagined by us was already there to be examined'.

The two positions seem like neat and symmetrical inversions of one another, and in fact that very symmetry is revealing: Needham's claim is surely and fundamentally impossible to square with the open-ended, change-your-mind spirit of ethnographic enquiry. At the very least, the view that what anthropologists are there to do is add gristle to the skeletons of philosophy's already-imagined 'tribes' is a paltry defence of an enterprise founded in part at least on the idea that doing fieldwork involves the possibility that one might in fact encounter things one had not imagined before, and that may change one's mind.

All of which is to wonder whether Wittgenstein's therapy might possibly, sometimes, be worse than the disease it cures, as far as anthropology is concerned. Is it possible to become so concerned about the value of 'looking and seeing' as an approach, the value of the concrete, the specific, the particular, the ordinary, and the everyday, the value of 'life' as a form, that all those things themselves come to take on a metaphysical weight that risks occluding any given instance of them?

What I'm trying to suggest is that sometimes anthropology's efforts to eschew metaphysics, and to avoid commitments that will trap us into an inability to change our minds, may themselves become obstacles to conceptual open-endedness and flexibility. That there is a risk of elevating such efforts to the level of metaphysical commitments themselves, repeating them to ourselves through our language until we no longer notice we cannot think otherwise.

One can imagine several costs to such an outcome, beyond a certain repetitiveness of conceptual language. To return to the specific issue of contextual form, Joel Robbins has forcefully articulated one such cost, which is that anthropology loses the possibility of 'finding promise in different ways of life', an idea itself grounded in the thought that 'there are profound differences between human lives lived out in different cultural surroundings' (2013: 456). Michael Degani frames this price neatly, too, as 'a sense that the ethnographic record is an archive of substantively different, not merely "recombinant", possibilities' (2025: 67).

As implied in the idea of 'cultural surroundings', and as Robbins makes clear in his call for an anthropology of values, the idea that 'difference' is anthropology's central focus requires a contextual frame of some kind to account for such difference (and see Heywood 2018a, 2018b). In this sense, one cost of the discipline's allergy to metaphysics is its progressive abandonment of formalist contextual frames ('culture', 'society', etc) in favour of formless alternatives such as 'ordinary life', that (at least apparently) eschew the kinds of commitment to a shape or form for context that come with older models, and partly for that very reason are designed to present the anthropologist's perspective as merely that of 'sensors recording events in high fidelity' (Degani 2025: 66). The anthropologist sees the truth of life as it is lived in all its granularity, and can sometimes connect such granularity to 'global' themes and events, but their capacity to speak clearly about what makes this 'ordinary life' different from that one – it's 'dimensionality', as Strathern puts it – is lost when the minimally granular ('the ordinary') and the maximally global ('life') exhaust what the discipline says about context. We lose 'the middle range of diversity' (Strathern 1992: 24).

To take a minor illustration of another potential cost, one apt for the themes of this book: it is often remarked with regret in contemporary anthropology that whilst it used to be the case that philosophers read anthropological work with interest and used (or misused) ethnographies in their arguments, the situation has been the other way around for some time now (see e.g. Robbins 2014: 69–70; Weiss 2024: 69). We'll see some evidence for the truth of both of these anecdotal claims in this book.

One might hear in this lament the implication that the problem of contemporary anthropology is that it fails to speak to broad philosophical issues; that anthropologists are not making clear and obvious enough the ways in which their work contributes to the kinds of conceptual questions that interest philosophers.

But what if the problem is the other way around? That anthropologists now sound, in some ways at least, so much like philosophers – often but not always of a particular stripe – that we are no longer interesting to them (cf. Jean-Klein and Riles 2005; Strathern 1987b)? That if anthropologists think of themselves as doing 'philosophy with the people in' (Ingold 2014), they risk giving precisely that same sense as given by Needham's remarks above, that all they do is add some intangible stratum of 'thickness' to what is already given to them by philosophy? Again, this sort of formulation of anthropology's purpose tends to erase the 'middle range', between the immediate ('people', whomever and wherever they are) and the abstract ('philosophy'), and, with that middle range, older forms of contextualism and relationality that would have interposed between the two.

This book is not a call for a return to or rejuvenation of such frames and forms of contextualism, though others writing today, as we will see at its conclusion, are making sophisticated and promising versions of such a call. As Sarah Green has put it, 'it may not be necessary to retain classical holism in order to develop coherent conceptual accounts; it might be enough to consider partial entanglements' (2014: 9). In this vein, this book is informed by a nostalgia for the relational dimensions such contextual forms gave anthropology the ability to speak to, a nostalgia already imagined thirty years ago in Strathern's epigraph to this introduction. This book is a plea for different kinds of silences and different forms of explicitness to those anthropologists have recently been used to rely upon. It tries to make manifest and evident some of what Wittgenstein might have called our disciplinary 'hinge propositions' of the last few decades, themselves deeply connected to Wittgenstein's ideas: the picture we have been repeating to ourselves. In doing so though it doesn't call for a different picture instead (or a new 'turn' cf. Laidlaw and Heywood 2013; Shah 2024).

Looking and seeing as an anthropologist must surely involve acknowledging one's conceptual commitments whilst refusing to allow them to calcify into dogma. The metaphysical anxieties that have driven anthropology's progressive abandonment of formal contextual models have perhaps prevented it from noticing the emergence of another picture to which it is now captive – that of formlessness itself. This book is an invitation to recognize the middle ground between rigid formalism and indistinct vitalism. By tracing how Wittgenstein's thought both parallels and influences anthropology's journal from structured context to formless 'life', I hope to show some of what anthropology has gained in this movement, what it has lost, and what possibilities remain open – if we can hold our commitments lightly enough to change our minds about them.

Part I

Logic: A Culture of Context

ONE

In the Background

... [the] strict and clear rules of the logical structure of propositions appear to us as something in the background.
– PI 102

Even readers unfamiliar with the details of any of Wittgenstein's arguments have probably gathered some sense of the monumental impact of the posthumously published *Philosophical Investigations* on philosophy and a host of other disciplines, including anthropology. It is almost invariably the Wittgenstein of the *Investigations* who appears in citations in social scientific or humanities scholarship, and it is from this book that many of Wittgenstein's most popular arguments come: the meaning of a word is its use in language; if a lion could talk, we wouldn't understand it; the beetle in the box. It is this Wittgenstein also who referred to himself as having adopted an 'anthropological perspective' precisely in the sense of taking a contextualizing approach to philosophical phenomena.

Yet to arrive at an understanding of the contextualism of this later Wittgenstein, we have first to put him in his own context. To do this, it's necessary to understand a text that is often left in the background of anthropological interpretations of Wittgenstein, but which the man himself considered, at the time it was written, to be his last word on philosophy, and which remained the only book of philosophy he published until his death: the *Tractatus Logico-Philosophicus*. But

In the Background

understanding the *Tractatus* is important not just as background context to the rest of Wittgenstein's work. It is also important for showing the wider culture of context from which both the *Tractatus* and early anthropological contextualism emerged, and for showing the connections between them.

For example, the same year (1922) saw the publication of the *Tractatus* and that of two other books with far-reaching effects on its discipline (cf. North 1999). Wittgenstein's book changed the face of philosophy, and the echoes of those changes still reverberate today (indeed, the text itself is still the subject of constant exegetical debate, a century on). Likewise, Malinowski's *Argonauts of the Western Pacific* is widely held up as the original ethnographic monograph, and to have instantiated for the first time the norms of fieldwork and writing that would define social anthropology for decades to come, and arguably still do to no small extent. Less well-known but similarly significant, Radcliffe-Brown's *The Andaman Islanders* exemplifies a very different kind of anthropological contextualism than *Argonauts*, one closer in many ways to that of the *Tractatus*.

The contexts in which Wittgenstein, Malinowski, and Radcliffe-Brown were writing, as well as their respective attitudes to these contexts, are also relevant to an understanding of the contextualism they each espoused. Such contexts were not entirely isomorphic despite their contemporaneity. For example, despite achieving their triumphs at the same time, the respective personal situations in which Malinowski and Wittgenstein found themselves in this period could hardly have been more different. Malinowski was gregarious and empire-building, and in 1922 he was in the process of laying the foundations for the reputation he would soon achieve as the founder of modern social anthropology. Wittgenstein, by contrast, was solitary and found it difficult to communicate with others. By the time the *Tractatus* was published, he had resolved to give up philosophy entirely in favour of a more 'ordinary' life as a schoolteacher in the Austrian Alps.

In the Background

Given Wittgenstein's problems with people it should not be too surprising that Ernest Gellner describes the *Tractatus* as 'a poem to solitude' (1998: 46). Gellner's engagement with the *Tractatus* is a rare instance of a direct anthropological reading of the text, and he goes on to argue – strikingly, for our purposes – that its central proposition is deceptively simple: *'There is no such thing as culture'* (1998: 68; italics in original). Given this apparently anti-anthropological spirit, it shouldn't surprise us to find that where the *Tractatus* has appeared in passing elsewhere in anthropological literature, it has received similarly short shrift. In a *Cultural Anthropology* commentary on Wittgenstein's 'Remarks on Frazer' from 1989, Thomas de Zengotita declares that the *Tractatus* 'gave ultimate expression to logical positivism [sic] and its style of mind' (1989: 391), and in a much more recent collection on the same topic, Carlo Severi characterizes the book as aiming 'to formulate a perfect, modern vision of Platonism' (2018: 78), and Veena Das notes in passing the ways in which the 'Remarks' and later work by Wittgenstein constituted a 'departure' from the *Tractatus*'s monochrome approach to philosophy (2018: 155).

All of that is to say that not only has the *Tractatus* rarely been invoked in anthropology, it has often been treated by anthropologists as the opposite of inspiring material. Where it appears in anthropology, it usually does so – as in most of the cases above – in order to serve as a foil against which to contrast Wittgenstein's later work, from which we are supposed to be able to learn a great deal. The *Tractatus* is generally viewed as anti-contextualist, as epitomized by Gellner's characterization.

That alone makes it worth trying to come to some understanding of the text itself, if only to grasp what it is about it that anthropologists tend to reject in favour of its future siblings in the family of Wittgenstein's philosophy. It's also worth trying to do so in order to understand the striking oddness of the fact that the author of a 'poem to solitude', the 'ultimate expression of logical positivism', and a 'modern

In the Background

vision of Platonism' should also have been of such influence and significance for anthropology, a discipline that would seem unlikely to welcome the advocate of any of those positions. Indeed, the *Tractatus* obviously has a bearing on the later work of Wittgenstein from which anthropologists have preferred to draw: it is part of the latter's context and background, in other words. But the exact nature of that bearing is a matter of some controversy, and I'll try to outline some of the interpretative disagreements that have gone on and still go on about the precise relationship between the Wittgenstein of the *Tractatus* and the Wittgenstein of the *Philosophical Investigations*. Such controversy also reveals something of the depths of feeling Wittgenstein's work produces in philosophers (and, occasionally, anthropologists).

What we'll observe in this chapter is that whilst Gellner's view and the wider anthropological eschewal of the *Tractatus* are understandable, they miss a great deal about the ways in which the *Tractatus* shows certain affinities with anthropological thinking about context, especially from this period. Whilst in some ways the particular form that context takes in the *Tractatus* is not one that contemporary anthropologists will feel much resonance with, it is a form that has as much of an important role to play in the history of anthropology as it does in the history of Wittgenstein's philosophy, and understanding how he came to change his view on that form will help us understand the intertwined nature of those histories.

Contexts of Creation

The interpretation of the *Tractatus* has become hard to separate from the context of its creation and its author's life, a point we'll return to often in this chapter. Born into one of the wealthiest families in the Austro-Hungarian Empire, Wittgenstein's early life was marked by both extraordinary privilege and by profound personal tragedy. This combination, as well as the wider context of the dying embers of the

Habsburg regime, the rationalistic pessimism of pre-war Vienna, the war itself, and Wittgenstein's loneliness and solitude during the war, have all become crucial contexts through which the *Tractatus* has been understood and received.

Wittgenstein had finished the *Tractatus* in 1918 while on leave from the Austrian army, but the first publisher to whom he sent it, Austrian Georg Jahoda, declined to take it up. An armistice between Italy and the Austrians was signed only a few days after Wittgenstein received this news, and he would spend the following ten months as a prisoner of war in Italian captivity. Over the course of that time, he sent the book to a number of people he hoped would understand and appreciate it, only to find that they did not, at least not in a manner he thought appropriate: Gottlob Frege, the renowned German logician, wrote that he couldn't make proper headway with the manuscript because he couldn't make sense of Wittgenstein's language and terminology; Bertrand Russell, Wittgenstein's mentor at Cambridge, clearly went to considerable effort to try to follow Wittgenstein's arguments (and believed himself to have succeeded), but Wittgenstein was deeply dissatisfied with Russell's interpretation and unhappy with the 'Introduction' Russell would go on to write for the published version of the text.

It would still be some time before that version would see the light of day. Another Austrian publisher, Wilhelm Braümuller, offered to publish the text if Wittgenstein paid for the costs of doing so, an offer the latter refused. Frege declined to endorse the text for publication in a German philosophical journal, both because he didn't understand it and because it was too long for such a medium. Wittgenstein then tried the publisher of a German literary journal, who strung him along for some time, before trying Reclam, who agreed to consider publishing the book thanks to Russell's 'Introduction', only to decline it when Wittgenstein suggested he didn't want the Introduction included.

The book was finally published first in German, almost by accident, in late 1921. While travelling in China, Russell had left his copy of the text with a mathematician and friend of his, Dorothy Wrinch, asking her to seek a publisher for it. She tried and failed with an approach to Cambridge University Press and then wrote to a number of German editors, one of whom, Wilhelm Ostwald, responded positively (again, thanks mainly to Russell's endorsement). As this was happening with little input from Wittgenstein himself, Russell's 'Introduction' (translated into German) was included in the Ostwald version, which otherwise consisted of a simple reproduction of Wittgenstein's original German manuscript, misprints, and typographical errors to boot. Wittgenstein 'was horrified. He regarded it, so he told [his friend Paul] Engelmann, as a "pirated edition"' (Monk 1991: 205).

In the eventual publisher of the English translation of the book, we find one of the first direct connections between Wittgenstein and anthropology. C. K. Ogden was a well-known personality in Cambridge and beyond, having been a student at Magdalene College associated with the Bloomsbury Group, subsequently editing a literary magazine and working as a bookseller and editor for Kegan Paul. Ogden already knew Wittgenstein, having in fact been present by chance at the fabled first meeting of 'an unknown German [sic], speaking very little English but refusing to speak German' and Russell at Trinity in 1911 when Wittgenstein first arrived in Cambridge (Monk 1991: 38). He would also co-edit (with literary theorist I. A Richards) a book called *The Meaning of Meaning* a year later (1923), which included an appendix by the young Bronislaw Malinowski, and about which we will have more to say later. The series in which he published the *Tractatus* (the International Library of Psychology, Philosophy and Scientific Method) also contained the anthropologist and psychologist W. H. R. Rivers's *Conflict and Dream* (1923).

Ogden presumably required little persuasion when Russell suggested he publish the *Tractatus* – as it was soon titled, at G. E. Moore's suggestion, and against Ogden's own wishes – with Kegan Paul. The translation was done by an undergraduate friend of Ogden's at King's,

Contexts of Creation

Frank Ramsey, who would later become a friend of Wittgenstein and one of the most brilliant polymaths of the twentieth century before his tragic early death (see Misak 2020).

Ray Monk reports that Kegan Paul expressed a wish to include some biographical and contextual details about Wittgenstein in the book, and to note among other things that it was partially put together in a prisoner of war camp. Perhaps Wittgenstein's reply to this suggestion illustrates something of his views on context in this period.

Do as you please, . . . only I can't for my life see the point of it. Why should the general reviewer know my age? Is it as much to say: you can't expect more of a young chap, especially when he writes a book in such a noise as must have been on the Austrian front? (Monk 1991: 208)

One possible reason for Wittgenstein's wishing to avoid contextualizing the *Tractatus* in this way is that he was deeply unhappy during the period in which he wrote it. But this unhappiness persisted throughout his life, and we'll have cause to return periodically to the particular manner in which it often manifested itself: as a dissatisfaction with philosophy and academia, and a yearning for something more 'real' and more 'ordinary' in their place.

He was miserable, lonely, and depressed as a soldier in the First World War, during which an early version of the *Tractatus* was composed alongside a personal diary detailing his misery and loneliness at great length, together with a clearly overwhelming concern about sex, sexuality, and his own sinfulness (see Perloff 2022). He seemed to loathe most of his fellow soldiers ('a bunch of delinquents'; 'no enthusiasm for anything, unbelievably crude, stupid and malicious'; 'a mass of scoundrels' – Monk 1991: 120) while also feeling intensely that fighting alongside them would be a spiritual and transformative experience and was therefore virtuous. To make matters worse, just before the end of the war, Wittgenstein learned of the death, in an air accident, of his closest friend, David Pinsent, a man with whom he was clearly in love. The *Tractatus* was dedicated to Pinsent's memory. Whether for this reason or another, or indeed many such, Wittgenstein entertained thoughts of suicide on several occasions during the war and in its aftermath.

Indeed, much of Wittgenstein's life was unhappy and filled with feelings of angst and loneliness despite the fact that he was born into incredible privilege in Vienna, the scion of the second wealthiest family in the entire Austro-Hungarian Empire, and one of the wealthiest in the world. The artist Gustav Klimt painted Ludwig's sister Margarete on the occasion of her marriage in 1905, and Brahms and Mahler among others were guests at family soirées. Ludwig's brother Paul became a concert pianist, despite losing an arm in the First World War, and it was for Paul that Ravel wrote his 'Piano Concerto for the Left-Hand'. Despite this privilege, Ludwig was far from the only unhappy member of the family: three of his four brothers – Hans, Rudi, and Kurt – had all committed suicide by the time Wittgenstein was writing the *Tractatus*.

A number of commentators on Wittgenstein have sought to contextualize him in the dying embers of the Empire and cosmopolitan Vienna, as well with reference to his family's Jewish roots. Allan Janik and Stephen Toulmin situate the famous eschewal of ethics and other 'mystical' elements from the *Tractatus* firmly in the rationalistic pessimism of Viennese intellectual context (1973). Ernest Gellner sees the entire span of Wittgenstein's career as boiling down essentially to a pendulum swing between the two extreme choices posed by the 'Habsburg Dilemma': either the individualist solitude of the cosmopolitan Viennese, as Gellner interprets the *Tractatus*, or the uncritical communalism of the ethnic nationalist, as he finds it in Wittgenstein's later work (1998). Ray Monk notes the enduring influence of Viennese philosopher and Jewish anti-semite and misogynist Otto Weininger on Wittgenstein, who first encountered Weininger's book *Sex and Character* as a schoolboy, but would return often to its characteristically

Viennese themes of pessimism about the modern age and of the 'duty of genius', as Monk subtitled his biography of Wittgenstein (Monk 1991: 19–25). Meanwhile, in comparing the biographies of Wittgenstein and another Habsburg refugee, Karl Popper, David Edmonds and John Eldinow have examined the Wittgenstein family's troubled relationship with its own roots, including the fact that they paid an astonishing sum of money (equivalent to 2 per cent of the entire Austrian national gold reserves) to the Nazis in 1939 to have themselves declared of Aryan descent (2001).

However it affected his life and work, Wittgenstein himself escaped from Vienna fairly early on. He went first to technical school in Berlin at the age of seventeen for two years, and then on to the University of Manchester to study aeronautics. It was whilst studying for this degree that he encountered Russell's *Principles of Mathematics*, and, via Russell, Frege's groundbreaking work on logic. Russell and Frege inaugurated what we know today as 'analytic philosophy' and the associated prominence of logic in Anglo-American versions of the discipline. Though anthropologists sometimes write of Anglo-American philosophy as if this was all it had ever been, the dominant approach to philosophy in Britain before Russell was, in fact, a version of Hegelian idealism, and it is hard to overstate the impact of the revolution Russell instigated. Formal logic and mathematics, and particularly Fregean logic, became indispensable instruments in a philosophy that believed they provided a conceptual clarity missing from ordinary language.

The classic example is the way in which Russell was thought to have solved the problem of how it is that we can meaningfully refer to entities that don't exist, as in the phrase, 'the present King of France is bald'. This proposition is not true because there is not a King of France. On the other hand, to say that it is false seems wrong also, since it is not the case that the present King of France has a full head of hair. Russell essentially rewrote ('analysed') ordinary language descriptions ('a man', 'some man', 'every man', 'all men', etc.) in logical form to point

In the Background

to the component parts they contain. This reveals, among other things, that we can understand the phrase 'the present King of France is bald' without being obliged to assent to French monarchism because 'the present King of France' is really a description, not the subject of the proposition, and thus itself either true or false. In other words, 'the present King of France' in the phrase 'the present King of France is bald' sounds like it refers to something real in the world, but in fact it asserts something, namely that there is a thing (and only one thing) that is the present King of France. One can think this assertion both meaningful and false, and thus also understand why someone (who might think it true) would add to it as a description the quality of being bald.

The question of the baldness or otherwise of non-existent French monarchs may seem arcane, but it is important to understand the revolutionary effect that this kind of logical analysis had on philosophy, if only to understand how Wittgenstein came to write the *Tractatus*. Russell is effectively showing that the simplest of ordinary expressions ('the man', or even just proper names like 'Bertrand' or 'Ludwig') contain logical complexity that is opaque without the technique of analysis; we think we know what we mean when we use such expressions but only logic can show what is really at stake.

While still at Manchester and captivated by the elegance of logical analysis, Wittgenstein entered into correspondence with Frege, who suggested he seek to study under Russell. With no prior introduction, he appeared in Russell's rooms in Trinity College, Cambridge, in 1911, and over the course of the next two years, the two men became extremely close. Though at first irritated by Wittgenstein's peculiar manners and the ferocity and intensity of his personality, by early 1912, he was won over and Wittgenstein enrolled as a student at Cambridge, where he impressed (and/or terrified and appalled) a great many others too, including the philosopher G. E. Moore and the economist John Maynard Keynes.

Contexts of Creation

Within the space of his first year, not only had it become obvious that Russell regarded Wittgenstein as his intellectual heir and natural successor in the fields of logic and philosophy, but – in a way unclear at this point to Russell himself – Wittgenstein had begun to stake out positions of his own, not all of which would coincide with those of his mentor. They would often have fierce disagreements, especially over the increasingly non-academic direction Russell's work was taking, as he began to write more for popular consumption and to explore questions of religion and ethics that the *Tractatus* would banish to silence. Russell himself was clearly ambivalent about some of this work and so was often cut deeply by Wittgenstein's brutal criticisms, as others were. As Monk puts it,

Wittgenstein was not one to debate his most fundamental convictions. Dialogue with him was possible only if one shared those convictions... To one who did not share his fundamental outlook, his utterances – whether on logic or on ethics – would, as likely as not, remain unintelligible. (Monk 1991: 53)

By 1913, Russell had effectively abandoned the field of logic entirely to Wittgenstein, and the two men were growing increasingly apart as Wittgenstein sought both to build on and supersede Russell's work on logic whilst thoroughly failing to show any sympathy or understanding for the latter's desire to write about metaphysical, political, and ethical – rather than solely logical – questions. By the end of the year, Wittgenstein had become so consumed with logic that he decided to leave Cambridge and 'exile himself', as David Pinsent, with whom he was travelling at this point, put it, to Norway. Pinsent records Wittgenstein's reasons as being firstly to do with his ability to concentrate solely and exclusively on logic in the absence of distraction, and secondly out of a desire to justify his feelings of contempt for most of the lesser mortals around him by achieving greatness in isolation (Monk

In the Background

1991: 89). As Monk puts it, 'if he is to behave like Beethoven, he ought, like Beethoven, to produce really great work' (Monk 1991).

Wittgenstein lived in the small village of Skjolden until mid-1914, at which point he returned to Vienna, intending to go back to Norway in the autumn, an intention frustrated by the outbreak of war. In this immediate pre-war period, we get some of the first glimpses of the *Tractatus* from a set of notes he ungraciously dictated to Russell in Cambridge just before his departure for Norway and a further set he dictated to Moore when the latter came to visit him in Norway.

By the time of Moore's visit, Wittgenstein and Russell had quarrelled by letter, with Wittgenstein declaring that he wished neither to write to nor see Russell again. Thus Moore – by all accounts, despite his brilliant intelligence, a preternaturally good person with an almost childlike innocence – became a sort of substitute for Russell, and Wittgenstein browbeat him, against his own better judgement, into coming to visit him in Norway in early 1914. In the wake of this visit, Wittgenstein insisted that upon returning to Cambridge, Moore should try to submit the notes he had taken in Norway as a thesis for Wittgenstein's BA degree. The university refused to accept notes – as indeed they were, without scholarly attributions – as eligible to be a thesis, and when Moore wrote to explain this, Wittgenstein responded with an outrageously rude letter in which he blamed Moore for the university's failure to recognize his genius and cut off relations with him, just as he had done with Russell. Though in time he would, to varying degrees, reconcile with both Moore and Russell, this period found Wittgenstein intellectually isolated, a situation that would only worsen with the outbreak of war and his enlistment in the Austrian army in August 1914.

No surprise, perhaps, then that *Tractatus* should seem to Gellner a 'poem to solitude'. In fact though, at the heart of the *Tractatus* lies a radical reconceptualization of logic's relationship to human understanding. While Russell and Frege saw logic as in some ways a realm of absolute truth to be discovered, Wittgenstein came to see it as something more like a context through which we give form to our experience. This shift emerges through his treatment of several key philosophical problems, and understanding it helps us to see why the *Tractatus*, despite its apparently anti-contextual metaphysics, may have more connections with anthropological thinking than has been generally recognized.

All That Is the Case

The text of the book consists of seven numbered basic propositions, with all other paragraphs labelled as decimal extensions of one or other proposition (though the precise nature of the way in which this extension is supposed to be understood is not always clear). So, famously, proposition no. 1 is:

1. The world is all that is the case.

Which is then followed by

1.1. The world is the totality of facts, not of things.
1.11 The world is determined by the facts, and by their being *all* the facts.[1]

These examples are characteristic of the assertive, rather than argumentative, style of much of the book and also of its metaphysical tone. Over the course of most of the following propositions and their subsets, it outlines an austere universe of 'complexes' made up of 'simple' objects, 'states of affairs' made up of combinations of objects, and existing states of affairs as 'facts'. 'A logical picture of facts is a thought', as proposition no. 3 runs, and a proposition is the expression of a thought.

Thanks to an insight that is supposed to have come to him after reading of a court case in France in which a model of a car accident was

In the Background

presented to the court to represent the facts of the accident (Monk 1991: 117–118), Wittgenstein develops what is often called his 'Picture theory of language', according to which propositions model reality thanks to the structural relationship between their elements matching up to the structural relationship between facts in the world. This capacity of propositions/pictures to model reality – to mimic its structure – he calls 'pictorial form' (also 'logical form' and also 'logico-pictorial form' – the point is that it is a matter of form). What pictures cannot model though is the pictorial form itself – their own capacity to represent – a point to which we will return. Propositions about complexes can be analysed, with logic, and completely, into 'elementary propositions' about states of affairs (or 'atomic facts' as the Ramsey/Ogden translation calls them).

As a universe, this might seem both far too austere and too simplistically representationalist to have any connection to anthropology. But over the course of outlining this universe, Wittgenstein makes a number of important arguments in relation to logic and analytic philosophy that would have significant effects. In several of these arguments we can see a shift from an understanding of logic as content to one of logic as context.

Wittgenstein's treatment of Russell's Theory of Types, for example, reveals this reconceptualization of logic's role. Russell had introduced the Theory of Types in order to cope with his eponymous paradox in set theory, more widely known in Russell's lay formulation of the barber's paradox: the barber is the man who shaves all and only those men who do not shave themselves. Does the barber shave himself? On the one hand, he cannot, for he shaves only those who do not shave themselves; on the other hand, if he does not, he becomes one of the 'all men who do not shave themselves' class and should therefore be shaved by the barber (himself). When posed in set theoretical form, the paradox had significant implications for the philosophy of mathematics and for logic more broadly, which depend on the notion of classes or sets. If therefore the 'set of all sets that do not belong to themselves' cannot be said to be either a member of itself or not without contradiction, there must be some serious deficiency in the logic at hand.

Russell's 'Theory of Types' purported to solve this problem essentially by introducing hierarchical distinctions into the logical system between different types of objects; thus the barber and the man to be shaved become different sorts of things.

For Wittgenstein, this wasn't just an awkward solution – it revealed a basic misunderstanding of logic's nature. Formulated in Wittgenstein's language, one should not have to – indeed one is unable to – 'say' things about the meanings of signs in logic, since there is no meta-language 'above' that of logic in which to do so; one should not have to say of logic that in this particular place it refers to distinct sorts of entities or distinct types of things. The problem, Wittgenstein thought, must be instead with the ways in which the logic is 'shown'; accordingly, he disposes of Russell's paradox by pointing out that the equivalents in logical notation of 'barber' and 'man to be shaved' are doing different things in the contexts in which they appear in the relevant propositions.[2] Thinking they are doing the same job (or needing to assert that they are different kinds of objects) is like mistaking a noun for a verb in a sentence – it violates the rules of grammar. Once you accept this, then the paradox disappears.

This marks a crucial shift from seeing logic as a set of rules that could be right or wrong to seeing it as the context within which we determine rightness and wrongness at all. Logic becomes not a thing in the world to be discovered, but rather the form through which we experience the world as meaningful.

Though there is some dispute as to whether C. S. Peirce or other philosophers got there first, the *Tractatus* is also widely credited with introducing truth tables, now used in a wide variety of mathematical and logical domains. Truth tables represent another crucial step in Wittgenstein's reconceptualization of logic as context rather than content. The metaphysical status of logical operators such as 'and', 'or', etc.

In the Background

P	Q	P^Q
T	T	T
T	F	F
F	T	F
F	F	F

Figure 1.1: Truth table for basic compound 'and' statements (^).

had long been a matter of philosophical confusion. Were they representative of something in the way that other symbols are? If so, of what? Are there unseen entities or objects floating around in the universe that correspond somehow to 'and', 'or', 'not', etc.? Whatever they are, they were the foundations of Russellian and Fregean logic. The genius of truth tables lay in showing how such operations could be understood without reference to any metaphysical entities at all.

Wittgenstein's view that elementary propositions about 'atomic facts' form the basis of all other propositions and that 'atomic facts' are independent of one another, means that one can understand the sense of any proposition (by which he means the conditions under which it would be true or false) if one understands the possible combinations of truth or falsity of its elementary propositions. For example, the statement 'Wittgenstein invented truth tables and tortured generations of undergraduate philosophers', when formulated in logical notation, involves the symbol for the conjunction 'and'. But such a conjunction is unnecessary if we can simply represent the possible combinations of truth and falsity of the statement's component parts, and which combinations yield truth or falsity of the statement overall. Wittgenstein may not have invented truth tables, but he may still have tortured philosophy undergraduates, as in the third row of the table, as shown in Figure 1.1.

The significance of this move goes far beyond technical innovation. By showing how logical operations could be reduced to patterns of truth and falsity, Wittgenstein removes their metaphysical mystery and reduces it to a matter of form. We don't need to imagine logic as a realm of abstract entities or eternal truths. Instead, we can see it as the form through which we organize our experience – the context that makes meaningful statements possible at all.

In keeping with some of what has already been said, Wittgenstein's view was that the form of logic could not itself be represented (or 'said'), just as pictures cannot represent the way in which they are representative; logical constants such as 'and' give the misleading impression that the relation they represent has a meaning, whereas what they really do is 'show' that relation. Truth tables show the relation with no 'saying' at all.[3]

The Context of Logic

What I have said so far should give a clear sense of how much the *Tractatus* is in dialogue with the questions of logical analysis that had preoccupied Russell, and to that extent how far it may seem from anthropological concerns. This distance is visible in Russell's own interpretation of the *Tractatus*, outlined in the 'Introduction' Wittgenstein so detested, which largely focuses on the parts of the texts I have so far outlined.

Russell declares the book to be about the search for 'a logically perfect language' (just as was his own work and that of Frege's). Such a perfect language would come in the form of an ideal logical notation and would have little interest in the vagaries of actual usage in any given context, just as does the *Tractatus* itself: at one point, Wittgenstein refers to 'the enormously complicated nature' of the 'silent adjustments' upon which 'everyday language' is built (4.002). As Michael North points out, this Ramsey/Ogden translation of '*stillschweigenbenden Abmachungen*' ('silent adjustments') has the air of implying 'something faulty in colloquial language' (1999: 38; and see Gellner 1998: 69). The subsequent Pears and McGuinness translation, written with an awareness of Wittgenstein's later work, amends this to 'tacit conventions'. Russell's

In the Background

own view on the 'errors' of actual language use and how to approach them is nicely captured in the following:

When a savage shows that he is muddle-headed as to the muddle in his head, it is assumed that we ought to learn to be equally muddle-headed, and that no clear account of his muddle is possible. This favouritism seems to indicate a bias in favour of muddle... Savages are muddled as to what is going on, whether inside or outside them, and their account is not to be accepted. (quoted in North 1999: 32)

The contrast between this view and that expressed in the notes Wittgenstein will later make on Frazer's *Golden Bough* is a very sharp one, as we will see. Even in 1922 though, Russell's interpretation of the *Tractatus* appears a rather partial one. For what the discussions of logic and analysis in the text we have met so far build up to is a far-reaching attack on the entire vision of logic that underpinned Russell's views (and those of other analytic philosophers), one which will lead into what are sometimes called the 'mystical' dimensions of the book. This attack also reveals the extent of the contextualism we have already met several times in Wittgenstein's presentation of logic – logic *is* context in the *Tractatus*.

By means of both complex logical argument (partly with the aid of truth tables) and more allusive suggestion, Wittgenstein comes to the view that 'all logical propositions say the same thing, to wit nothing' (5.43). Heralded by the distinction between 'saying' and 'showing' we have already met, the position he arrives at – *pace* Russell, Frege, and a great many others of the period – is that logic is not a thing out there in the world with laws to be discovered, with the capacity to define rationality and irrationality, or provide us with fundamental constants. Logic is rather the way we have of giving form to our experience: it is our context. It has nothing to do with the world whatsoever, and is therefore inherently tautologous – a logical proposition 'says' nothing at all; it rather 'shows' your own thinking to you. As he puts it, 'our

The Context of Logic

fundamental principle is that whenever a question can be decided by logic at all it must be possible to decide it without more ado. (And if we get into a position where we have to look at the world for an answer to such a problem, that shows that we are on a completely wrong track.)' (5.551). Hence also why 'In a certain sense, we cannot make mistakes in logic' (5.473) and why 'we cannot give a sign the wrong sense' (5.4732): Because the framework of logic is *ours* but also how we inhabit experience, then it simply is what we do that has sense to us. It shows us what has sense to us (what may be true or may not be true), but it does not tell us truth or falsehood.

That making ('saying') such claims themselves is difficult is also a part of the point of the *Tractatus*, the point of its peculiar structure and tone, part of the point of the 'saying' and 'showing' distinction, the point that 'pictures' of reality cannot themselves show the relationship between picture and reality (pictorial form).

Much of what I have described so far of the book was already written by late 1915 (Monk 1991: 134). In early 1916, Wittgenstein was sent to the front to serve with an artillery unit fighting against the Russians, as he himself had long desired. As in many other comparable situations in his life, however, the fulfilment of his desires brought him no happiness (not that they were likely intended by him to do so). He spent a great deal of time contemplating the possibility of his imminent death, and as usual, loathed the people around him: he characterized his fellow soldiers (who he thought resented him for actively volunteering for army service) as 'a company of vile and stupid people ... malicious and heartless. It is almost impossible to find a trace of humanity in them' (Monk 1991: 139). Lonelier even than he had been as a soldier before this point, and clearly, confronted by battle, in an existential frame of mind, his philosophical notes begin to exhibit a concern with the nature of the self, one which correlates with a longstanding interest he had in Schopenhauer, and many of them carry over into the final version of the *Tractatus*. This concern with the self is likely what motivated Gellner's 'poem to solitude' characterization.

We have seen above how Wittgenstein saw logic as tied up with our capacity to represent the world as it appears to us, seeing logic as a 'mirror-image of the world' (6.13). This leads him on to the famous aphorism that '*The limits of my language* mean the limits of my world' (5.6; italics in original) and he goes on to extend this notion of 'limit' to the self: 'the world is *my* world: this is manifest in the fact that the limits of *language* (of that language which alone I understand) mean the limits of *my* world' (5.62; italics in original).

As with several aspects of this final section of the book, interpretations of these sections are controversial. At first glance, they might seem to support anti-contextualist readings of the *Tractatus*. So, Russell, for example, has Wittgenstein endorsing solipsism, on the basis that one cannot think about or say anything about what is beyond 'the limits of my world.' This endorsement is qualified, in accordance with what Wittgenstein has already said about language and logic's capacity to reflect on their own limits, by the fact that this solipsistic claim cannot itself be said (only shown). In other words, solipsism is quite right that there is nothing in the world beyond one's own awareness of it, but as an attempt to put oneself beyond this awareness, to examine it from an external position, this argument is itself impossible.

The Ramsey/Ogden translation makes these points sound even more solipsistic by rendering the key passage as 'the language which only I understand', as opposed to 'the only language which I understand', seeming to imply that the self can know only its own version of the world.

In fact though, Wittgenstein's point is much more subtle than Russell conveys. It is that there is no substantial difference between solipsism and realism: that, as he says, 'the world is my world', does not make it any less of a world, and both doctrines are equally mistaken in imagining their ability to step outside of the self-world relation and represent it. This is not a claim about being trapped in private solipsism, but rather about the nature of any contextual understanding. We cannot use logic to examine logic itself, just as we cannot use language to get 'outside' language. This is an important point, because it shows the anti-metaphyscial, antifoundationalist character of Wittgenstein's thought even in this early period, and this antifoundationalist character will only intensify over the years, as we will see.

In line with this view, and again with the repeated emphasis on the inability of language to represent things beyond itself, the *Tractatus* ends by declaring that ethics 'cannot be put into words' (6.421), for, like logic and language, it does not consist of laws to be discovered but pervades the world ('my world'); thus actions and the exercise of the will are not in themselves or in their consequences good or bad, but instantiate the world as it is for us. So 'the world of the happy man is a different one from that of the unhappy man' (6.43). Propositions that claim to be about ethics (and thus about the limits of the world as it is), are, like propositions about logic, or about the relation between logic and the world, in fact nonsense. Ethics, like other 'problems of life' 'cannot be put into words. *They make themselves manifest.* They are what is mystical' (6.522; italics in original).

The book ends with what must be several of the most hotly debated lines in contemporary philosophy: the penultimate proposition runs,

My propositions serve as elucidations in the following way: anyone who understands me eventually recognizes them as nonsensical, when he has used them – as steps – to climb up beyond them. (He must, so to speak, throw away the ladder after he has climbed up it.).

He must transcend these propositions and then he will see the world aright. (6.54)

As we'll see, these lines have occasioned decades of debate over their correct interpretation. The final proposition (7), famously declares, in the pleasantly archaic Ramsey/Ogden original, 'Whereof one cannot speak, thereof one must be silent.'

In the Background

Even this short sketch of the text should convey some of the problems of interpretation it presents. On the one hand, there is the extensive outline of the universe of logical atomism: atomic facts, complexes, elementary propositions, etc. All this will no doubt seem dry and uninspiring to anthropologists and perhaps also familiar as a sort of caricature of philosophical atomism from Democritus through to David Hume: an ordered universe exists, and it is philosophy's task to represent and mirror this universe (Gellner 1998: 47). In some ways, this was the interpretation Russell put forward in his 'Introduction' to the book, which as we have seen favours the straightforwardly analytical portions of it and glances somewhat askance at its 'mystical' portions.[4]

On the other hand, however, there is the apparent undoing of much of this 'realism' in the remarks about logic's capacity to represent the world, and to do anything beyond express in a certain form our intuitions about the world. There is further the repeated insistence regarding the inability of logic (and language) to say anything about these capacities of its own or anything at all about the form of the relationship between itself and the world; in other words, and this is of course reinforced by the text of the penultimate proposition cited above, it would appear that Wittgenstein is both making a set of metaphysical claims about logic, the world, and the relation between the two, and also insisting that it is precisely these sorts of claims that we should regard as nonsensical.

The positivist reading may have looked plausible to Russell and to logical positivists in the 1930s (and to at least one anthropological interpreter – see Zengotita 1989), but it would not be popular to many of those who came to an appreciation of Wittgenstein's philosophy through his later work, who would focus much more squarely on the question of the 'limits of language.'

It is hard to explain in detail why this is without presenting in comparable detail the later work in question, which I will go on to describe in subsequent chapters. Some readers may already be familiar with the broad outlines of the distinction between 'early' and 'later Wittgenstein', and we have already encountered Veena Das and other anthropologists situating that later work as a more profitable departure from the *Tractatus*.[5] Even a glance at a copy of the *Philosophical Investigations* will show what an ocean separates it in terms of form from the austere logical structure of the *Tractatus*, and the 'meaning is use' doctrine many have taken from the *Investigations* seems an obviously far cry from that of the 'Picture theory of language' we met above. Wittgenstein himself frequently referred back critically to the *Tractatus* in his later writing, so the idea that his thought changed in some regard at least is hard to dispute.

A great deal else has been disputed, however, and briefly explaining some of these disputes serves both to highlight a few of the problems intrinsic to the 'early' vs 'later' Wittgenstein distinction, whilst also illustrating the depth of feeling that can be involved in the project of interpreting Wittgenstein's intentions.

For most of the latter part of the twentieth century, the dominant interpretation of the *Tractatus*, inaugurated by Wittgenstein's students Elizabeth Anscombe (e.g. 1959) and Peter Geach (e.g. 1976), and subsequently maintained by a range of scholars, most notably Peter Hacker (1972), has been what is today sometimes called the 'traditional' or 'ineffabilistic' reading.[6] This reading tends to hold to some version or another of the idea that the *Tractatus* conveys a set of important ideas about the nature of logic and propositions, but that amongst those ideas is the insight – encapsulated in 6.54 – that because 'ideas about the nature of logic and propositions' cannot themselves be put sensibly into logical language, the propositions of the *Tractatus* are in fact some variant of nonsense. In John Koethe's words, themselves paraphrasing Wittgenstein, 'The limits of language are thus drawn from inside language' (2003: 200). One simple way of putting this – a formulation with which most though not all of its advocates would disagree (Bronzo 2012: 57; Koethe 2003: 190; cf. McGuinness 1988) – would be that the

In the Background

Tractatus 'shows' us the limits of language in the course of illustrating why one cannot 'say' them.

This reading obviously involves the view that the *Tractatus* makes a positive contribution to philosophy, in the sense that even though precisely what it says might be 'nonsense' in some fashion or another, in saying it the text does – somehow – succeed in teaching us a set of important things about the nature of language and logic. Thus to this reading, the *Tractatus* can be said to resemble traditional philosophy at least insofar as we learn something substantive from it about the nature of things.

Partly for this reason, this view has also contributed, at least to some extent, to readings of Wittgenstein's oeuvre as a whole that very radically differentiate the *Tractatus* from later work like the *Philosophical Investigations*. In the latter text, formal logic barely appears, and it is hard to read it as setting out any kind of substantive theory or doctrine of propositions or language (beyond the 'meaning is use' idea, which Wittgenstein would certainly have wished to deny was a theory or doctrine). No doubt this reading – in which the *Tractatus* is at least at some level about saying something definitive about logic – has contributed to anthropologists' aversion to the book, even as they have been drawn to the later work, or even, as in Gellner's case, when they have not.

However, for the past three decades or so debates about the interpretation of the *Tractatus* have been reignited thanks to the emergence of what is now often called the 'resolute' reading of the book, a reading associated in particular with James Conant and Cora Diamond, the latter of whom has also had some influence on anthropological readings of later Wittgenstein (see e.g. Conant 1989; Conant and Diamond 2004; Diamond 1988).[7] Delightfully, much of the controversy revolves around exactly how we should understand the word 'nonsense.'

The resolute reading takes off from the position that the traditional reading appears to be committed to a strange idea of the notion of nonsense. That is, the traditional reading seems to acknowledge that Wittgenstein must have genuinely meant proposition 6.54, and thus that we are supposed to understand the main body of the *Tractatus* as composed of nonsense; and yet it also wants to say that we learn something from this nonsense. It thus seems to imply that the *Tractatus* is a special kind of nonsense, 'ineffable', as it is often described, that cannot be sensibly said and yet can somehow be conveyed. As we have already seen, some – though not most – versions of the traditional reading simply say that what the *Tractatus* 'says' is nonsense but that what it 'shows' is a set of important philosophical ideas about meaning, logic, and language.

By contrast, the resolute reading insists on reading 6.54 'resolutely': that is, by taking Wittgenstein at face value, and by seeing the propositions that precede it in the *Tractatus* as nonsense in the straightforward sense of the term, no more sensical than saying 'Wittgenstein is raining'.

The point of this reading is to assert that Wittgenstein is not trying to gesture at metaphysical or ineffable truths in the *Tractatus* that are so deep as to be unsayable. He is instead indicating the futility of looking for any such truths in the first place, including those that appear to emerge from the *Tractatus* (whether by being said or by being shown, and, to some extent at least, including the saying and showing distinction itself as well).

However, despite insisting that we take the propositions of the *Tractatus* to be nonsense in what is called an 'austere' sense (in the sense of their being straightforwardly without sense or meaning, rather than ineffable nonsense), proponents of the resolute reading nevertheless also argue that this nonsense performs an elucidatory function upon the reader, that is, precisely by indicating its own nonsensical nature by its conclusion (Conant 1989; Diamond 1988).

This may sound, in fact, very much like a special kind of ineffable nonsense, and one that does indeed convey meaning, unlike 'Wittgenstein is raining'. Proponents generally get around this problem by arguing that what is semantically meaningless may nevertheless still have psychological effects. Yet alone this could be read to imply that 'the sentences of the *Tractatus* could be aptly replaced by a very studious kick in the head that brings about the same 'psychological effects'' (Bronzo 2012: 62–63). Diamond argues instead that the effect of the sentences of the *Tractatus* is a rational one – unlike the effect of a kick in the head – but functions in a manner like that of a riddle, in which the steps that lead up to the resolution of the puzzle don't have sense in themselves until one gets there (Diamond 1988). This view of the *Tractatus* is very much related to the wider views on Wittgenstein's work of American philosopher Stanley Cavell, who has had a significant influence on anthropological views on Wittgenstein and whom we will meet in more depth later in this book.

There is now a vast corpus of literature devoted to debating these interpretations, and it is beyond my ability here to give anything like an adequate summary of either. Any attempt at adjudicating between them is also obviously beyond our purposes. The two interconnected issues I want to highlight about them are: firstly, their implications for how we should understand Wittgenstein's work as a whole; and secondly, the ways in which 'Wittgenstein as a whole' – his life and intellectual biography – has itself become a crucial context through which his work must be read.

Consider first how the 'traditional' reading emerged. Many of its exemplars – Anscombe and Geach, for instance – were students or associates of the later Wittgenstein at Cambridge. Their interpretation of the *Tractatus* was inevitably shaped by their personal experience of its author in the 1940s, decades after its writing. This biographical context surely isn't incidental to the traditional reading – it helps explain why these interpreters might have wished to work so hard to reconcile the *Tractatus* with Wittgenstein's later philosophy, even at the cost of some philosophical tension. It is difficult without incoherence to think that Wittgenstein was both right in most of what he says in the *Tractatus* and also right in saying it is nonsense. Yet that is more or less what the traditional reading does say.

The resolute reading, by contrast, might seem less biographically contexualist in its insistence on taking Wittgenstein wholly at his word in 6.54 and by reading the rest of the book in the very particular way prescribed by Conant and Diamond (as elucidatory nonsense). Yet it too has clear implications for Wittgenstein's overall intellectual trajectory that go beyond the *Tractatus*. In some ways, indeed it is much more radically contextualist than the traditional reading insofar as it demands the *Tractatus* be read in the light of Wittgenstein's later work, and indeed be upheld as an example of antimetaphysical and antiphilosophical continuity in Wittgenstein's thought. For this reason, the resolute reading is often said (and sometimes frames itself – e.g. Crary and Read 2000) to challenge the entire distinction between 'early' and 'late' Wittgenstein by subsuming the former into the latter.[8]

My point here is not to establish any philosophical problem with either reading, but rather to note the effort undertaken in order to avoid having to say that Wittgenstein was wrong, and wrong by his own lights. It is those lights, moreover, which are often the criteria against which right and wrong are assessed; in other words, in these debates the *Tractatus* is frequently being measured not against the yardstick of contemporary counterarguments or the perspectives of other philosophers on similar questions, but against the yardstick of Wittgenstein himself, albeit older and wiser, at least apparently in some respects.

Somewhat ironically then, for a man who refused to include any biographical details in the *Tractatus* for his publisher on the basis that they couldn't be relevant, Wittgenstein has in a sense become his own context (has indeed spawned a universe of exegetical books and specialist journals), within which what is stake is correct interpretation of Wittgenstein's intentions as read against the background of his life and work. So whilst the sense of 'disproportionality' of comparing Wittgenstein with social anthropology outlined in this book's

In the Background

Introduction is important, there is also a sense in which Wittgenstein is now an entire discipline unto himself.

The Opposite of Anthropology

What though of Gellner's charge against the *Tractatus* as a 'poem to solitude', the metaphysical and solipsistic musings of an extraordinarily lonely man who felt himself facing the universe by himself; who clearly thought himself, to his enormous frustration, unable to communicate with many of those he found around him, and so developed a philosophy in which 'If there are other people (this is not explicitly denied, though the *Tractatus* comes very close to implying it) they are irrelevant' (Gellner 1998: 64)? And what of Gellner's contention that the *Tractatus* is essentially anti-culturalist and so, far from being of relevance to anthropology, the *Tractatus* is in this sense its opposite?

One can see why a reader might come to this conclusion. The austerity of Wittgenstein's apparent metaphysics – of a world of simple objects, atomic facts, elementary propositions – does not seem friendly to the presence of actual people. When Wittgenstein does speak of subjects, it is almost invariably in the first person singular or plural ('we' and 'I'), and we've met the apparent (though restricted) endorsement of solipsism and the potential for the 'limits of language are the limits of my world' argument to sound as if it is meant to apply to a private language, to a language 'I alone' can understand.[9]

Whilst Gellner may have reason to read the *Tractatus* as anti-culturalist, that is not quite the same thing as it being anti-contextualist. It is true that the book seems little if at all concerned with the ways in which contextual worlds may differ (though note the aside quoted earlier about the world of the happy man and the world of the unhappy man). But as we've seen, it also attacks the foundationalist approach to logic of Russell, Frege, and other dominant voices in philosophy of the time, seemingly in favour instead of a view of language and logic that

The Opposite of Anthropology

sees them as wrapped up with experience, and arguing for the impossibility of stepping outside of such experience. 'The limits of my language mean the limits of my world' is in that sense a contexualist claim if it is anything, and in translations other than the Ramsey/Ogden version the subsequent remark about 'language I understand' comes out much more culturalist ('language which alone I understand') than solipsistic ('language which I alone understand'). The resolute reading brings to the fore the problems with attempting to make such strongly contextualist claims: if we are so tightly bound to our language (understood in the broadest contextual sense), then how could we ever step outside of it enough to understand others – as Wittgenstein often failed to do – or even far enough to see the sense of this claim itself? These are also issues to which we will return in subsequent chapters. The key point I wish to make for now is that context – in the shape of a formalist approach to logic – in fact plays a key role in the *Tractatus* despite its apparently atomistic metaphysics. And whilst such formalism and logicism may seem as anti-anthropological as solipsism today, that was not true at the time the *Tractatus* was written, as we'll see in the next chapter.

To compare context in the *Tractatus* with context in anthropology more fully, it will help to examine what was going on in the latter discipline at the same time as Wittgenstein was writing the book he then imagined to be his (or rather, *the*) final word on philosophy. Indeed, we'll leave Wittgenstein as he himself left philosophy in the wake of the First World War, having first given away the vast fortune he had inherited upon his father's death, and then decided to train to be a schoolteacher, since there was nothing more to be said about philosophy. By the end of the war, Wittgenstein's own context had changed radically, and so had he. The Austro-Hungarian Empire into which he had been born was no more, and in Monk's words, Wittgenstein had over the previous four years 'faced death, experienced a religious awakening, taken responsibility for the lives of others, and endured long periods of close confinement in the company of the sort of people he would not previously have shared a railway carriage with. All this had made him a different person – had given him a new identity' (Monk 1991: 170).

His world though was still not that of the happy man. Despairing at the failure of people he at least claimed to respect, like Russell and Frege, to appreciate the *Tractatus*, still utterly heartbroken by Pinsent's death, and at sea as a thirty-seven-year-old man re-training to be a schoolteacher among teenagers, he continued to contemplate suicide. After a year of such training, he was, at his own request, posted to a small, poor, mountainous village south of Vienna called Trattenbach. Whilst enthusiastic at first about his new life, he soon – as usual – came to loathe the people around him, and his liberal use of corporal punishment, among other things, did not endear him to his charges' parents. By the time the *Tractatus* was published, he had moved on, first to a secondary school in which he stayed 'barely a month' (Monk 1991: 212), and then to another village called Puchberg. He was in Puchberg – whose inhabitants he described to Russell as only three-quarters human (Monk 1991) – when he received a copy of Ogden and Richards's *The Meaning of Meaning*, which contained an appendix written by a rising star in anthropology named Bronislaw Malinowski.

TWO

The Gods of Context

> It is obvious that an imagined world, however different from the real one, must have *something* – a form – in common with it.
> – TLP 2.022

In his appendix to *The Meaning of Meaning*, Malinowski coined what Hilary Henson calls 'the really rather strange phrase "context of situation"' (1974: 52), arguing that language was primarily 'a mode of action' rather than representation and that meaning could only be understood through its function in context. In other words, at the same time as Wittgenstein was elaborating on the – at least superficially – representationalist and atomistic 'picture theory of meaning', Malinowski was arguing instead for a contextualist understanding of language; for the idea that meaning is embedded in context, and that people use language to practical effect, not (just) to represent.

Though Wittgenstein's response to *The Meaning of Meaning* was characteristically scathing – he wrote to Russell declaring it 'a miserable book' – the parallels between his later ideas about context and those emerging in anthropology are striking. Where Malinowski insisted that 'the meaning of a word must always be gathered, not from a passive contemplation of this word, but from an analysis of its functions, with reference to the given culture' (1923: 309), Wittgenstein would later famously insist that 'the meaning of a word is its use in the language' (*PI* 43).

The Gods of Context

This overlap was no mere coincidence. Both men were products of the intellectual ferment of the dying Austro-Hungarian Empire, and both found themselves reimagining their respective disciplines in ways that would place context at their heart. We'll look in detail at some of these overlaps later in this chapter.

Yet if Malinowski to some extent parallels the work of the later Wittgenstein, which we'll go on to examine in subsequent chapters, it is in the work of A. R. Radcliffe-Brown that the most intriguing parallels between 'early' Wittgenstein and early anthropological cultures of context emerge. Radcliffe-Brown's vision of social structure as context bore striking resemblance to Wittgenstein's treatment of logical form in the *Tractatus*. For both men, understanding required grasping not just isolated elements but the formal relations between them – whether those elements were social institutions or logical propositions.

These complex overlaps and parallels become particularly clear when we examine the publication of three major works in 1922: Wittgenstein's *Tractatus*, Malinowski's *Argonauts of the Western Pacific*, and Radcliffe-Brown's *The Andaman Islanders*. Each, in its own way, wrestled with questions of how context shapes meaning, though they arrived at strikingly different answers. While Malinowski's approach to context remained largely unsystematic – focused on rich description of lived experience in a relatively formless fashion – Radcliffe-Brown developed a formal theory of social structure that echoed in many ways the philosophical thinking about logic we have just encountered in the *Tractatus*. It did so, I suggest, because it emerged from the same culture of context from which did the *Tractatus*.

The Cambridge School

The roots of these parallel developments in thinking about context may be traceable to an even earlier connection between Wittgenstein and anthropology than that of *The Meaning of Meaning*. Whilst at Trinity in

1912, Wittgenstein briefly came under the influence of Charles S. Myers, who, like Radcliffe-Brown, was a fellow in moral sciences at Trinity College (McGuinness 1988: 125–126; Monk 1991: 49–50). Whilst initially trained as a physician, Myers went on to study psychology with W. H. R. Rivers as the latter was developing the pioneering approaches to anthropological methods we discuss below (Langham 1981; North 1999: 44–45). Not only had Myers been a participant in the fabled Torres Straits expedition led by Alfred Haddon, but he very nearly took Rivers's place on it (Stocking 1983: 108–109). By 1912, he had become interested in cultural variation in perceptions of rhythm and tone, partly thanks to musical material he had gathered on the Torres expedition. Accordingly, he seems to have recruited Wittgenstein and David Pinsent as a subjects and assistants in a series of experiments throughout 1912–1913 that aimed to investigate differences in the ways in which people hear stress on musical notes (see Guter 2020).

Though Wittgenstein would make some reference to these experiments in much later lectures on the philosophy of psychology (see e.g. AWL), and though, as we will see, he would regularly draw parallels between music and logic in his work (McGuinness 1988: 127), what is really worth noting about this encounter is that it would have brought Wittgenstein into the orbit of a man who was at that very moment collaborating – with Rivers, Haddon, and Malinowski's later sponsor C. G. Seligman – on the seminal fourth edition of *Notes and Queries on Anthropology* (North 1999: 44–45; Stocking 1995: 121–122; Urry 1972). This was a methodological treatise that anticipated much of what Malinowski would later claim for himself in the way of innovation, including a central focus on context and contextualization (Langham 1981; Stocking 1983: 89–93; Urry 1972).

Notes and Queries was originally developed by the social evolutionist E. B. Tylor as a handbook to aid *Travellers and Residents in Uncivilized Lands* in the process of collecting and systematizing information they could then send back to 'armchair' anthropologists in Britain.

The Gods of Context

Structured largely in accord with Tylor's categorizations of societies in his *Primitive Culture* (Stocking 1995: 85), *Notes and Queries* accompanied Haddon on his first expedition to the Torres Straits in 1888, alongside a similar questionnaire printed by Sir James Frazer (Stocking 1995: 100). Both these bits of methodological toolkit were primarily focused on eliciting answers to standardized questions that had been developed to fit evolutionary theoretical assumptions, and so not very much concerned with context at all.

That first expedition to the Torres Straits already established Haddon as an unusual mixture, for the time, of observer and trained scientist. He had studied natural sciences at Cambridge and the putative purpose of his first visit to the Torres Straits was to recreate the kind of wide-ranging biological and zoological study Darwin had carried out on his voyage on the *Beagle*. As it transpired though, he returned with a rich array of ethnographic material, which he published according to the form prescribed in the early versions of *Notes and Queries*. Over the next decade, together with Rivers, Haddon was instrumental in establishing anthropology as a discipline at Cambridge, and by 1898 had accumulated the funds and personnel – including Rivers, Myers, and Seligman – for a new Torres Straits expedition.

Although, as Stocking describes, the Cambridge Torres Straits expedition was still a far cry in many ways from modern anthropological fieldwork (1995: 111), and, of course, it was not the only example of anthropological fieldwork from this period (see Stocking 1983 for a survey), it was instrumental in the development of anthropological ideas about contextualization in a number of ways. Most obviously, it was so in heralding what would become a dominant concern on the part of its protagonists and those they influenced for 'concrete' and 'intensive' field study, a concern exemplified by the fourth edition of *Notes and Queries* they were editing whilst Wittgenstein was working with Myers. Indeed, as well as sections from *Notes and Queries*, Wittgenstein is likely to have read some of Myers's contributions on 'primitive music' to the ethnographic publications that resulted from the expedition and heard a paper Myers delivered to the Moral Sciences Club at Cambridge (McGuinness 1988: 127).

Langham calls the fourth edition of *Notes and Queries* 'the first clear statement of what later came to be identified as the procedural and theoretical basis of British Social Anthropology' (Langham 1981: 327), and it is obvious that both Malinowski and Radcliffe-Brown were products of the 'school' that emerged from the Torres Straits expedition and its methodological advances. Stocking shows how the fourth edition was in many ways 'a programmatic systematisation of the ethnographic experience of the Cambridge School' (1995: 121), particularly the experience of Rivers. During the Torres expedition, Rivers developed what he called the 'genealogical method', a way of eliciting kin and affinal relationships between ethnographic subjects that would later become fundamental to structural-functionalist anthropology. The method was perceived to be a significant innovation because it approached abstract problems such as social organization by means of concrete, contextualized facts such as how one person was related to another, and also because over time Rivers came to believe, and enshrined in *Notes and Queries*, that a whole gamut of sociological data could be appended to people's positions on a genealogical grid, which, taken together would reveal 'laws regulating the lives of the people which they have probably never formulated themselves' (Stocking 1983: 86–88).

More broadly, Rivers's endorsement of what he called 'intensive study' was shot through with a concern for contextualization: he insisted on the use of 'native terms' wherever there was a possibility of mistranslation, a possibility the consciousness of which was itself comparatively novel; he emphasized the importance of observing rituals and events first-hand, rather than only working on the basis of reports; and – with a holism Malinowski would later echo – he cautioned against specialization in particular subsets of ethnographic data, given that '[i]n

The Gods of Context

a "rude" culture, the domains civilized men designated as politics, religion, education, art, and technology were interdependent and inseparable' (Stocking 1995: 123). Rivers was not the only contextualizer either: R. R. Marett, writing in the *Notes* on religion, for example, argued that a ritual must be '"taken in its concrete entirety" amid "the whole complex of conditions" in which it is performed and experienced' (North 1999: 45; Stocking 1983: 91).

But perhaps Rivers encapsulated the contextualizing spirit of the Cambridge School best in a separate piece from 1913, where he wrote:

> The essence of intensive work ... is limitation in extent combined with intensity and thoroughness. A typical piece of intensive work is one in which the worker lives for a year or so among a community ... and studies every detail of their life and culture; in which he comes to know every member of the community personally; in which he is not content with generalized information, but studies every feature of life and custom in concrete detail and by means of the vernacular language... It is only by such work that it is possible to discover the incomplete and even misleading character of much of the vast mass of survey work which forms the existing material of anthropology. (Quoted in Kuper 1973: 7)

This is a far cry from the *Notes and Queries* Tylor had designed, and, as Stocking points out, what Rivers was advocating in 1913 and earlier 'was just what Malinowski did in the Trobriands' a few years later (1983: 97; and see Young 2004: 334–335 on Malinowski's use of *Notes and Queries* in the field).

The Cambridge School, in other words, represents a distinct culture of context – one that saw scientific observation and logical structure as naturally complementary. And the wider culture of contextualism in which the School emerged shaped both Radcliffe-Brown's (and, in a different way, Malinowski's) anthropology, as well as Wittgenstein's early thinking about logical context. Rivers's emphasis on 'concrete method' and systematic tabulation exemplifies this distinctive approach in many ways: context was something to be methodically observed and logically structured.

One of the first things Malinowski did upon reaching London in 1910 was to travel to visit Rivers and Haddon in Cambridge (Young 2004: 165), and on that visit, or if not, shortly thereafter at the London School of Economics (LSE), Malinowski would have encountered A. R. 'Anarchy' Brown, a Fellow at Trinity and another rising star trained in the mould of the Cambridge School.

Radcliffe-Brown had arrived at Trinity as an undergraduate in 1901 and read moral sciences under Haddon, Myers, and Rivers. After a research expedition to the Andaman Islands in 1906, he won a fellowship despite having acquired an eccentric reputation in college, as one of his contemporaries described:

Brown, Anarchy Brown, as he was often called, for he had been a declared Anarchist, had a peculiar reputation at Trinity. In spite of his having passed all examinations with distinction and being a Scholar and Fellow of the college, there were many of the erudite who looked on him with suspicion. He was too dramatic a personality to fit easily into the conservative life of a college. (Grant Watson 1946: 84–85, cited in Kuper 1973: 39)

Given the obvious parallels with Wittgenstein's personality and own later reputation for peculiarity at Trinity – not to mention their mutual connection through Myers – one imagines their meeting would have produced an interesting encounter. There is no evidence either way as to whether or not they did meet, but Radcliffe-Brown's absence on fieldwork in Australia for much of Wittgenstein's pre-war years at Trinity may have deprived them of the opportunity.

The Andaman Islanders, based on the research Radcliffe-Brown carried out between 1906 and 1908, was published the same year as *Argonauts* (and the *Tractatus*), by which time Radcliffe-Brown was at the University of Cape Town, having spent, just like Wittgenstein, a brief and unhappy period as a schoolmaster. Though *The Andaman*

The Gods of Context

Islanders languishes in comparative obscurity relative to *Argonauts*, its more famous cousin, it is in some ways an even more instructive example of the ways in which contextual formalism was emerging as the key device of modern anthropology.[1]

In a passage that echoes famous remarks on 'imponderabilia' in the Introduction to *Argonauts*, despite both authors' private problems with fieldwork, Radcliffe-Brown declares that,

> Living, as he must, in daily contact with the people he is studying, the field ethnologist comes gradually to 'understand' them, if we may use the term. He acquires a series of multitudinous impressions, each slight and often vague, that guide him in his dealings with them... This general impression it is impossible to analyse, and so to record and convey to others. Yet it may be of the greatest service when it comes to interpreting the beliefs and practices of a primitive society. (1964 [1922]: 230–231)

In Radcliffe-Brown's case, the commitment to contextualization in the book emerged as well thanks to the influence of Émile Durkheim, to whose views on the importance of social context he became converted after having carried out the actual research. As Kuper notes, it was 'the view that meaning and purpose of customs should be understood in their contemporary context ... that he set out to demonstrate' (1973: 43), and as Michael North describes, *The Andaman Islanders* displays 'the massively difficult anthropological practice of translating [cultural phenomena] by recreating around them, like a Potemkin village, a simulacrum of their original context' (1999: 46). Indeed, one of the things that is notable about *The Andaman Islanders* is that, alongside *Argonauts*, it is one of the first examples of monographic form in anthropology, that is, of a fusion of description and interpretation (Boon 1983; Strathern 1987a). More so than *Argonauts*, if anything, it is context that is both the material described and at the same time the answer to what that material means.

The Cambridge School

North provides the best exegesis of this facet of *The Andaman Islanders*:

> At first glance, there seems to be an agreement between the point of view of the field anthropologist and that of the Andaman Islanders so complete as to be a little suspicious. Just as field anthropology finds meaning in the contextual relationships of social practices and derives its authority from the observance of them, Andaman society finds meaning in social cohesion itself and bases its religion on propitiation of 'that power on the interaction of the different manifestations of which the well-being of the society depends'. (1999: 47)

In other words, context not only explains Andaman society, it is their God.

On the other hand, as North points out,

> there is also a very great difference between the point of view of the anthropologist and that of his subjects, because they cannot possibly know, as he does, that context is their god... In fact, they pursue the very form of anthropology that *The Andaman Islanders* is meant to dethrone forever, the simple collection of uncoordinated facts. Like the anthropologist who studies 'one isolated custom' after another, the Andamans 'regard each little story as independent, and do not consciously compare one with another. (1999: 47–48)

Though Radcliffe-Brown's views and ways of expounding them would develop over the course of his life, in this contrast between ethnographic subjects for whom context is god, and the anthropologist whose ability to see context where his interlocutors do not makes him godlike, we already have the germ of something that both connects and differentiates early anthropological ideas about context from those of Wittgenstein. As we'll see, Radcliffe-Brown's structural-functionalism contains a number of elements that resemble the Russellian views on logic that we have met in the *Tractatus* – indeed both Radcliffe-Brown

71

The Gods of Context

and some of his disciples made use of formal logical notation – and there is good evidence to suggest that Russell (and his collaborator, Alfred North Whitehead) had a very direct influence on Radcliffe-Brown's thinking, even if evidence of their interaction while at Trinity together remains frustratingly sparse (Singer 1984). But, as we've already seen, whilst Russellian views on logic may be the foundation of the *Tractatus*, they are also an object of its critique. Wittgenstein's contextualism, unlike that of Radcliffe-Brown, is not self-excepting, and we are supposed to read the *Tractatus* as nonsense to the extent to which it purports to take an external, godlike view of the relationship between logic and the world. In this respect, we can already begin to imagine the ways in which, for later generations of anthropologists, including plenty today, Wittgenstein will feel like closer kin than some of their own disciplinary ancestors. Wittgenstein's formalism contains the seeds of its own undoing. Radcliffe-Brown's would be undone by others.

The Logic of Context

Despite this important difference, it's in Radcliffe-Brown's work that we see the clearest anthropological parallel to Wittgenstein's treatment of logic as context. Writing at the same time, from a similar intellectual context, and indeed at times from the very same place (Trinity, Cambridge), both men sought to understand how formal relations between elements – whether social institutions or logical propositions – create frameworks of meaning.

It's sometimes remarked that the school of anthropological thought with which Radcliffe-Brown is most closely associated, structural-functionalism, is a singular set of ideas that pulls in mutually opposed directions. On the one hand, it tends towards either a mechanical and/or tautological functionalist view of social phenomena as existing in order to perpetuate themselves; on the other it emphasizes a structural view of social

The Logic of Context

phenomena as logically interrelated according to specific patterns of form. This division is also sometimes reflected in commentary on the different approaches to certain social phenomena – such as, most famously, totemism (see Lévi-Strauss 1963) – that Radcliffe-Brown himself took, approaches which seemed sometimes to emphasize one pole and sometimes to emphasize the other. This was so much so that Claude Lévi-Strauss famously claimed Radcliffe-Brown's 'second' theory of totemism as an early version of Lévi-Strauss's own structuralist form of argumentation, precisely because it seemed to emphasize what Edmund Leach would call a 'mathematical-logical view of structure' over any purported function, and in place of organic or mechanical analogies.

Radcliffe-Brown himself seems to have seen no contradiction between the two emphases (see e.g. 1941), and in some ways both tendencies are worthy of exploration here. On the functional side, for example, whilst Radcliffe-Brown is sometimes caricatured as naively scientific in his search for social laws (which, as many critics have noted, yielded meagre results), both George Stocking and Matei Candea make clear, in different ways, how important were notions of 'meaning' and 'understanding' to Radcliffe-Brown's method (Candea 2018: 86–87; Stocking 1983: 329). As early as *The Andaman Islanders*, in fact, Radcliffe-Brown was effectively equating meaning with function (use) (e.g. 1922: 324), and, as Candea makes clear, this was in service of a contextualized sense of 'understanding' (2018: 87). While Radcliffe-Brown would later be accused by Leach (1961) of trying to turn anthropology into a kind of 'butterfly collecting' with his various typologies of different societies, such typologies were supposed to yield a kind of interpretation, a way of seeing the meaning/use of a certain social phenomenon in a particular context. We'll have much more to say about meaning and use when we come to later aspects of Wittgenstein's philosophy.

For present purposes, I want to focus more on the role of structure as context in Radcliffe-Brown's work, and particularly on its relationship to logic in Wittgenstein's. The concept of social structure (and the

The Gods of Context

related one of structural form) was crucial in systematizing the ways in which early anthropologists conceived of context, and they bear comparison with contemporary ideas in philosophy. They also form a significant contrast to the way in which context emerges in the work of Malinowski, though that too, as we'll find, may be productively compared with contextualization in Wittgenstein, and in some ways has had a far longer intellectual shelf life.

Milton Singer, an anthropologist who studied philosophy under Carnap at Chicago, has suggested that Radcliffe-Brown was, in fact, directly influenced by the views on logic of Russell and Whitehead (1984).[2] Singer unearthed a revised copy of Radcliffe-Brown's seminal *A Natural Science of Society* that contains extensive references to Russell; Fred Eggan, who was a student of Radcliffe-Brown's at Chicago, confirmed the latter's interest in contemporary philosophy and found the Russell connection highly plausible (and himself cited Whitehead as an influence on Radcliffe-Brown in his obituary for the latter); the anthropologist Max Gluckman and philosopher Dorothy Emmet, who both attended a series of lectures and seminars Radcliffe-Brown delivered in Manchester and Oxford in the late 1930s and early 1940s, both remember extensive discussions of Russell and Whitehead on Radcliffe-Brown's part; and M. N. Srinivas, a student of Radcliffe-Brown's at Oxford in the 1940s, recalls the latter speaking of the influence of both on his ideas (see Singer 1984: 69–85).

Exactly how far such influence stretched and whether it was a consequence of undergraduate exposure at Trinity or later reading we will likely never know and is not of particular concern to arguments here. What is hard to dispute is the presence of resemblances between this extremely influential early theorist of context in anthropology and the ideas about logic and logical structure to be found in the *Tractatus* and its antecedents.

The most obvious resemblance is to be found in the overt formalism of some of Radcliffe-Brown's ideas, a formalism by no means unique to him alone in the historical arc of anthropology but which he in many ways epitomizes and which marks one great gulf between him and Malinowski. For Radcliffe-Brown context is not, largely speaking, an amorphous background of sociological detail despite the remarks above about the impossibility of analysing general impressions; it is a structured set of systematic relations of behaviour and attitudes between people in formal roles, just as logic, for Russell, Whitehead, Frege, and at least to some extent Wittgenstein, is a set of structured relations between formal elements.

This resemblance is at its clearest perhaps in Radcliffe-Brown's distinction between social structure and structural form, famously made, among other places, in a letter to Lévi-Strauss (see also 1952: 192; and see Evans-Pritchard 1950: 122). A social structure is a system of actually existing relations between a given set of individuals. Structural form, on the other hand, is the particular morphology involved in that system. The form will (or may) persist despite changes in the composition of the set of individuals, and it may be visible across more than one social structure. 'Radcliffe-Brown's concept of "structural form"', as Singer argues, 'is, in other words, a specialized application of Russell's logico-mathematical concept of "the structure of a relation" as the class of all relations similar to the given relation' (Singer 1984: 32).

Another analogy would be one which Wittgenstein himself uses in the *Tractatus* in order to illustrate his own notion of pictorial form, an analogy one imagines him making at least partly in the light of Myers and his musical experiments: 'a gramophone record, the musical idea, the written notes, and the sound-waves, all stand to one another in the same internal relation of depicting that holds between language and the world. They are all constructed according to a common logical pattern' (*TLP* 4.014).

All this, together with his Durkheimianism, is what allowed Radcliffe-Brown to distinguish between his discipline and psychology: the particular motivations or personalities of people inhabiting social roles were unimportant to anthropology in comparison to the roles themselves. He himself made an analogy with chemistry and atoms (one does not need to know the internal structure of an atom to understand its relationship to other atoms 1957: 48–51) but in many ways the analogy with logic is happier: the purpose of formal logical notation (a, b, c, etc.) is to abstract the relations it describes from the specificities of mathematical number. The point of Russellian logical analysis 'is not the intrinsic nature of our terms, but the logical nature of their interrelations' (Russell 1971 [1919]: 59, cited in Singer 1984: 27).

That this is a happier analogy is evident from the fact that Radcliffe-Brown was a prominent early advocate of the use of logical notation in the analysis of kinship (e.g. 1930), and though his particular system was not the one eventually adopted as standard in the discipline, it very much resembles it.[3] In fact, the ways in which such forms of notation were seen as advantageous over particular linguistic kinship terminologies resembles in some ways Wittgenstein's views on the role of saying versus showing in logic, and both were directly inspired by logic and mathematics (see Wilson 2018): one could, and people did, try to 'say' such relations (as in 'f. bro' for father's brother, 'FBD' for father's brother's daughter), but logical notation allowed one to 'show' them, with – it was thought – less risk of importing misleading semantics.

The predilection for logical notation and formalism on the part of anthropologists of this period was perhaps taken furthest in the work of Siegfried Nadel. In further parallels with philosophical developments of this period, Nadel was Viennese, like Wittgenstein, and indeed studied first with Moritz Schlick, the founder of the Vienna Circle and a collaborator of Wittgenstein's, before moving to anthropology and studying with Malinowski at the LSE. Despite his training with Malinowski – who thought logical notation a bloodless abstraction – Nadel's work came to epitomize what would later be seen as the formalist excesses of Radcliffe-Brown's structural-functionalism. As Candea describes, his *Theory of Social Structure* (1957) is an attempt to devise anthropology's very own form of complex logical notation that would be capable of expressing the range of relationships and attributes of social roles, and be advantageous, just like the Russellian analysis we met in the last chapter, by 'making visible some entailments which would not have been discovered if the situation had merely been described in conventional language' (2022: 74).

Though such formalist extremes were criticized by other anthropologists at the time, even some of their critics could also see the value in the abstractions of logic. Edmund Leach, for example, derided Nadel's logic as 'mathematics', with the inverted commas (1976: 133), but famously went on to put forward his own version of anthropological algebra in a text we will return to later for its Wittgensteinian echoes, *Rethinking Anthropology*, justifying it, again in language that resembles Wittgenstein's saying versus showing distinction, with reference to the avoidance of the need for semantics:

I am not telling you to become mathematicians. All I am asking is: Don't start off your argument with a lot of value loaded concepts which prejudge the whole issue. The merit of putting a statement into an algebraic form is that one letter of the alphabet is as good or bad as any other. Put the same statement into concept language, with words like paternity and filiation stuck in the middle of it, and God help you! (1961: 17; see also Candea 2022; Corsin-Jimenez 2003).

Leach is also interesting in having read a logical formalism into Radcliffe-Brown from his very earliest work on the Andaman Islands. Whilst some, such as Kuper (1973: 43), have considered *The Andaman Islanders* a more or less mechanical and colourless application of Durkheim's views on function, Leach detects in it the same capacity for identifying patterns of structural form that we find very explicitly in Radcliffe-Brown's much later so-called second theory of totemism. Leach argues that 'the mathematical-logical' view of structure was present in Radcliffe-Brown's work from the beginning, rather than

The Gods of Context

appearing out of thin air in later life (1971), an argument that fits with the idea Radcliffe-Brown was influenced by Russell and Whitehead at Trinity, and in this view of structure we find further echoes of Wittgenstein.

The Durkheimian concern for function is very evident in *The Andaman Islanders*, for example in the sense of a concern with the ways in which 'myths and legends serve to express certain ways of thinking and feeling about the society and its relation to the world of nature, and thereby to maintain these ways of thought and feeling and pass them on to succeeding generations' (1922: 405). This is more or less what we have seen North referring to in suggesting that in this way 'context is god' both for the anthropologist and the Andaman Islanders themselves. This also marks the text as an early example of criticism of what Radcliffe-Brown (and others after him) calls Frazerian 'intellectualist' approaches to myth (1922: 233), which make belief, rather than practice, primary, and which we'll meet Wittgenstein making similar criticisms of in his 'Remarks' on Frazer's *Golden Bough*.

However, as he would continue to be for the remainder of his career, Radcliffe-Brown was also carefully interested in the particular details of how social life and the natural order were connected in such myths, and these particular details led to claims that were much less tautological than the thought that myths and rituals are simply instances of society worshipping itself.

For example, Radcliffe-Brown describes Andaman conceptions of the order of nature as being dominated by the same forces as those of social life: solidarity or opposition, where the former leads to benefit and happiness and the latter to disintegration. So, his account is not merely of Andaman Island society finding ways to value social cohesion and its own continuance, but also of the ways in which it 'projects' its view of the social order into the natural world. Yet it also does the reverse, 'naturalizing' certain structural forms, most famously the so-called 'calendar of scents', in which the female life cycle and associated ritual

The Logic of Context

processes mirror successive seasons of distinct floral blossoming and associated odours (1922: 311–312). In other words, relations in nature are analogized with relations in society, just as they will be in Radcliffe-Brown's second theory of totemism, in which, as Lévi-Strauss will put it, animals are good to think, not just to eat (1963).

The interest for our purposes of such ideas is the way in which they suggest that the structural form (to use Radcliffe-Brown's later terminology) of social relations mirrors the structural form of the world. As we've seen in the last chapter and above, Wittgenstein's tractarian notion of 'pictorial form' is based precisely on the idea that the structural relationships between the elements of a picture/language mirror the structural relationships between elements of reality. Indeed, the very language of 'projection' Radcliffe-Brown uses echoes Wittgenstein's characterization of the 'projective relation' between logic and the world in the *Tractatus*.

All of this is to say that whilst North, Kuper, and others are quite right to identify *The Andaman Islanders* as vitally concerned with context and indeed formatively so in anthropology, and thus in that sense already of relevance to our focus, the book – and Radcliffe-Brown's work more widely – is concerned with context in a more than straightforwardly Durkheimian functionalist sense. What I've been trying to show is that for Radcliffe-Brown, context is structured in a manner directly comparable to the ways in which logic is structured for Wittgenstein and the philosophers from whom Wittgenstein learnt the most. This is true in the sense that when Radcliffe-Brown and later structural-functionalists contextualize they do so structurally – by putting behaviour, ideas, and people within a set of logical relations; thus the idea that formal relations between variable elements are what reveal the meaning of phenomena is in this way at the heart of both early Wittgenstein and early anthropology. It is also true in the more complex sense that the key structural-functionalist notion of structural form in many ways resembles the Wittgensteinian concept of pictorial form in being a kind of morphology, an abstraction from any particular set of relations between elements in order to isolate the form of relation itself.

Singer raises some of these issues to highlight the ways in which Radcliffe-Brown was to some extent a 'structuralist' *avant la lettre*. As we've seen, Lévi-Strauss made a similar point in his reading of Radcliffe-Brown's views on totemism. But to ask these questions solely in terms of the relation between structural-functionalism and structuralism is to obscure the wider culture of context of which both form a part (and see Pettit 1972 for a discussion of Wittgenstein and structuralism).

Indeed, my point is not so much about Radcliffe-Brown and Wittgenstein in particular as it is to illustrate that their contextualizing itself shares a context. Others, such as D'Arcy Thompson (see e.g. 1917), who emerge from the same context as Wittgenstein and Radcliffe-Brown, are similarly concerned with morphology, and will go on to influence the morphology of structuralism, as we'll see in Chapters 3 and 4.

Moreover, as I suggested earlier on, there is at least one striking difference between Radcliffe-Brown's and Wittgenstein's views on the structure of context, and that is that while we know the problem of how the observer of such structural context would themselves be subject to it in some form preoccupied Wittgenstein, this reflexivity is largely absent from Radcliffe-Brown, as one might expect from the committedly empiricist author of *A Natural Science of Society*.

There is a hint of such considerations in Radcliffe-Brown's views on what Candea calls, following Richard Handler, 'the problem of units' (Candea 2018; Handler 2009): despite Radcliffe-Brown's reputation for scientific realism, he expressed concern about the issue of what might or might not 'count' as a society, a context, suggesting in some places that a simple relation between two people might be sufficient, and elsewhere wondering, 'Is the British Empire a society, or a collection of societies?' (1940: 4–5, cited in Candea 2018: 36). This question of what he also calls the 'continuity' of social relations and their endless spread in some ways echoes the problem of tractarian solipsism raised in the last chapter – what is the 'unit' of context: the individual? A wider network of individuals? Or is there one 'continuous' context?

The question of reflexivity, and of the author/observer's own contextualization, is also of significant relevance to Malinowski, the man perhaps most responsible for anthropology's character as the contextualizing discipline *par excellence*. But if Radcliffe-Brown's formal approach to context echoed the *Tractatus* in some important respects, Malinowski's more fluid vision anticipated aspects of Wittgenstein's later work. The contrast will help us understand both changes in anthropological thinking about context and their complex relationship to developments in Wittgenstein's philosophy.

A Spirit of Life and Growth

The status of Malinowski and his *Argonauts of the Western Pacific* as 'charter-myths' for modern social anthropology is so well-established it requires little rehearsal, nor does the fact that much of this mythical status turns on Malinowski's foundation of 'the ethnographic method' and its capacity for contextualization (Firth 1957; Leach 1966; Kuper 1973; Stocking 1983, 1995; Strathern 1987a; Young 2004). What also requires little rehearsal is the fact that the myth in question bears only a passing relation to history.

Here is the irreverent summary of the Malinowski myth in its original form that Adam Kuper provided barely a half-century after *Argonauts* was published:

Malinowski, a brilliant young Polish student, becomes ill when on the point of entering a professional career in science... He is told he is too ill to continue his scientific research. In despair he decides to divert himself with an English classic, chooses *The Golden Bough*, and is at once bound in the service of Frazerian anthropology. In due course he sets off for England . . . and becomes a student at the LSE. After precociously solving the problems of Australian aboriginal family organization he finds himself in Australia with an anthropological mission when the First World War erupts. He is an Austrian citizen, an enemy alien, and may be interned. Fortunately he is permitted to spend his internment in the Trobriand islands. There he passes the war inventing intensive fieldwork by participant observation, working through the vernacular, and living as one of the people in total isolation from European contacts. After the war he returns to England, and in the face of pigheaded opposition from reactionary evolutionists and mad diffusionists he builds up a group of dedicated disciples who go forth etc. etc. (1973 [1983]: 10).

Very much unlike young Wittgenstein, in other words, Malinowski was quite happy to contextualize his work in his own biography, albeit usually in a manner that would prove advantageous to his career and his vision for his discipline (Leach 1966). The oft-heard description of Malinowski's narrative of himself as a 'charter-myth' for anthropology is a sly wink at one of Malinowski's own arguments about the ways in which social institutions often validate themselves on the basis of a myth of origin (e.g. Stocking 1983: 109–110), and hence itself a form of contextualization, reflexively performed by anthropologists upon themselves.

We know Wittgenstein read at least one text containing an essay by Malinowski, Ogden and Richards's *The Meaning of Meaning*. Malinowski's biographer Michael Young is of the view that his subject, on the other hand, never met nor read Wittgenstein (2004: 49), a view we have no reason to reject. However, as we've already seen, the biographical and intellectual overlap between the two men is substantial, and in noting the absence of direct influence Young like many others is also making the point that this absence is somewhat remarkable given the similarity of some aspects of their thought.

Ernest Gellner sketches out the major lines of biographical overlap, advancing a book-length argument to the effect that both men's views were products of what he calls 'the Habsburg dilemma', the tension between the rootless cosmopolitanism of elite Vienna and the romanticized ethnic communitarianism of Imperial hinterlands (1998). Both, of course, were also émigrés to Britain, with Wittgenstein arriving only a few years before Malinowski, and both remained somewhat exotic figures in British society for the rest of their lives.

There are also a number of clear overlaps in intellectual influence, perhaps unsurprisingly given that Malinowski first studied philosophy. Leach, in a survey of epistemological influences on Malinowski, awards primacy to the pragmatism of William James (1957: 121), and Young too notes the influence of James on Malinowski (2004: 82–85).[4]

American pragmatism was also a significant influence not only on Wittgenstein but on the wider philosophical set of approaches within which context became important, including J. L. Austin and Ordinary Language Philosophy. Indeed, Cheryl Misak has recently made a set of strong claims regarding the fact that the shift in Wittgenstein's views from the *Tractatus* to the *Philosophical Investigations* can be attributed in no small part to his readings in pragmatism under the influence of his friend Frank Ramsey, whom we met briefly in the last chapter as the first translator of the *Tractatus* and will meet again in the next (2016). Similarly, a recent – and so far the only – intellectual biography of Austin by M. W. Rowe describes pragmatism as having had a profoundly formative effect on Austin's ideas on language and use (2023: 118–122). Though this is not the place to advance this case, it is perhaps in pragmatism that we find an apical ancestor of the concern for context in a number of different disciplines in the twentieth century.

Gellner is sceptical of the primacy of influence on Malinowski Leach attributes to pragmatism, arguing that the philosophy of Ernst Mach is likely to have been more formative (1998: 129 see also Young 2004: 85), though the two are hardly mutually exclusive positions given that James and Mach met, read, and were influenced by one another, and Peirce certainly read Mach (see e.g. Banks 2014; Holton 1992).

The Gods of Context

Mach was undoubtedly a very significant influence on Malinowski in his early studies, as a number of sources make clear (Staley 2023; Thornton 1985; Young 2004: 82–88), and he was so in a number of ways, not least on Malinowski's empiricism and also on his holistic approach to phenomena. Malinowski's dissertation was an intervention in Machian epistemology, and Young argues that Malinowski took from Mach the idea that 'functional relations between things, not phenomena in themselves, constituted the proper study of science' (2004: 87). That will echo with some of the preceding discussion of the importance of 'mathematico-logical relations', and indeed Mach was also something of an influence on Wittgenstein.[5]

The other major influence on Malinowski, foreshadowed in the version of his myth we heard from Kuper, is Sir James Frazer and his *Golden Bough*. Young reports Frazer as Malinowski's preferred answer to the question of why he became an anthropologist (2004: 3), citing the story Malinowski told in his 1925 Frazer Lecture at the University of Liverpool, of being too ill to continue with his philosophical studies, and seizing on *The Golden Bough* as entertainment and subsequent conversion to the ideas of the man Malinowski acknowledged in the same lecture as his 'master' (1948). The particular relation between Frazer, Malinowski, and Wittgenstein is one we'll explore further both in this chapter and the next, given the importance of Wittgenstein's 'Remarks' on *The Golden Bough* for later generations of anthropologists.

The relationship is complex enough even as far as Frazer and Malinowski go. Despite what Young describes as Malinowski's 'quasi-filial' relationship with Frazer (at least after the former's return to England in 1920; before this, they seem to have only met once, shortly after Malinowski came to London in 1910), almost as soon as Malinowski set foot on anthropological territory, he began to attack Frazer's ideas. This shouldn't surprise us too much, given that Malinowski was trained by the same sort of men and in the same sort of views as Radcliffe-Brown – Haddon introduced him to Seligman, under whom he worked at the LSE, and the thoroughgoing empiricism he had learnt from Mach and others would have found a welcome home in the environment of anthropology of the time, suffused as it was by the new excitement over Rivers's 'concrete methods'. Malinowski's early publications before his fieldwork are all devastating critiques of Frazer's positions on questions of religion and kinship, some from a fairly Durkheimian position, concerned with contextualizing instead of abstracting social institutions like the family (Stocking 1995: 248–250; Young 2004: 227–233). Durkheimian collectivism could not long survive Malinowski's basic methodological individualism, and he soon abandoned it (Leach 1957: 127; Young 2004: 237–240), but the concern with context would never disappear.

A great deal has been written about the vagaries of Malinowski's Trobriand fieldwork – sponsored by Seligman – that produced *Argonauts*, as well as about the relationship of the monographic text to Malinowski's posthumously published private fieldwork diaries (1967). The diaries certainly reveal the struggles Malinowski faced in dealing with the problem of reflexivity we met in the case of Radcliffe-Brown, and his failures – to put it mildly – in overcoming such problems. He was clearly aware of them, however, even somewhat self-servingly noting in *Argonauts* the ways in which his 'slavonic nature' was 'more naturally savage than that of Western Europeans', thus leaving him better placed to understand life in the Trobriands (1922: 21). Clifford Geertz, whom we'll meet in more depth later, has characterized the entirety of Malinowski's oeuvre as an oscillation between 'High Romance' and 'High Science' (1988: 79), pointing to the ways in which Malinowski seems to alternate between insisting on the contextualized nature of all social phenomena and on the need for the anthropologist to de-contextualize such phenomena in order fully to understand them. On the latter side, he quotes a passage from Malinowski's brilliant early essay on 'Baloma', the Trobriand matrilineal spirits, in which Malinowski demands that we see the 'facts' of fieldwork '*sub specie aeternitatis*', echoing exactly Wittgenstein's characterization of the mystical ability

The Gods of Context

to see the world as a limited whole, only seemingly without a sense of the difficulty of this enterprise (1988: 81).

A great deal has also been written about *Argonauts* itself. Within that, a substantial sub-genre of writing exists on the relationship between Malinowski and Frazer the book exhibits (e.g. Boon 1983; Leach 1966; Stocking 1983; Strathern 1987a), beyond the laudatory preface Frazer wrote for it. This is unsurprising given that *Argonauts*'s reputation rests in no small part on a mythical contrast between it and *The Golden Bough*, one that turns largely on the question of context. For that reason, and because we will meet *The Golden Bough* again in Wittgenstein's notes on it, it is helpful to rehearse some of this contrast as it bears on the emergence of contextualization as the defining characteristic of modern anthropology and Malinowski's particular version of it.

Frazer, as numerous historians of anthropology and his own biographer have noted, is an embarrassment to the discipline. By 1890, he had said virtually everything of note he would ever say as regards anthropology, and for the next fifty years, 'he simply went on repeating himself' (Leach 1966: 562). Whether his comparatively limited theorizations are attributed to the influence of Tylor (Stocking 1995) or W. Robertson Smith (Leach 1966), his ideas are rarely seen as original even when historicized (Strathern 1987a). By the period we have been concerned with in this chapter, most academic anthropologists had largely ceased to engage with his work despite its enormous *bien pensant* cachet in its time. Most damningly, as far as the modern discipline goes – and in contrast to the Cambridge School that influenced Radcliffe-Brown and Malinowski – he is the quintessential 'armchair anthropologist', the issuer of questionnaires to actual fieldworkers like Haddon, who rightly displace him when they turn out to be better anthropologists as well as better ethnographers. When William James met him in Rome and asked whether he had ever met a 'savage', Frazer is said to have responded, 'but heaven forbid!' (Stocking 1995: 148; Young 2004: 229). As the epitome of everything opposed to the modern anthropologist, his magnum opus, the thirteen-volume encyclopaedia that constitutes *The Golden Bough*, is usually thought of as the epitome of everything opposed to the modern monograph: an enormous compendium of ethnographic facts abstracted from their context by a man who knew nothing of such context and arbitrarily arranged in service of social evolutionism.

Argonauts, on the other hand, is built on contextualization. It begins with a famous series of methodological injunctions for carrying out proper fieldwork in order to understand social context: 'One of the first conditions of acceptable Ethnographic fieldwork certainly is that it should deal with the totality of all social, cultural and psychological aspects of the community, for they are so interwoven that not one can be understood without taking into consideration all the others' (1964 [1922]: xvi). However unlike his fieldwork, which may really have been to the myth Malinowski liked to paint of it, it was certainly inspired by the approach to 'concrete method' Rivers, Haddon, and Myers were detailing in the *Notes and Queries* while Wittgenstein was working with Myers. Moreover, it was undertaken with an unprecedented level of intensity, certainly far more successfully than was Radcliffe-Brown's Andaman sojourn: 'No professional anthropologist had ever before spent two full years studying a single tribal group, actually living in a native village and sharing the native way of life' (Leach 1966: 565).

As well as building on Rivers's 'genealogical method' by advocating for the 'charting' and systematization of a whole range of social phenomena (on the basis that they were interconnected), Malinowski also famously insisted on the need to attend to 'the imponderabilia of actual life' (1922: 20):

In working out the rules and regularities of native custom, and in obtaining a precise formula for them from the collection of data and native statements, we find that this very precision is foreign to real life, which never

The Gods of Context

adheres rigidly to any rules. It must be supplemented by the observation of the manner in which a given custom is carried out, or the behaviour of the natives in obeying the rules so exactly formulated by the ethnographer, of the very exceptions which in sociological phenomena almost always occur. (1922: 11)

Elsewhere, he put it like this:

We portray the wood after a fashion. It suits our sketchy methods well enough to represent it as a dead mass of colour. But we have not sought, so far, to render the subtle values of the individual trees. Yet only by doing so can we hope to do justice to the spirit of the wood, which is a spirit of life and growth (quoted in Kuper 1973: 18).

As Kuper notes sardonically, this is not 'a wood in which Frazer's sacred grove was likely to be hidden'.

As we have seen, on the other hand, there is every reason to be suspicious of the mythical narrative in which Malinowski revolutionizes anthropology by introducing fieldwork as a methodology and thus also by standing handmaiden to the birth of the modern discipline as one that shows how social phenomena make sense in relation to one another within a contextual frame. Before Malinowski, Haddon, Rivers, Seligman, Radcliffe-Brown, and others conducted fieldwork, albeit less intensively, and urged it on the discipline as a whole. Before Malinowski, Radcliffe-Brown under Durkheim's influence certainly, but also others such as Marett, as quoted earlier, were speaking of the importance of seeing rituals within 'their whole complex of conditions', and of interpreting 'social life as a whole'.

Yet the mythical contrast between *Argonauts* and *The Golden Bough* remains extraordinarily powerful in British social anthropology today. Speaking in her Frazer Lecture of 1986, and clearly cognizant of the critical historical scholarship on Malinowski, Marilyn Strathern suggested that in spite of that scholarship there are still good reasons to

A Spirit of Life and Growth

think of Malinowski as inaugurating the epoch of modernist anthropology, reasons that turn on the question of context. For Strathern, it is not the contextualizing theory of functionalism that makes Malinowski revolutionary, or the contextualizing practice of fieldwork. Rather, as for James Boon (1982), it is the organization and presentation of the text:

the importance of setting things in their social context came to be universally underlined in anthropology at large by the disparagement of Frazer's disregard for context, for the new ideas in question had acquired a double identity: the organising analytical ideas of the anthropologists were themselves contextualised by putting into *their* social context the indigenous ideas through which people organised their experiences. Contexts could be compared. (1987a: 259)

One of the key devices by which this is accomplished, she argues is 'the discovery of the ordinary in the bizarre, civilisation under savagery' (1987a: 260). 'Making sense', as she notes following Leach, was about making 'commonsense', just as Malinowski is clear that 'the field Ethnographer has seriously and soberly to cover the full extent of the phenomena in each aspect of tribal culture studied, making no difference between what is commonplace or drab, or ordinary, and what strikes him as astonishing and out-of-the-way' (1922: 11). We'll return to notions of 'the ordinary' and their connection to Wittgenstein in later chapters.

Despite this textual novelty, however, it is often remarked – including by Strathern (1987a: 259) – that Malinowski's rhetorical style in *Argonauts* is in many ways redolent of Frazer's. Malinowski himself acknowledged this debt in a letter to Frazer in 1917 in which he says that it is 'through the study of your works that I have come to realize the paramount importance of vividness and colour in descriptions of life' (Stocking 1983: 106). As Strathern notes in fact, to accuse Frazer of decontextualizing is only partially correct:

The Gods of Context

> Every instance is placed. Frazer faithfully ascribes particular customs to particular people. There is respect for these specific origins, as there would be in establishing the different authorship of classical or biblical manuscripts. But the effect of piling example upon example achieves the opposite. One has long since lost any sense of specificity about the Israelites, let alone distinctiveness about the Torres Straits or Melanesia. In fact, there is a counter-specificity in his demonstration of similarity. (1987a: 255)[6]

As the literary theorist Stanley Hyman has noted (1959), drawing on the ideas of Kenneth Burke – who, together with Wittgenstein, will later be a significant influence on Clifford Geertz – Frazer is the master of the 'scene/act ratio', the presentation of 'exotic but generically human experience within a vividly recreated landscape', a technique that Stocking and others have shown was also characteristic of Malinowski (North 1999: 51; Stocking 1983: 93; 104–110). *Argonauts* is full of imaginative and colourful dramatic descriptions of actions and their settings, so much so that Malinowski at one point begs the readers forgiveness: 'frequent references to the scenery have not been given only to enliven the narrative, or even to enable the reader to visualise the setting of the native customs. I have attempted to show how the scene of his actions appears actually to the native, to describe his impressions and feelings with regard to it' (1922: 298). Hence also the famously repeated instances of what Stocking calls 'the author/reader equation', in which the reader is placed not only amidst the 'native's' scenery, but amidst that of the ethnographer: 'Imagine yourself set down ...' etc,, etc.

In fact, it is this sort of Frazerian context – scenery, colour, and a broadly literary attempt to convey life as it is lived – that is characteristic of *Argonauts*, rather than the analytical, formal, comparative sense of context that Strathern invokes. Malinowski, in fact, hardly ever engaged in comparison.[7] He spent virtually his entire career writing about a single society, and his holism entailed a radical rejection of the Radcliffe-Brownian view that one might isolate parts of a society's structural form in order to compare them with parts from another society. This is somewhat ironic given that, as Kuper points out, his monographs focused on particular institutions in Trobriand society, and 'he never produced a single coherent statement of Trobriand "culture" as a whole'. Yet Kuper surely also hits on the explanation for this irony when he says,

Perhaps he could not, for despite his insistence upon interconnections he lacked the notion of a system. His monographs recall the spiritual, 'the toe bone is connected to the foot bone, The foot bone is connected to the ankle bone,' etc – very just, but not a theory of anatomy. (1973: 24)

Whilst later in life he may have regretted this certain absence of system and sought unsuccessfully to correct it – and perhaps more successfully to instil other approaches in his students – it is undoubtedly as characteristic of him and of what he means to anthropology as is his mythical status as the original contextualizer.[8] Even during his lifetime his barely theorized biological functionalism – in which social institutions served the (biological) needs of individuals – was thought naïve by his own students, had hardly any traceable impacts on the history of the discipline; and for what it was it gave him no theoretical tools with which to conceive of the form of context beyond Frazerian scenery. He had no equivalent of Radcliffe-Brown's 'structural form' (Gregory Bateson once despaired at being unable to find a single instance of the word 'logic' in *Coral Gardens*) and no picture of what context was, except what it *actually* was in the Trobriands. At one point in *Argonauts*, he notes the prevalence of ideas of 'custom' in any given society and the ways in which they compel obedience. Lest the reader infer any Durkheimian overtones of clearly identifiable social structure however, he quickly continues,

systems of social philosophy have been built to explain and interpret or misinterpret this general principle... most of these systems, especially those evoking the Phantom of Collective Soul are futile, to my mind, in so far as they try to explain in the terms of a hypothesis that which is most fundamental in sociology, and can therefore be reduced to nothing else, but

The Gods of Context

must be simply recognised and accepted as the basis of our science. (1964 [1922]: 327)

Context, in other words, is most definitely there, but the endeavour of trying to give it a single form or cause is a fool's errand. But alongside his linguistic pragmatism, this contextual antiformalism foreshadows significant facets of both later Wittgensteinian and later anthropological approaches to form and context, as we'll see.

Scenery and Austerity

So we have two seemingly very different forms of context to compare with that of Wittgenstein in two books that appear in the same year as the *Tractatus*. One, that in *The Andaman Islanders*, resembles, at least in some regards, the austere universe of logical relations between elements that populate the *Tractatus*. The other, that of *Argonauts*, seems far removed from this universe, instead a colourful but formless world of seafaring adventure in which an attempt is made to show not the morphology of a seashell but the 'subtle value of individual trees' in order to depict 'a spirit of life and growth'.

Malinowski's formless organicism is, of course, closer to later anthropological contextualism than the formalist logicism of Radcliffe-Brown. Indeed, the remainder of the story of this book is a story of the multiplication, collapse, and disintegration of form, both in anthropological contextualism and in Wittgenstein's philosophy. Somewhat ironically, if in this chapter we have seen the ways in which a certain kind of structural anthropology looks to some extent to have been influenced by early Wittgenstein or at least by some of early Wittgenstein's influences, when later Wittgenstein himself comes to adopt what he calls the '*ethnologische Betrachtungsweise*', or 'anthropological point of view', that point of view turns out to look much more like Malinowski's than Radcliffe-Brown's.

Part II

Language: Contexts in Question

THREE

A Gesture to Anthropology

> Once I wrote, 'a proposition is laid against reality like a ruler...' I now prefer to say that a *system of propositions* is laid against reality like a ruler.
> – WVC 64

In the last two chapters, we saw some of the close parallels that exist between Wittgenstein's early work and the development of British social anthropology. In particular, we saw how a definite and particular vision of the importance of context emerged as crucial to both, as indeed it did in a number of other areas of intellectual life in this period of what Peter Burke calls a 'contextual turn' (2002). In the cases of Wittgenstein and (a significant strand, though by no means all of) anthropology, this vision of context was highly structured, logical, and formalist in character. The parameters, shape, and character of context were clear.

Beginning from this part, the remainder of this book is in many ways the story of the disintegration of this clarity about context, and the disappearance of its formal, structured character in both Wittgenstein's philosophy and in anthropology, as well as the ways in which those disappearances related to one another.

This is not to say that context becomes less important to either Wittgenstein or anthropology – if anything, the reverse. But correlated with this increasing importance is a decreasing explicitness about what 'context' or its equivalent concepts actually mean. This begins with a

A Gesture to Anthropology

shift we'll see in this part of the book, from logic to language as a model of context, one tied into a broader linguistic turn in philosophy and the social sciences.

Tracing this disintegration of clarity in Wittgenstein's case in particular means coming to grips with a period of his life and work that – with the notable exception of the 'Remarks on Frazer' – is even more rarely engaged with by anthropologists than the *Tractatus* and has historically received less attention from philosophers than his more famous 'early' or 'late' periods. This is what we might call his 'transitional' period.[1]

Examining the character of Wittgenstein's philosophy in the early 1930s, by which point it clearly differed – in some respects – from the *Tractatus* but did not yet fully resemble – in all respects – the *Philosophical Investigations* is important. Doing so will show us the beginnings of the shift in conceptualization of context that will find their endpoint in Wittgenstein's later work, or what he sometimes called his 'anthropological perspective'. It will also show us the ways in which the nature of this shift parallels similar shifts in anthropology. It is not only that Wittgenstein's famous early and late philosophies resemble parts of the history of anthropology, in other words; it is also that what I will continue to call, for want of better terminology, his transition between the two resembles a historical anthropological transition as well. We will meet this anthropological transition in the next chapter.

A final good reason for examining this 'middle' or transitional period is that whilst it was happening Wittgenstein was reading anthropology. More specifically, and somewhat ironically given how much, as we will see, this version of Wittgenstein sounds like an anthropologist of today, he was reading the quintessential anthropologist of yesterday: Frazer.[2]

Frazer the Savage

Either in 1930 or 1931, Wittgenstein asked his student and friend Maurice Drury to get a copy of *The Golden Bough* for him out of the

Cambridge Union library, and Drury subsequently read a small portion of the first volume aloud to Wittgenstein.³ Beginning on June 19, 1931, Wittgenstein wrote a series of remarks on Frazer's material that ran to about ten pages. The version of these remarks that was eventually published in 1967 also contained a second set of notes, which Rush Rhees suggests was written separately, 'not earlier than 1936 and probably after 1948'. The 'Remarks' as a whole are famously critical of Frazer, particularly of his depiction of magic and ritual as being based on mistaken ideas about the nature of the world and cause and effect.

Unlike the *Tractatus*, Wittgenstein's major published work in his lifetime, these sparse and somewhat disjointed comments have received a large amount of anthropological attention. Mary Douglas discussed them in her assessment of Frazer (1978); Rodney Needham cited them frequently and devoted a chapter of his book *Exemplars* to them (1985); Stanley Tambiah draws on them at some length in his 1984 Morgan Lectures, later published as *Magic, Science, Religion, and the Scope of Rationality* (1990); Thomas de Zengotita wrote an essay about them in *Cultural Anthropology* (1989); and more recently an entire book of essays has been published alongside a new translation of them (da Col and Palmié 2018).

With some exceptions (e.g. Palmié 2018), and somewhat ironically given the topic, there is sometimes a tendency in this commentary to take the 'Remarks on Frazer' out of context. Perhaps unsurprisingly, anthropologists have found Wittgenstein's critiques of Frazer highly congenial and to confirm their owns views of Frazer's work as impoverished and unsympathetic, and this, together with the 'reverential' approach towards the 'later' Wittgenstein that is sometimes adopted in the discipline (Laugier 2018a: 209), goes some way towards explaining the fact that sometimes the commentary on the 'Remarks' seems to proceed from the assumption that because they were written by the author of the *Philosophical Investigations*, they must contain comparable wisdom and that the proper task of the commentator is to correctly

A Gesture to Anthropology

interpret and distil that wisdom. This is despite the fact that, as Palmié notes, the 'Remarks' 'really are just that: disjointed notes, never meant for publication' (2018: 3), and despite the fact that they were written at a particular point – two quite separate particular points, in fact – in Wittgenstein's philosophical trajectory. The majority of the notes were written in the period we are concerned with in this chapter, not later, when Wittgenstein was more confirmed in the views that would later find expression in the *Philosophical Investigations*.[4]

A number of commentators do, however, note, even if only in passing, the anthropological context in which the remarks were written: de Zengotita, for example, points out the congruence between Wittgenstein's points about 'savage practicality' and Malinowski: 'The same savage who, apparently in order to kill his enemy, sticks his knife through a picture of him, really does build his hut out of wood and cuts his arrow with skill and not in effigy' (RFGB, 10). To treat magic as error, in other words, is (usually) to misunderstand its role in life, a suggestion anthropologists were more than capable of making themselves by this period, and that Edward Evans-Pritchard would make particularly forcefully just a few years after Wittgenstein wrote his remarks, as we'll see in the next chapter.

Then, of course, there is Wittgenstein's critique of Frazer's evolutionist explanations, which again would have likely appeared largely redundant to anthropologists of this period. Stephan Palmié captures the fact that there is nothing, in fact, very anthropologically novel in Wittgenstein's disagreements with Frazer when he says, 'Putting the matter bluntly, what had been the "persuasive fictions" (Strathern 1987a) of anthropology in, say 1900, had stopped being persuasive by the 1930s' (2018: 5). Indeed, we might even speculate that Wittgenstein himself had heard such critical views of Frazer expressed as far back as his time with Myers in the early 1910s; certainly this time spent around Myers (and the possibility that Wittgenstein later read Malinowski) is good reason to suppose that Wittgenstein was not reading Frazer in the belief that the *Golden Bough* represented cutting edge anthropological work, and indeed he may have known perfectly well that some of his 'Remarks' were quite in tune with what many anthropologists of his own time thought of Frazer. One doesn't, in fact, even need to be an anthropologist to see, as Wittgenstein did, that 'When the adoption of a child is carried out in a way that the mother pulls the child through her clothes, then is it not crazy to think that there is an *error*, and that she believes to have born the child?' (RFBG, 11). In other words, there is nothing particularly secret (or even very 'untimely and farsighted' – McGee 2023: 21–22) about the wisdom that some of Frazer's implied claims about what people believe about their magic are patently absurd.

Rather than focus on Wittgenstein's critiques of Frazer, here I want instead to draw out other points from them that relate to the wider set of arguments in this book. The first is the simple fact of the possibility of reading them as in some way reflective, anticipatory, and/or prophetic for developments in anthropology. What I mean by this is that rather than interpret such a possibility as evidence for Wittgenstein's brilliance in being able to see then what we in our own brilliance see now, it should instead lead us to ask how it is – both in the narrow sense of intellectual history and in the wider sense of 'family resemblances' between ideas – that such a possibility exists, and whether it is simply accidental that it does. We've already seen one set of connections in the form of Wittgenstein's early exposure to the Cambridge School of anthropology that suggests this possibility is less than accidental, and we'll encounter further such connections when we examine Wittgenstein's own later influence on anthropology. But crucially, and in an appropriately Wittgensteinian spirit, seeing such connections requires starting from the actual context in which the 'Remarks' were written, rather than from a presentism that takes this possibility as a happy accident rather than a matter of genuine historical relations.

This leads on to the second point that is worth drawing out from the 'Remarks'. It is entirely understandable that they are often interpreted by anthropologists in the light of the *Philosophical Investigations*. This is

A Gesture to Anthropology

understandable both because most of Wittgenstein's work is usually interpreted by anthropologists in the light of the *Philosophical Investigations* because the latter is the source of much of Wittgenstein's influence on the discipline (as well as being his most famous work) but also because the 'Remarks' themselves, like much that Wittgenstein wrote in this period, represent a transitional stage in Wittgenstein's trajectory. This is not so much between the *Tractatus* and the *Philosophical Investigations* (as in Severi 2018) as it is between what some call the 'calculus' conception that dominated his thought of the early 1930s, and the 'anthropological perspective' that he would describe as characterizing his later views.

Put simply, the 'Remarks' are not evidence for a single and overarching contextualism that dominates all of Wittgenstein's post-Tractarian views and explains his affinity for anthropology; rather, they are, like the other work described in this chapter and this book more broadly, evidence for the shifting and varied views on the form of context Wittgenstein adopted, views that were both influenced by and an influence upon anthropology at different times.

Out of the Ordinary

So, to put the 'Remarks' in their proper context means understanding how Wittgenstein's thought was shifting at the time in which they were written, perhaps partly through their writing, but certainly also under the influence of other factors.

The most orthodox interpretation of Wittgenstein's transitional period is that it began at some point shortly after his return to Cambridge in January 1929, a return marked by Keynes's memorable description: 'Well, God has arrived. I met him on the 5.15 train.'

Entirely predictably, Wittgenstein's career as a schoolteacher had been a short and disastrous failure for reasons it's briefly worth marking as they return us to an important biographical theme in Wittgenstein with significance for later arguments. As at many times in his life, he seems to have seized on teaching as a way of doing what Monk refers to as 'joining the ranks': escaping from the rarefied air of philosophy, or from his extraordinarily privileged background, to what he saw as a more 'real', and more ordinary life, of the kind he would later urge on many of his own students. But as on most of the occasions on which he tried it, this desire was frustrated by his basic incapacity to live the kind of life he viewed as 'ordinary': not only was he not, in a range of respects, a very 'ordinary' person, but he was also often very bad at interacting with people he thought of as 'ordinary'.

We've already met his contemptuous attitude to his fellow soldiers in the Austrian army, and to the inhabitants of Puchberg, one of the rural villages to which he insisted on being posted as a teacher. This attitude persisted at other such postings, and he was eventually forced to resign after physically assaulting a young boy who then collapsed. Charges of brutality were levelled against him (Monk 1991: 234), and though he was acquitted, the experience of having caused the boy's collapse, of the subsequent hearing, and of the humiliation of lying during the trial about how often he beat his young charges, set Wittgenstein firmly against the possibility of any future in the teaching profession.

These experiences didn't, however, at first persuade him to return to philosophy at Cambridge or to his home in Vienna. After resigning his last posting in April 1926, his initial move was to try to join a monastery, an outcome judiciously thwarted by a Father Superior whom Monk describes as 'obviously perceptive' as regards Wittgenstein's motivations and suitability for the calling. He was, though, employed for a few months as a gardener at the monastery, and this period seems to have given him sufficient strength to choose to return to his family in Vienna at the end of the summer.[5]

In Vienna, Wittgenstein took the first tentative steps towards a return to philosophy, prompted by his sister Gretl's suggestion that he meet Moritz Schlick, the founder of the Vienna Circle (and supervisor of

Siegfried Nadel). Schlick had already tried to arrange a meeting with Wittgenstein through Frank Ramsey in 1924 after reading the *Tractatus*, but hadn't succeeded, so he was delighted at the prospect when Gretl wrote to him in 1927. The initial meeting was a success, and though Wittgenstein couldn't be persuaded to attend the wider Circle itself, he did start to meet with a smaller and more select group, chosen by Schlick and instructed in advance, according to Rudolf Carnap, one of its members, 'to let Wittgenstein talk and then ask only very cautiously for the necessary elucidations' (Monk 1991: 242–244).

As we saw in Chapter 1, various members of the Circle had seen in aspects of the *Tractatus* – not least its apparent dismissal of metaphysics – a great treatise of logical positivism, their preferred philosophical approach. They were thus somewhat taken aback to find Wittgenstein quoting Indian poetry at them, and arriving at philosophical conclusions not by means of discussion and doubt but seemingly by intuition and inspiration. Despite this mismatch, his interactions with the Circle effected a reconciliation with Ramsey – with whom he had quarrelled in 1925 – and the resumption of contact with Keynes, who had been pressing him to return to Cambridge ever since his initial departure. After a short bout of illness over the winter, Wittgenstein returned to Cambridge and to full-time philosophy in late 1928.

As soon as he returned to Cambridge, Wittgenstein began to spend considerable periods of time in the company of two men, both of whom would have a significant influence on this transitional period in his thought.

The first was Ramsey, whom we've met as the original translator of the *Tractatus*, and an extraordinarily gifted undergraduate at King's College. Ramsey himself is a remarkable character, whose biography and astonishingly extensive impact on several different academic disciplines in a life prematurely cut short at the age of twenty-six have been brilliantly documented by Cheryl Misak (2020). Among other striking qualities, he seems to have been one of the few people in Wittgenstein's orbit so secure in himself and his own ideas and beliefs that he could comfortably discourse with Wittgenstein without being either browbeaten into discipleship or becoming tired enough with the latter's imperious style to end the friendship.

Equally comparatively unusual is the respect and esteem in which Wittgenstein seems to have held Ramsey despite describing him as a 'bourgeois thinker' (Monk 1991: 246). Indeed, there was a great deal of common-sense pragmatism about Ramsey that may well have struck the mystically inclined Wittgenstein as 'bourgeois', but Misak has made the case for his philosophical pragmatism being a substantial influence on Wittgenstein's transition (Misak 2016), a case worth noting in brief both for its explanation of the transition period under discussion and also because it returns us to the idea of pragmatism as an apical ancestor of sorts to the contextualism at issue in this book.

Ramsey had won a fellowship by the time of Wittgenstein's return and was put in the somewhat strange position of acting as Wittgenstein's PhD supervisor despite being twenty-five years old to Wittgenstein's forty. But this relationship was not to last. Wittgenstein's thesis – which was in fact the already published *Tractatus* – was submitted by June and passed by Russell and Moore as examiners in a farce of a viva that concluded with Wittgenstein patting them both on the shoulder and saying, 'Don't worry, I know you'll never understand it.' And, tragically, Ramsey was dead of an infectious disease by January 1930, with Wittgenstein at his hospital bedside. The strength of feeling Wittgenstein had for Ramsey is demonstrated by the rare privilege of his influence being acknowledged in several of the pieces of work Wittgenstein composed over the subsequent years, including in the posthumously published *Philosophical Investigations*.

The precise extent of this influence is the subject of some debate. Misak makes an extensive argument for the indirect influence of American pragmatism – particularly that of Peirce – on later Wittgenstein through Ramsey's interpretation of Peirce's work (2016).

A Gesture to Anthropology

Ramsey had read pragmatists like James, Lewis, and Santayana, as a student, and noted the relevance of Peirce's type-token distinction to the *Tractatus* in his review of the latter in 1923.[6] Misak's case for understanding much of Ramsey's own later philosophy as pragmatist in orientation is convincing. The idea that Ramsey's views had a significant effect on Wittgenstein also seems more than plausible, given Wittgenstein's own words on the matter of Ramsey's influence, though as those words were far from consistently positive about Ramsey's philosophy that effect seems likely to have been complex and multifaceted, rather than a simple question of cause and effect.

The second figure whom Wittgenstein came to know in this period was an Italian economist at Trinity named Piero Sraffa. Born in Turin and raised in an academic family, Sraffa was only a few years older than Ramsey when he met Wittgenstein, but his work in economics had already made a significant impression on leaders in his field such as Keynes. It was Keynes who invited Sraffa to come to Cambridge in 1927, when the political climate in Italy was making it an increasingly dangerous place to be friends with prominent socialists and critical of regime economic policy: Sraffa was close to Antonio Gramsci (sending him the materials with which to write his *Prison Notebooks* after his arrest), was a former co-editor of the prominent leftist journal *L'Ordine Nuovo*, and had also published critical articles in the press about the state of the Italian banking system. According to Sraffa's student Amartya Sen, Mussolini personally sent telegrams to Sraffa's father, the Rector of Bocconi University in Milan, demanding the retraction of these pieces.

The nature of Sraffa's influence on Wittgenstein's transition is in some sense much harder to specify than in Ramsey's case because it didn't emerge through conversation about technical philosophy. Unlike Ramsey, Sraffa was not an expert in mathematics or in logic, though he clearly spent a great deal of time with Wittgenstein in this period, and continued to do so until around 1946 (albeit with some breaks), discussing the latter's ideas. In another sense though, Sraffa's influence is easier to pinpoint because it has been condensed into an anecdote that has achieved mythical status among students of Wittgenstein's biography.

The anecdote is present in two forms in Norman Malcolm's touching memoir of his time as Wittgenstein's student and friend (Malcolm 1958: 69). Malcolm himself didn't meet Wittgenstein until 1938, so the story is told as one Wittgenstein himself recounted to Malcolm long after it happened. In the first and more famous form, in Malcolm's text, Sraffa and Wittgenstein are travelling together on a train and Wittgenstein is insisting – in accord with the argument in the *Tractatus* we have met – that propositions share a 'logical form' with the state of affairs they describe, in the sense that the elements of a picture relate to one another in the same way in which the elements they depict do. In response, Sraffa is supposed to have made the Neapolitan gesture in which the hand flicks outwards from under the chin, and asked, 'What is the logical form of that?'

A footnote in Malcolm's text retells the story from the recollections of another of Wittgenstein's students, G. H. von Wright, who arrived in Cambridge in 1939, and therefore is also recollecting Wittgenstein's own narration, rather than the event itself. In von Wright's version, the issue is 'grammar', rather than 'logical form', a distinction that speaks to the process of Wittgenstein's transition in this period, as we will see.

The anecdote has achieved mythical form partly because it seems neatly to condense the entirety of Wittgenstein's transition from the logical analysis of the *Tractatus* to the 'meaning is use' idea of the *Philosophical Investigations* in a few lines, and this chapter will outline the ways in which both the general moral of the story and its specific versions do indeed seem to capture much of the spirit of this shift. Another reason it has achieved mythical status is that, in addition to acknowledging a debt to Ramsey, the *Philosophical Investigations* begins

A Gesture to Anthropology

by noting that it is 'even more' indebted to Sraffa's criticism, and that it was to '*this* stimulus [to which it owed] the most consequential ideas of this book'. Particularly notable for our purposes is a remark along these lines Wittgenstein made to another student, Rush Rhees, in which he claimed to owe to Sraffa the 'anthropological' perspective on philosophical problems that he saw as characterizing his later work (Monk 1991: 261; and see Engelmann 2013; Gebauer 2017; Hacker 2013; Medina 2003; Munz 2017; Pichler 2018).[7]

In Between Pictures

The story of the transition from Wittgenstein's thinking in the *Tractatus* to that of his thinking in the *Philosophical Investigations* can be and has been told in a number of different ways, and as we've seen there's extensive disagreement even about the extent and nature of the transition itself. The way in which I relate it here is thus one amongst many such possible ways, but it's one that I think makes clearest the connection of this transitional period to the themes of this book, as well as laying the groundwork for an explanation of what Wittgenstein might have meant by an 'anthropological perspective'.

One simple form in which the transitional narrative often appears – a form in which we have seen it appear in some anthropological writing (e.g. Gellner 1998) – is as a straightforward shift away from the austere and representationalist metaphysics of the *Tractatus*. To this view, the early Wittgenstein held to a naïvely logical vision of language and meaning, such that he thought there were things called 'elementary' or 'atomic' propositions that represented basic bits of reality, and meaning was the correct alignment of such propositions with reality. To get to the *Philosophical Investigations*, all Wittgenstein had to do was abandon this set of presuppositions in favour of a contextualism in which meaning is not a matter of words representing reality but of their use in practice.

Though there are some echoes of truth in this picture of Wittgenstein's early philosophy, the *Tractatus* is far more complex than it is given credit for in this narrative, and ideas about context – understood in a certain sense – already play a role in it. Indeed, as I'll try to describe here, to understand Wittgenstein's transition it's crucial to understand the ways in which Wittgenstein's thinking about context shifted gradually – rather than in the abrupt fashion imagined in the simple story above – over the course of this period of his life. These shifts in how he understood context, I want to suggest, are in many ways at the heart of the wider shift in his philosophy. They will also have ramifications for the ways in which his later work – that inspired by his 'anthropological perspective' – is taken up in anthropology itself, as we'll see.

In the simple form of the transitional narrative, the key elements of the *Tractatus* that Wittgenstein abandons are its logical atomism and its metaphysical realism: that is, the idea that there are certain things in the world ('objects', 'states of affairs', etc.) and that logic and language function by correctly representing those things. But even if one accepts that the *Tractatus* is in some sense realist in its approach to facts in the world, the way in which it conceives of 'representation' is much more complicated than a simple view of correspondence between language and reality – the idea of shared 'logical form' refers instead to common structures of relations between propositions and facts, and this sharing of form is understood as an internal, rather than an external, relation (hence Wittgenstein's tendency to use the word 'projection').[8]

However one interprets the *Tractatus*, what is not in doubt is that already by July of 1929 Wittgenstein had abandoned the idea that 'atomic' or 'elementary' propositions are independent of one another, as we know from the single piece of philosophical writing he published after the *Tractatus*, a paper called 'Some Remarks on Logical Form', which he was due to give at the Joint Session of the Mind Association and the Aristotelian Society that year (Wittgenstein 1929). In that paper, he responds to some criticisms of the *Tractatus* aimed at it by Ramsey in the first published review of the work (1923).

Ramsey had pointed out, roughly speaking, that in the *Tractatus* Wittgenstein had claimed that the only kind of necessity and impossibility is logical necessity and impossibility, hence the idea of truth tables – the view that one can show or display the truth or falsity of combinations of independent atomic propositions. Atomic propositions must be independently true or false for it to be the case that the truth or falsity of their combination results only from their logical connection. Put another way, one doesn't need to know anything about elementary propositions P or Q to know that if both are true then the proposition 'P and Q' is also true: that is a logical necessity. If, on the other hand, there is something in the natures of P and Q that connects them and causes their truth or falsity to depend upon one another, then we have left the realm of logic and seemingly entered that of metaphysics or science.

At the same time though, Wittgenstein claims in the *Tractatus* that propositions such as 'this is both red and blue' are also impossible. He had tried to argue that they were logically impossible, and thus that propositions like 'this is red' cannot be atomic (independent) propositions – if they were, then there would be nothing logically impossible about combining them. Yet attempts at breaking down propositions like 'this is red' and 'this is blue' into component parts in the notational logic of the *Tractatus* fail: they yield absurdities like 'units' of redness in a manner that ought to allow one to ask 'which' unit is in question.

In 'Some Remarks on Logical Form', Wittgenstein changes his mind. Atomic propositions, or at least those of a certain form, he suggests, are dependent upon one another because the truth of one excludes the truth of others. This may sound simple – and obvious – but it is in fact crucial to the changing significance of context (broadly understood) in Wittgenstein's philosophy.

This dependence of propositions about colour upon one another is not a matter of metaphysics. Unsurprisingly, Wittgenstein is still unwilling to make his logic depend on something about the nature of the entities in question. Instead, the dependence is a matter of the propositions' relative existence in what he will start to call 'logical space', 'logical syntax', 'geometry', or – as in the second version of the Sraffa anecdote – 'grammar'.

Some hints of a concern with understanding the place of logical phenomena in a wider linguistic context are already present in, for example, the Tractarian critique of the Theory of Types discussed earlier. But abandoning the idea of the independence of atomic propositions will put this question centre stage. As Wittgenstein himself said in a conversation with members of the Vienna Circle in late 1929 and early 1930, 'What was wrong about my conception [in the *Tractatus*] was that I believed that the syntax of logical constants could be laid down without paying attention to the inner connection of propositions.' Or again, elsewhere, 'Once I wrote [in the *Tractatus*], "a proposition is laid against reality like a ruler..." I now prefer to say that a *system of propositions* is laid against reality like a ruler' (Monk 1991: 284–286).

The point can be illustrated with reference to Ramsey's issue with colour, an issue Wittgenstein himself continued to focus on. To say that a point in the visual landscape is red is also to 'say', as it were, that it is not any of the other possible hues it may have been. The 'space' or the 'grammar' of colour gives the claim a certain context: all the possible shades that point may have been. So, a proposition to the effect that it is one such hue is 'complete' in the sense that it is also (in some sense) a proposition to the effect that it is none of the others: 'If someone asks us "What is the temperature outside?" and we said "Eighty degrees", and now he were to ask us again, "Is it ninety degrees?" we should answer, "I told you it was eighty"...Thus, when asked, we say what the time is, and not also what it isn't.' (Wittgenstein 1929: 167).

When Wittgenstein calls these relations between possible uses of words 'inner connections' his claim is that such relations are internal, not external. The notion of 'internal relations' is here brought out in direct counterpoint to the 'causal' understanding of language held at this point by Russell and also set out by Ogden and Richards in *The Meaning of Meaning*, which also appears in the more simplistic versions of Malinowski's 'meaning as use' claim: the causal view of meaning sees words as externally (causally) related to their effects on the average hearer – so the meaning of a word is the effect it produces.

By 'internal relation', Wittgenstein instead means that concepts of colour, for example, presuppose one another: built into those concepts are qualities that imply the possibility of being otherwise, of being darker, lighter, brighter, dimmer, etc. So, '[I]f everything I saw were red and I could describe it, then I should also be able to construct the proposition that it was not red. This presupposes the possibility of other colours. Or else red is something that I cannot describe – then I have no proposition either and there is nothing I can deny...' (in WVC: 88–89; see also Blank 2007, 2008, 2011). The same applies to our conceptions of space, time, sound, etc., which all have their own spaces of logical possibility, or grammar. Meaning is not given by the effect of words but by their place in grammar.

So, if it is in some loose sense comprehensible that Gellner read the *Tractatus* as a 'poem to solitude', a story about one man and 'the logic of our language', writ large, already by 1929 that reading of Wittgenstein's philosophy is no longer at all a plausible one. Language and logic are now composed of multiple different fields of grammar, fields of grammar that define their meaning by virtue of setting out possibilities. Any given proposition is thus defined both by what it is and what it is not. Context here is still structured, formalized, and logical, but it also now multiple.

Anthropological readers will note the resemblance to structuralism, one we'll explore in much greater depth in the next chapter. There is no evidence Wittgenstein was acquainted with structural linguistics at this point. On the other hand, others in his orbit were, and some have suggested Ogden introduced some of Saussure's ideas to Wittgenstein (Harris 1988: 1).[9] It's also striking, as Stephan Palmié has noted, that both Edmund Leach and Rodney Needham, two prominent anthropologists who acknowledged the influence of Wittgenstein, were also very much influenced by French structuralism (Palmié 2018: 14; and see Lambek 2018: 187; Tambiah 1990). Indeed, regardless of the presence or absence of direct connection between Wittgenstein and Lévi-Strauss, it is clear that both emerged from the same 'context of context' this book describes: in addition to linguistics, Lévi-Strauss was influenced by similar ideas about mathematical logic to those we have seen influencing Radcliffe-Brown in the last chapter – ideas from cybernetics and information theory, as well as the game theory of von Neumann and Morgenstern (see e.g. Geoghegan 2020, 2022; Hénaff and Doran 2013; Le Roux 2009). Indeed, these latter ideas themselves emerged in many ways from the philosophy of logic we've been examining: Misak, for example, calls von Neumann and Morgenstern's 1944 *Theory of Games and Economic Behaviour* 'a near recreation' of an earlier but unpublished paper by Ramsey (2020: 274).

In some important senses, Wittgenstein's early views on grammar are a continuation of his positions in the *Tractatus*. When he speaks at this point about 'rules of grammar', he is talking about 'direct descendants of the "rules of logical syntax" of the *Tractatus*. Like the rules of logical syntax, rules of grammar determine the bounds of sense' (Baker and Hacker 1985: 40). What is at stake is still a system – or a 'calculus', as Wittgenstein sometimes calls it – of language. Thus, for example, in his response to Ramsey on colour, he draws a simple diagram of a system of x and y coordinates to represent a visual field, with his point being that any particular coloured patch within it can be represented by 'statements of numbers which have their significance relative to the system of co-ordinates and the unit chosen' (1929: 165). The 'calculus' conception of language present in the early parts of Wittgenstein's transitional period is still in other words very much committed to a contextual formalism: to exactness, and to the view that meaning in language is relative to a certain set of clearly specifiable logical variables.

A Gesture to Anthropology

Yet this view also differs significantly from the *Tractatus* in a number of important respects. One of the most obvious respects in which it does so is the pluralization of context. It is not possible to read this Wittgenstein, as Russell had read the author of the *Tractatus*, as in search of a logically perfect form of notation, because the 'logical space', 'geometry', 'calculus', or 'grammar' of, say, colour, is not the same 'logical space' as that of, say, sound, and it is a mistake to confuse them, even if they share the same form, that is are all 'logical spaces' or forms of grammar (Stern 2018: 29). There are thus different 'clusters' or 'systems' of context here, rather than independent 'elementary propositions' within a transcendent logic, and the systems are connected together because of their content, nor merely their logical form, in somewhat similar fashion to the ways in which actual grammarians might classify words according to their roles verbs, nouns, adjectives, etc:

I could explain things in this way: the colour of this patch is called 'red', the shape 'circle'. And here the words 'colour' and 'shape' stand for kinds of application (grammatical rules) and really signify/really are kinds of words, such as 'adjective', 'noun.' One could perfectly well introduce 'colour-word,' 'shape-word' into (ordinary) grammar to stand alongside the latter terms... (BT, 32)

Another crucial and related departure from the *Tractatus* is the disappearance of any trace of realism, and the emergence of the concomitant idea of the 'autonomy of grammar'. The *Tractatus* advanced the view that a shared 'logical form' between language and reality is what gives language meaning, as well as the idea that elementary propositions correspond to 'atomic facts' in the world. On Wittgenstein's new views, in contrast, the grammatical rules that tell us that, for example, one cannot say 'this is both red and blue' are just that: grammatical. They are conventions about the roles words play in systems of language and they tell us what roles such words may or may not play. They do not describe a reality to which we have access outside of the systems of language they form a part of, though in a sense this too is an extension of the claim in the *Tractatus* about the 'limits of language' as the limits of the world. If though the *Tractatus* nevertheless sought to 'show' something ineffable about the connection between language and world, Wittgenstein's work in this period begins to abandon the idea that there is something mysterious about the formal equivalence between the shape of the world and the shape of language:

It is also incorrect to say that the agreement (and lack of agreement) between proposition and world/reality is *created* arbitrarily by coordinating them. For how is this coordination to be expressed? It consists of the proposition 'p' saying that *this particular thing* is the case. But how does this 'this particular thing' get expressed? If through another proposition, then we gain nothing in the process; but if through reality, then *the latter* must already have been articulated – understood – in a particular way. (BT, 189)

In other words, we understand/articulate reality through the same grammatical rules by which we articulate propositions. Reality 'corresponds' with language and logic in the same way in which '5' 'corresponds' with '2+3': it is built into the rules, internal to the system, that it does so (Engelmann 2013: 123). Hence in a certain sense, the idea of language as a 'calculus' – we 'calculate' the truth or falsity of propositions based on the grammatical rules with which we live. Hence also the idea that what these rules really tell us is how to distinguish between 'sense' and 'nonsense', not 'truth' or 'falsity' in the sense of correspondence with an external world.[10]

Rules play a vital role in the calculus view of language Wittgenstein adopts at this point: they demarcate the boundary between sense and nonsense, and elucidating them is all that Wittgenstein thinks philosophy can do. Philosophy has no special access to reality, and Wittgenstein has already been clear in the *Tractatus* about his views on metaphysics. So providing what he calls a 'perspicuous representation' of language as a calculus or 'game' (another analogy introduced at this point) by showing how its rules work is the best one can hope for. Not that this project is unimportant – without an understanding of such rules we fail to see 'the system in our language', and thus fall into misleading nonsense.

It is at this point that Wittgenstein's reflections on the method of philosophy become – and remain – fully committed to the project of 'description', as opposed to 'discovery': to leaving 'everything as it is' (BT, 418). The rules of grammar are out there in actually existing language, not buried in a hitherto undiscovered logical notation. To be elucidated, they need only be properly shown and tabulated, in the manner that the game of chess is elucidated by enumerating its rules: 'Someone describing the game of chess neither lists the properties of the chess men nor does he talk about the usefulness and use of the game of chess' (BT, 192).

Note that this is quite different from the 'meaning is use' idea we will find later in the *Philosophical Investigations*. Indeed, claims like this come as part of an ongoing critique of Russell's, as well as Ogden's and Richards's, views of language as purposive and as a tool with which to cause effects. Wittgenstein's view at this point is that the rules of grammar, in his sense, are utterly fundamental to language, and that a language without rules is not a language at all. Thus rules are primary, not any particular use to which language is put (Stern 2018):

Couldn't I look at language as a social institution that is subject to certain rules because otherwise it wouldn't be effective? But here's the problem: I cannot make this last claim; I cannot give any justification of the rules, not even like this. I can only describe them as a game that people play. (BT, 191)

As suggested by the idea of philosophy as description, and of it 'leaving everything as it is', Wittgenstein is not thinking of the rules in question here as equivalent to the ideas he had about logic and logical form in the *Tractatus*. These rules are not metaphysical laws of logic, and they do not yield generalities about the correct form propositions must take. They are not *a priori*, because any grammatical rule exists inside a wider system of such rules, the outside of which we can never reach.

So, in a certain sense we can say that Wittgenstein's concern with context has become pluralized in this period, as distinct from that of the *Tractatus*, in that he is now speaking not of 'the logic of our language' but of different sorts of language, different sorts of 'game' – that of colour, for instance, as opposed to that of space. We can also say that he is certainly aiming at least to discard what traces of metaphysics there were in the *Tractatus*, whether of realism or of the transcendental nature of logic. And we can say that Wittgenstein has begun to try to aim at something like an 'ethnographic', descriptivist method of doing philosophy, in which what is sought is what he calls 'synoptic presentation', not theory or explanation.

The Persistence of Form

At the same time, and as implied by the idea of a 'system in our language' that we miss without attention to rules, there is more than a trace of the metaphysical in the status Wittgenstein ascribes to rules of grammar at this point. The idea of a 'system', or the idea that different kinds of logical spaces (colour, shape, sound, etc.) all share the quality of having 'rules', suggests a formal equivalence between those rules, even if their content is different. This is indicated in some of Wittgenstein's writing from this period, in which for example he writes as if there is a distinction between the grammar of 'logical spaces' and the grammar of 'logical constants' such as 'and', 'not', 'or', etc., in a way that suggests a formal universality of the latter despite the variability of the former – in the same passage he compares logical constants to a chessboard, a necessary part of the game of chess, an analogy he later admits is misleading (Engelmann 2013: 130–131).

A Gesture to Anthropology

This is also implied by the fact that Wittgenstein seems to be using the terms 'grammar' and 'rules of grammar' in a rather special sense, one that suggests they carry particular philosophical import, rather than just 'leaving things as they are'. We have seen earlier an attempt on his part to suggest that what he means by grammar and what an actual grammarian might mean by grammar are not different in kind, but both Sraffa and Moore would pick him up on this question.

In 1932, Sraffa pointed out to Wittgenstein that if by 'grammar' he meant nothing more than the actual description of how language is in fact used, then that would appear to be equivalent to saying that meaning is use (Engelmann 2013: 117–118). If grammar is just real usage, then its 'rules' are nothing more than descriptions of matters of fact. If that were true, it would entail Wittgenstein having to reject the idea of the 'autonomy of grammar' as well as the hard boundary between sense and nonsense, both of which collapse with the idea that the rules of grammar are merely the contingent result of observations of real usage, whatever that happens to be.

At the point in his trajectory we are presently concerned with though, Wittgenstein is still unwilling to concede this. In response, he points out 'the ambiguity of the word "description." Sometimes we speak of the description of a real house or tree, etc., and sometimes of the description of a shape, a structure, etc., of a notation, a game' (BT, 245). In other words, he thinks the object he sees himself as describing has a systematic quality to it, a clear form or shape, as also in the idea of a calculus or tabulation of the rules of grammar. Indeed, the idea of a certain morphology to grammar beyond any actually existing instance is highly reminiscent of Radcliffe-Brown's distinction between structural form and social structure, as well as of the Tractarian notion of 'logical form'.

In the same year, Moore too raised some objections to Wittgenstein's use of the word 'grammar' whilst attending his lectures. He could not understand, he said, how the sentence 'Three men was working' and the claim that 'this is both red and blue' could be grammatical errors in the

The Persistence of Form

same sense (Stern 2018; and see Monk 1991: 322–323). The former, for example, is clearly not nonsense – it may be ungrammatical but it is comprehensible, whereas Wittgenstein seems to want to say that the latter is necessarily impossible. In his initial response, Wittgenstein insists that there is no difference between the kind of rule at issue, only in the philosophical consequences of the different mistakes. Even if true, this would still suggest that Wittgenstein is using 'grammar' in a distinctly 'un-ordinary' sense of the word, and we will return to Moore's objection shortly.

So, whilst Wittgenstein is clearly of the view that there are different rules of grammar for different domains of life, the very idea of 'rules of grammar' would seem to transcend them all. Moreover, the rules of grammar seem to have a certain formal, structured, and systematic quality insofar as they are all capable of being systematically tabulated, and of course the very notion of 'rules' implies a systematic and formal status. This is reflected in Wittgenstein's concern in this period for exactitude and completeness of understanding in language, in which to understand language is to read off the place of symbols within the wider structure in which they sit. This either happens or it doesn't, and there is no place in this conception for ambiguity or amorphous half-understanding. This view of the rules of grammar will persist into later interpretations of the meaning is use formulation of the *Philosophical Investigations*, in which some have read Wittgenstein narrowly to mean syntactical use in the context of a meaningful sentence (e.g. Hacker 1972).[11]

Furthermore, these very commitments – or at least apparent commitments – to ideas about the nature of rules of grammar would seem to suggest that more than mere 'synoptic presentation' is going on. The formal and morphological equivalence between logical spaces Wittgenstein wants to insist on and the structure of grammatical rules and the ways in which they determine choices about the use of alternative signs within a given logical space all point to the persistence of the idea that the form context takes in shaping what we say and do has regularity to it: that, indeed, there is one form, that of grammar as calculus.

Gesture and Primitive Language

Given that Wittgenstein may have already abandoned the idea of 'logical form' by 1929, it seems unlikely that Sraffa's Neapolitan gesture would have had much significance for him in this regard. Malcolm's telling of the anecdote in some ways reinforces the fairly simplistic narrative of Wittgenstein's transition in which he goes from logician to anthropologist in an instant thanks to the realization that a gesture is unlike a logical proposition and requires a background against which to be understood. In reality, as we've been seeing, Wittgenstein's views on the nature of context shifted gradually and in stages, and within the same text 'one' Wittgenstein is often arguing with another (Pichler 2018).

von Wright's version, in which Sraffa's point is that the gesture has no 'grammar', in the sense we have been exploring, is a more plausible one. This is partly because, in his pursuit of a descriptivist philosophy, it tallies with the way in which Wittgenstein is increasingly coming to focus on real or fictitious concrete examples of what he will later come to call 'language-games' in his philosophy, a focus he will go on to elevate into a core principle of his work. Indeed, this too may even have been partly at Sraffa's urging – a note from him to Wittgenstein written in 1932 reads: 'We should give up the generalities and take particular cases, from which we started' (Engelmann 2013: 158). Interestingly, then, Wittgenstein's shift to his 'anthropological perspective' begins in a sense from his imaginings of what he sometimes calls 'primitive tribes' or 'societies'.

In his writings and lectures from this period, he begins to imagine what he calls 'primitive languages', by which he means languages with restrictions inherent to them, such as the language of children, or invented

Gesture and Primitive Language

languages with particular artificial constraints, or, indeed, gestural language. Clearly, a gesture like Sraffa's, or the way in which a young child speaks, does not have a grammar in any sense we might normally use the word, nor in the sense in which Wittgenstein is using it. Initially, however, Wittgenstein in some respects wants to show that such 'primitive' forms of language may be translated into complex ones that do possess the structural characteristics he thinks at this point are necessarily inherent to language (see e.g. Harris 2010). So, one can, of course, 'translate' Sraffa's Neapolitan gesture into a sentence with the kind of morphology that allows its sense to be understood according to grammatical rules that together form a complex system or logical space made up of contrasting possibilities like the colour system. At the same time though, the very idea that this would be a 'translation' suggests that with this account we would have failed to say anything about the language of gesture itself – as if we had tried to explain German by translating it into English, without saying anything about its internal grammar.

A language of gesture though, like other kinds of 'primitive language', has no internal grammar. There is no set of rules that defines its space of possibility and allows for meaning to emerge through distinction. If such languages are indeed languages – and they clearly are insofar as they successfully communicate – then Wittgenstein's dictum at this point that a language without grammar is no language at all falls apart, as, it would seem, does the idea that language is defined by the singular logical form taken by the context we need to understand it.

Indeed, the problem is made more acute by the fact that the boundary between these sorts of primitive languages or language-games and complex language is impossible to draw consistently. The language of children, for example, is a part of our own language, not sharply distinguished from it:

Think also of teaching a child to understand words by showing it objects and uttering words. The child is given ostensive explanations and then it

A Gesture to Anthropology

understands the words. – But what is the criterion of understanding here? Surely, that the child applies the words correctly. Does it guess the rules? – Indeed we must ask ourselves whether we are to call these signs and utterances of words 'definitions' at all. The language game is still very simple and the ostensive definition has not the same role in this language-game as in more developed ones. (For instance, the child cannot yet ask "What is that called?"). But there is no sharp boundary between primitive forms and more complicated ones. (PG, 26)

It is this sort of insight that will lead Wittgenstein later to speak of language as a 'family resemblance' concept, one made up of a range of structures, none of which need share any one specific morphological or structural attributes. As Wittgenstein will say of all this in late 1933, 'What is then our concept of system if it is not a cloud cuckoo land?' (Engelmann 2013: 167).

Sraffa was, of course, likely far from the only influence on Wittgenstein's shift in this regard, and accounting for some other potential influences leads us back to ideas about 'use'. We've met Moore's point about the distinct sense in which Wittgenstein seemed to have been using the word 'grammar'. A part of what Moore is trying to say in pointing this out is that there seems to be something distinctly non-arbitrary about the idea that a point in space cannot be both blue and red, in a way there is not about the rule that one should say 'were' rather than 'was' when speaking of plural subjects in the past tense.

Initially, as we've seen, Wittgenstein is inclined to insist the rules are of the same kind – grammar, after all, he thought, is 'autonomous' and so we shouldn't have to invoke the nature of the world to justify the rule about colour. Yet in the revisions on notes made a few days after Moore delivered his objections in 1932, we find Wittgenstein saying:

The rules of grammar are arbitrary and not arbitrary, in the same sense as is the choice of a unit of measurement. This is also expressed by saying that these rules are 'practical' or 'impractical', 'useful' or 'useless', but not 'true' or 'false'. (BT, 236)

Whether or not the introduction of seemingly pragmatist criteria of 'practicality' is down to Moore or to Ramsey or to Sraffa or to all or none of them isn't germane to our concerns. The point is that in these remarks and elsewhere at this time – around 1933–1934 – Wittgenstein stops denigrating causal theories of meaning and starts to see them as one among many ways of understanding varieties of language. Even the very simplest versions of such theories, such as the variant of Malinowski's in which meaning comes down only to immediate effect on the hearer, may characterize a certain sort of language-game, such as one made up of commands.

Beyond such specific instances, criteria of practicality imply a view of relevant context that is far, far broader than the systematic, formalist view of grammar and grammatical rules to which Wittgenstein had held. By 1933, in what would become the *Philosophical Grammar,* Wittgenstein is asking: 'Is meaning then really only the use of a word? Isn't it the way this meshes with our life?' (PG, 29). The introduction of the notion of 'life', gesturing as it does far beyond the morphology of language and yet without specifying particular boundaries or limits to its reach, heralds what will later become the famous – and oft-quoted by anthropologists – idea of 'form of life' as the relevant context with which to understand social phenomena. The notion of language as dynamic, practical, and active is what will later lead Wittgenstein to borrow Goethe's maxim from *Faust* as a motto for this philosophy: 'in the beginning was the deed' (Monk 1991: 306).

Yet another, and perhaps even more anthropological motto he would also express a wish to adopt came from *King Lear*: 'I'll teach you differences' (Monk 1991: 537). In a sense, this latter instance captures perfectly the move Wittgenstein makes (or tries to make, at least) when he shifts to his anthropological perspective. This shift constitutes a, and

A Gesture to Anthropology

perhaps in some sense *the*, final move in Wittgenstein's longstanding project of banishing metaphysics from his philosophy, insofar as it's an attempt to do away, not only with any particular vision (such as that in the *Tractatus*) of the general form of language or logic, but of the quest for such visions altogether – including even the comparatively loose notions of 'grammar' and 'calculus' he had been developing. In place of any such generality, Wittgenstein will now focus on the particular case – hence in part the notion of an 'anthropological perspective'.

Reading Frazer

It is in this period, when Wittgenstein began to insist on a descriptive approach to philosophy, to pepper his work with real or fictitious examples, to speak sometimes of an 'ethnological' or 'anthropological viewpoint', and to expand and render amorphous his view of the context in which we should situate language and practices in order to understand them, that he was also reading Frazer. We can now return to the 'Remarks' and read them in the light of their context.

One of the clearest respects in which the 'calculus' conception appears in the 'Remarks' is in the concern with morphology they exhibit. Wittgenstein is, as we've seen, famously critical of Frazer's evolutionist explanations of ritual in the 'Remarks':

A historical explanation, an explanation in the form of a hypothesis of development is only *one* kind of summary arrangement of the data – of their synopsis. It is equally possible to see the data in their relation to one another and to gather them into a general picture without doing so in the form of a hypothesis concerning temporal development. (RFGB, 20)

In fact, Wittgenstein is seemingly critical of the idea of any kind of explanation: 'Already the idea of explaining the practice – say the killing of the priest king – [235] seems to me wrong-headed' (RFGB, 1). In the place of such explanations, and in a manner bound to appeal to anthropologists suspicious of explanation (see Heywood and Candea 2023), he says, 'One can only resort to *description* here, and say: such is human life.' (RFGB, 3). In what exactly though does Wittgenstein think such description should consist in this first part of the 'Remarks' from 1931? What does 'the data in their relation to one another' mean?

[T]he principle according to which these practices are ordered [Rhees adds a footnote here that reads: 'That is, how they stand related to one another and what this depends on'] is a much more general one than [it appears] in Frazer's explanation, and it exists in our own soul, so that we could think up all the possibilities ourselves.[12] – We can thus readily imagine that, for instance, the king of a tribe becomes visible for no one, but also that every member of the tribe is obliged to see him. The latter will then certainly not occur in a manner more or less left to chance; instead, he will be *shown* to the people. Perhaps no one will be allowed to touch him, or perhaps they will be *compelled* to touch him. Think how after Schubert's death his brother cut Schubert's scores into small pieces and gave to his favorite pupils these pieces of a few bars. As a gesture of piety, this action is *just* as comprehensible as that of preserving the scores untouched and accessible to no one. And if Schubert's brother had burned the scores, this could still be understood as a gesture of piety.
  The ceremonial (hot or cold) as opposed to the haphazard (lukewarm) is what characterizes piety. (RFGB, 13 italics in original)

Note the phrase 'the principle according to which these practices are ordered', as well as Rhees's clarificatory footnote: 'That is, *how they stand related to one another*...' (my italics). Note also that the examples Wittgenstein proceeds to provide us with are contrasting possibilities: the king is invisible, or he is deliberately shown to all; he cannot be touched, or he must be touched; Schubert's scores are cut up and given to his favourite pupils, or they are left untouched and inaccessible, or indeed they are burned; the hot or the cold, rather than the lukewarm and haphazard.

A Gesture to Anthropology

The connections Wittgenstein has in mind here, in other words, are exactly the same kinds of connections that characterize his views on grammar, calculus, and logical syntax at this point – they are systematic connections, based on alternative possibilities from within a particular contextual space.

This becomes even clearer a little later:

'And so the chorus points to a secret law' is what one might want to say about Frazer's collection of facts. Now, I *can* represent this law, this idea, in the form of a hypothesis of development, but also in analogy to the schema of a plant, I can represent it as the schema of a religious ceremony, or again by grouping the facts alone in a 'perspicuous' presentation. (RFGB, 22; italics in original)

The reference to 'the secret law' comes from Goethe's 'The Metamorphosis of Plants', a significant and important influence on Wittgenstein alongside Goethe's wider morphological studies (see e.g. Monk 1991: 509–516; McGuinness 1988: 33–35). Goethe's 'secret law' of plant-life was not about its evolutionary development, but about its morphological similarity. He developed the notion of the *Urpflanze*, or 'original plant', which was not 'original' in developmental terms, but in formal terms – like Radcliffe-Brown's notion of 'structural form', it was not an actually existing plant, but a synoptic model that reveals formal analogies and differences between given cases, just as Wittgenstein's notions of the logical syntax of space, colour, time, etc. at this time did for those qualities.

Following directly on from this passage, Wittgenstein says,

For us the concept of perspicuous presentation is of fundamental importance. It designates our form of presentation, the way we see things. (A kind of "Weltanschauung" as it is apparently typical of our time. Spengler.) (RFGB, 22)

Palmié notes Wittgenstein's affinity for Spenglerian pessimism about progress (2018: 19), and this affinity is certainly present – as well as in references to other pessimists in Wittgenstein's work – and it is quite likely, as Palmié also suggests, that Wittgenstein would have agreed with Frazer's suggestion that the 'savage' practices he describes in the *Golden Bough* exist in latent form in 'civilised' society too. But the reference to Spengler here is also plausibly characterized by Hacker as one to Spengler's formalism: to the 'formal relations between [the life cycles of different cultures], conceived in terms of rise, maturation, and decline' (1992: 295). Indeed, in the idea that this formalism is 'a peculiar way of looking at phenomena, a kind of Weltanschauung characteristic of (some) thinkers in the early twentieth century (i.e. *his* [Wittgenstein's] times) in contrast with typical nineteenth-century positivist ways of looking at phenomena in evolutionary, developmental terms', Hacker interprets Wittgenstein to be in some ways making a similar point to that of this book about the 'context of contextualism'.

Spengler is not the only comparator invoked here. A short while after these discussions, Wittgenstein makes the remark from which the title of the recent collection of essays on Wittgenstein and Frazer is taken: 'A whole mythology is deposited in our language' (RFGB, 24). As Marco Bastianelli notes, this comment and others like it elsewhere on 'mythology' are usually interpreted 'negatively' – that is, as meaning that 'our' language possesses certain misleading properties that cause understanding to go astray if they are not taken into account (2013 and see Bouveresse 1977).

This is surely how references to 'myth' are meant sometimes in Wittgenstein's work, but far from always: in this particular case, when Wittgenstein makes more or less the same remark later in *The Big Typescript*, he acknowledges the German writer Paul Ernst, whom we know he read and admired (BT, 433; McGuinness 1988: 251–252). Like Spengler, Ernst was a pessimist conservative thinker (at least later in life), but also like Spengler, he was concerned with morphology: one of Ernst's most famous works is called *Weg zur Form* (The Road to Form) and the afterword he wrote to the 1910 edition of Grimm's fairytales

A Gesture to Anthropology

that Wittgenstein mentions specifically in a note in late 1930 contains, as Hacker notes, 'a similar conception of a principle of ordering ... of the inner character of folk-tales' (1992: 295). In other words, when Wittgenstein says that there is a 'mythology in our language', he probably means exactly what he means when he says there is a 'system in our language': that it operates according to certain structural and morphological principles.[13]

I'm not aiming to suggest that the entirety of the 'Remarks' is an unambiguous expression of Wittgenstein's so-called calculus conception of language; there's nothing about the second part of the 'Remarks', written much later, that expresses this, and the ideas in the first part can be interpreted in a number of ways. Indeed, as we've seen, Wittgenstein's transition from the calculus conception to the anthropological perspective was unlikely to have been a sharp and well-defined one, so it would make sense to find some ambiguity in this period. One obvious connection to the transition is the following remark: 'What we have in the ancient rites is the use of a highly cultivated gestural language' (RFGB, 26). The idea of a 'gestural language', and its connection to 'ancient rites', akin perhaps to the 'primitive languages' Wittgenstein will soon begin to imagine and describe, suggests that Sraffa's point about the inability of the calculus conception of context to capture everything about linguistic expression has already been made by this point.

What I'm aiming to suggest is that if all we see in the 'Remarks' is a generic contextualism on Wittgenstein's part and a pseudo-anthropological confirmation of all we think of Frazer's decontextualizing evolutionism today, we miss the much more specific and nuanced connections between his shifting and varied views and those we find in anthropology.

For example, we've already seen the structuralist echoes of Wittgenstein's calculus conception, and the fact that parts of the 'Remarks' in some ways resemble structuralist anthropology has also been noted. Palmié mentions it briefly but then dismisses it on the basis that there is a difference between 'morphology' and 'deep structure' (2018: 14).[14] Yet others might regard the distinction between 'structure' and 'morphology' as less than clear cut: Lévi-Strauss himself for example declared that he was more influenced by D'Arcy Thompson and Goethe's notions of form than he was by linguistic notions of structure (Lévi-Strauss and Eribon 1988: 158–159; see also Candea 2018: 112ff; Petitot 2009, as well as Green 2024). Similarly, Stanley Tambiah refers to some of the passages I have quoted above as an 'incomplete' version of the theories of differentiation developed by Saussure and 'exploited' by Lévi-Strauss, though he later notes that Wittgenstein 'artfully combines with another feature of symbolization familiar to Saussure and the later structuralists, that metaphorical and metonymical associations are "arbitrary" or "conventional" as well as "meaningful" and "rational": a king's sacred state is conveyed as much by his confinement from view as by his public display' (1990: 56C–59; and see also Lambek 2018: 187). We'll address these and other parallels in more depth in the next chapter.

The Character of Magic

By way of closing this chapter, I want to draw out the final point of interest for our purposes in the 'Remarks'. In his foreword to the original publication of the 'Remarks', Rhees notes that Wittgenstein began his notes on Frazer with three points that he later crossed out and did not have typed up into the manuscript with the others:

I now believe that it would be right to begin my book with remarks on metaphysics as a kind of magic.
    Where in doing so, however, I must neither speak out for magic, nor ridicule it.
    The depth of magic ought to be preserved. –
    Yes, here cancelling out magic has the character of magic itself.

A Gesture to Anthropology

For when I began earlier [i.e. in a prior work] to speak about the 'world' (and not of this tree or table), what else was I attempting than to conjure up something higher in my words. (in da Col and Palmié 2018: 30).

This specific set of remarks is often noted in anthropological commentary. De Zengotita is rather cross with Rhees for saying that he 'can see why' Wittgenstein crossed out these remarks, and attributes it, and Wittgenstein's crossing out, to philosophical prejudice about magical practices (1989: 390). Carlo Severi hears echoes of the *Tractatus* in them, though it seems clear that Wittgenstein is referring to the *Tractatus* somewhat self-critically when he refers to his 'earlier' speaking about the 'world' (2018: 78). Heonik Kwon interprets them this way and sees the comments as straightforwardly critical of metaphysics and of the work of Russell and others (2018: 95). This last is in some respects the easiest reading, and is very much in tune with the general anthropological characterization of Wittgenstein as a contextualizer and an anti-metaphysician *par excellence.*

As Marcus McGee points out though, Wittgenstein is quite specifically equating magic and metaphysics and therefore urging against the celebration or cancellation of either one (2023). Indeed, it seems plausible that this remark is helpfully read alongside a similar one written only a few months later: 'All that philosophy can do is to destroy idols; and that doesn't mean creating a new one, e.g: out of the absence of idols' (BT, 413).

By this reading, what he is doing in both passages is effectively pointing out the performative contradiction involved in the (metaphysical) critique of metaphysics, or the generalist insistence that there be no generalization in philosophy: 'cancelling out magic has the character of magic itself'.

The attempt to avoid this contradiction will characterize much of the later work we will examine in Chapter 5. Indeed, it is quite in line with that effort that Wittgenstein would go on to erase this passage: one can imagine him thinking that even stating the contradiction is to some extent a way of instantiating it, or at least undermines attempts to avoid it. As Ramsey famously quipped of the discussion of metaphysics in the *Tractatus*: if you can't say it, you can't say it, and you can't whistle it either.

The effort to avoid performative contradiction is also crucial to understanding the shifts in conceptualization of context we have seen taking place in this chapter. Pluralizing logical spaces, as we have seen Wittgenstein do here in the early stages of transition, is a way of pluralizing context, of moving further away from what are – arguably at least – metaphysical commitments in the *Tractatus* to a singular logic, writ large, as the context for otherwise independent propositions. And leaving behind the notion of 'logical space' entirely, or of 'grammar' as a transcendent metaphysical form for context, is a similar move, a way of defusing Sraffa's critique that grammar, if it is really just descriptive context and not metaphysical, should be unsystematic and formless. This is the path that will take us to the notion of 'form of life' in Chapter 5, and we'll examine in Chapter 6 how far anthropologists influenced by Wittgenstein have avoided saying, whistling, or conjuring up 'something higher' in their words.

FOUR

A Metaphysics of Magic

> How misleading Frazer's explanations are becomes clear, I think, from the fact that one could very well invent primitive practices oneself, and it would only be by chance if they were not actually found somewhere.
> – RFGB 13

As we saw in the Chapter 3, in the early 1930s Wittgenstein's contextualism changed its character. It became pluralized, as in the notion of distinct logical spaces for distinct phenomena, logical spaces governed by their own internal rules (often, as we saw, morphological rules of opposition and difference). The notion of 'grammar' and 'grammatical rules' came to occupy a key place in this philosophy, and for at least a time Wittgenstein seemed to consider such grammar and rules to have an autonomous existence and a determining character in relation to life. As in the idea of distinction between logical spaces, he also for a time seemed to consider them to be complete systems, sharing the form of 'grammar' but otherwise separate, and indeed to think that the confusion of such systems was the source of much philosophical error.

At the end of Chapter 3, we saw him coming to abandon several of these conclusions, but before we move on to the ideas of 'life', and 'form of life' as models of context that come to characterize his later 'anthropological perspective', in this chapter we'll examine the emergence of a comparable transition in anthropology, from logic to language, and the ways in which it was informed by Wittgenstein's work.

A Metaphysics of Magic

As Talal Asad has noted, from the 1950s onwards British social anthropology came increasingly to see itself as concerned with 'the translation of cultures' and to understand society and culture via language as a model (1986). Asad cites a paper of Godfrey Lienhardt's (1954) as one of the earliest examples of this tendency and notes that Lienhardt was a pupil of F. R. Leavis at Cambridge before going on to study anthropology with Edward Evans-Pritchard at Oxford (1986: 142). In fact, Lienhardt first studied with Evans-Pritchard in the brief year in which the latter taught at Cambridge in 1945, and we know this because Lienhardt once recollected that in this period he became interested in Wittgenstein 'by indirect contact':

The Meaning of Meaning as well as the meaning of meaning were (where E-P thought they would always remain) in the air. Malinowski himself [who taught Evans-Pritchard at the LSE] had contributed an appendix to the Ogden and Richards book. I wrote an essay for E-P ... in which I must have pursued the fashionable 'what exactly do we mean by ...' line. He was receptive, or appeared to be so, as always... Then he talked to me about the joy and excitement of extroversion to the ethnographic facts, and the danger, he said, of 'losing oneself in the minutiae of philosophical bunkum.' (1974)

We'll return shortly to the question of Evans-Pritchard's relation to linguistic philosophy. For now, I want to highlight the fact that already with Lienhardt we have some evidence of the connection between the rise of language as a model of cultural context and a familiarity with Wittgenstein and linguistic philosophy. This connection makes sense given that Wittgenstein and other philosophers concerned with language, like J. L. Austin at Oxford, were the driving forces in British philosophy in this period, and we should expect it to be the case that anthropologists studying and working in Oxford and Cambridge would come across their ideas, at least indirectly. However, these connections will become more direct and explicit as the chapter advances. Later,

A Metaphysics of Magic

we'll also return to Asad's essay and note that whilst critical of several aspects of this linguistic turn, his arguments themselves owe a debt to Wittgenstein too.

Language as a model for context in anthropology shared several features with language as a model for context in Wittgenstein's transitional philosophy, including some of those features Wittgenstein would go on to repudiate: most notably, the idea that contexts are in some sense discrete and distinct from one another, as languages often appear to us to be (hence the requirement of 'cultural translation'); and the idea that whilst they are discrete and distinct from one another, they may yet share a certain morphology (or 'grammar') that can be unearthed through analysis.

Both these issues become key problems in British social anthropology from the 1950s onwards. Indeed, whilst we'll examine later and different issues in anthropology related to Wittgenstein emerging in the United States in Chapter 6, traces of these two problems remain in a range of more contemporary anthropological debates.

We'll trace these connections through two important and contemporaneous developments, both of which emerge from and in relation to Wittgenstein's philosophy: anthropology's first explicit encounter with Wittgenstein took place posthumously and with a bang in the early 1960s in the form of the so-called 'rationality debates'. At the same time as the 'rationality debates' were beginning, and partly in relation to them, what Edwin Ardener later called the 'new anthropology' was also emerging with Wittgenstein's ghost lurking behind it (1971). Edmund Leach at Cambridge and Ardener and his colleague Rodney Needham at Oxford, among others, influenced by the ideas of Levi-Strauss, were introducing structuralism into British anthropology. We noted in the last chapter the affinities between structuralism writ large and Wittgenstein's transitional philosophy. In this chapter, we'll see the direct influence of this philosophy on British variants of structuralism. In other words, we'll see how two major shifts in mid-century British

A Metaphysics of Magic

anthropology were directly influenced by Wittgenstein's thought. Exactly which parts of his thought, though, is a complex question.

These two shifts map on to the two problems we noted earlier: at the heart of the 'rationality debates' is the question of the very possibility of cross-cultural understanding, exemplified in particular by the problem of the 'category mistake' – just how formalist, discrete, and complete should our models of context be? So much so that we should see 'understanding a primitive society', as one prominent contribution to those debates was titled, as a doomed endeavour? Similarly, at the heart of structuralism is a concern for morphology, as we have already seen in Wittgenstein's and Levi-Strauss's shared debt to Goethe and D'Arcy Thompson. Just as Wittgenstein moves in his transition from an atomistic approach to logical units to a systematic one, in which what is at issue are not 'elementary propositions' and their place in a singular logic, but 'systems of propositions', which share the form of grammar but are otherwise distinct, so anthropology moves from a vision of cultures as wholes from which parts can be extracted and compared to a morphological approach to cultures that sees them as like forms in which internal components are arranged in systematically different ways.[1]

Handwringing about relativism and the universalist certainties of structuralism may both seem as dead to anthropologists as Wittgenstein's transitional philosophy might seem to those of his present-day readers primarily interested in the *Philosophical Investigations*. But understanding both 'transitions', for want of a better word, is crucial to understanding what follows them. Wendy James, one of Evans-Pritchard's students at Oxford, once suggested that understanding the rationality debates was essential to understanding the distinctive character of mid-century British anthropology (2003: 41), but as Stephan Palmié has recently argued, the rationality debates also represent a foundational moment for a great many future anthropological questions, from debates around relativism to the recent

A Metaphysics of Magic

'ontological turn' (2022: 87, n. 3; and see Ulin 1988). And the problem of contextual form in both structuralism and the rationality debates will return us to the problem of the 'magic of metaphysics' we met at the end of the last chapter, and anthropology's ongoing attempts to eschew it, which will culminate in the radical antiformalism we'll meet in the final part of this book.

Systems and Structures

We've seen in Chapter 2 how the structural-functionalist anthropology of Radcliffe-Brown and Nadel resembled the logic of the *Tractatus* in its formalism (right down to the invention of a notational language for social roles). Another comparable aspect worth highlighting is mereology.

Candea describes Radcliffe-Brown's anthropology (quoting Salmon 2013: 195) as 'the art of subsuming' (2018: 89). That is, it moves upwards from particulars to generalities via classificatory categories. This involves an isomorphism of scale: bird totemism in New South Wales is 'an instance of' the principle of opposition, as also found in Heraclitus and 'the Yin-Yang philosophy of ancient China' (1951: 21). As Radcliffe-Brown puts it in diagnosing a difficulty of anthropological generalization in the wake of the Cambridge School critiques of Frazer we met in Chapter 2,

> The student is told that he must consider any feature of social life in its context, in its relation to the other features of the particular social system in which it is found. But he is often not taught to look at it in the wider context of human societies in general. (Radcliffe-Brown 1951: 15)

Note how the 'context' of a 'particular social system' and the 'context' of 'human societies in general' are transposable here, different only in scale. One should be able to 'look at' both – the form of context is not

Systems and Structures

a problem here, it is rather the place of things – 'features of social life' – within it that constitutes the question.

Nadel makes a comparable point at the beginning of his *Theory of Social Structure*, in which he will go on to set out his vision of a logical notation for social roles:

> Structures can be transposed irrespective of the concrete data manifesting it [sic]; differently expressed, the parts composing any structure can vary widely without changing the identity of the structure. Our definition [of social structure] should thus be rephrased as follows: structure indicates an ordered arrangement of parts, which can be treated as transposable, being relatively invariant, while the parts themselves are variable. This definition, incidentally, fully corresponds to the one logicians would apply in their field. (1957: 8)

Here we have an explicitly theorized version of Radcliffe-Brown's implication: there is a second-order conception of 'context' at work in anthropology of this period, even if largely only latent, and it is one that is basically invariant, both horizontally – across different 'concrete manifestations' – and vertically – up to 'human societies in general'.

Without returning in too much depth to the controversial task of interpreting the *Tractatus*, we might say that the Tractarian counterpart to the 'art of subsuming' is Russellian logical analysis. If the anthropological task in this period is to move 'up' from parts to wholes – wholes which are more or less formally identical to one another – the philosophical task in this period (not just for Wittgenstein but for any philosophy after Russell) is to move 'down' through analysis from the complexities of ordinary language to the purity of a logic composed of independent elementary propositions. The isomorphisms of scale mirror one another, and in both cases the 'levels' to which we are supposed to move share a singular form: as we saw in Chapter 2, 'logic' for Tractarian Wittgenstein is homogenous just as 'context' is for anthropologists, and indeed the two forms resemble one another in their composite character.

A Metaphysics of Magic

For both Wittgenstein and anthropology, this changes dramatically in the periods we're discussing in this part of the book. We've seen how, in the transitional period, Wittgenstein shifts from a concern with independent elementary propositions in a singular logic to systems of such propositions, forming 'logical spaces', in which propositions are defined by their relation to one another.

We've also already briefly seen some of the obvious parallels between this view of relations as having primacy over elements and anthropological structuralism, as well as the genealogical connections between the two in their roots in morphology (and see Candea 2018). We can now look in more detail at these parallels in terms of conceptualizations of context. Seeing these parallels with British structuralism is of particular relevance, given the explicit debt of the pioneers of British structuralism such as Rodney Needham to Wittgenstein.

Though an early disciple of Evans-Pritchard, Needham's major influences were both structuralism and Wittgenstein. He wore his Wittensteinianism on his sleeve, drawing on him often and explicitly (e.g. 1972, 1975, 1985), and authored a number of Wittgensteinian anthropological arguments, perhaps most famously and enduringly a critique of the notion of 'belief' as an internal state (1972). More pertinent for our purposes in this chapter is his essay on 'Polythetic categories' (1975), which, like an earlier comparable piece by Leach (1961), takes aim at the mereological imaginary of structural-functionalism that Leach famously called 'butterfly-collecting'.

Both Leach and Needham target what Candea calls 'typolology', that is, their objection is to forms of classification (such as 'matrilineal societies') that imply categories united – in a significant sense – by a shared characteristic. Their objections are manifold, but in Needham's case, he draws specifically on the later Wittgensteinian notion of 'family resemblance'. Roughly speaking, what Needham calls, using terminology from biology, 'monothetic sets', are equivalent to structural-functionalist imaginaries of anthropological classification: we say 'matrilineal societies' and we think that all members of the category will share at least one common predicate, and we likely hope that on this basis we can say something meaningful about other things they share or do not. 'Polythetic sets', on the other hand, are united by family resemblances: not by a single element, but by an overlapping and criss-crossing set of elements, such that any two members of the set may not, in fact, share any one characteristic with one another.

Leach's antecedent attack (in the inaugural Malinowski Lecture) is similar, as Needham notes in his essay. Assailing Radcliffe-Brown's project of 'comparing social structures' in the manner of putting seashells in a line according to structural type, Leach highlights the arbitrariness of the 'types' used: 'It *may* be that to create a class labelled *matrilineal societies* is as irrelevant for our understanding of social structure as the creation of a class of *blue butterflies* is irrelevant for the understanding of the anatomical structure of lepidoptera' (1961: 4; italics in original). Like Needham, Leach argued that anthropology's interest should not be in 'the interconnections between parts of a whole but with the principles of operation of partial systems' (1961: 6). Leach was certainly aware of Wittgenstein (see e.g. 1968, 1970, 1984) but the analogy he drew here was with mathematics – specifically topology – and its interest in 'generalised structural patterns' (1961: 7):

In the simplest case if there be a relationship p which is intimately associated with another relationship q then in a topological study we shall not concern ourselves with the particular characteristics of p and q but with their mutual characteristics, i.e. with the algebraic ratio p/q (Leach 1961: 8).

Leach's point here, as we saw in an earlier chapter, is not at all about quantification but about logical relations – the form that a particular system takes. As he goes on, nearly echoing Wittgenstein of the transitional period:

A Metaphysics of Magic

I readily admit that, in any given social system, we shall always find some kind of notion of corporate kinship which stands opposed to some kind of notion of marriage alliance as p is to q, but what we can usefully compare as between different societies are not these particular ps and qs (regarded as separate institutions) but the ratio of p to q considered as a mathematical function. Or, in non-metrical language, we need to think of the relationships which link children to their parents and the parents to one another as constituting a 'neighbourhood system' – a topological space. (Leach 1961: 26)

In other words, just as we saw Wittgenstein of the transitional period move from a concern with independent elementary propositions and their place in an overarching logic to a focus on the form of particular logical spaces and the interdependent relation of propositions within those spaces, so with Needham and Leach we see a shift from a focus on the character of the 'parts' of a social system to one on the variable relations that make up the form of such systems.

In a sense, we can think of the shift in both cases as one involving both a more concrete *and* a more abstract, formalist conceptualization of context. Logic as context in Wittgenstein becomes pluralized: instead of atomistic elementary propositions existing in the same context of logic, we now have different and distinct 'logical spaces' and attention to the concrete and systematic relations within them. At the same time, as we noted in the last chapter, the metaphysical weight with which the concepts of 'grammar' or 'syntax' are still invested in this transitional period is precisely what allows Wittgenstein to speak of forms like 'logical spaces': they may be governed by different rules of grammar, but the notion of 'rules of grammar' transcends them (at this point in his thinking).

In the same way, having inveighed against the abstractions of 'monothetic categories' and classificatory terminology in anthropology that bears no relation to concrete reality, Needham concludes his 'Polythetic categories' essay by asserting that such criticisms do not apply to

Systems and Structures

relational concepts such as 'symmetry', 'alternation', 'transitivity', 'complementarity', etc, or to analysis by reference to logical possibilities ... Here we have formal properties which can be defined in purely formal terms, e.g., in the notation of symbolic logic, without reference to any classes of entities, however the classes may be composed, or to the characteristic empirical features of their members. (1975: 365)

A generalized formal logic of relations, in other words, governs structuralist contexts, just as it does Wittgenstein's transitional logical spaces. The point is even clearer in Leach, though without the references to Wittgenstein, as he couches the entirety of his argument as a plea for 'generalization' through logical variables in place of 'comparison' across elements.

As we saw with structural-functionalism and Tractarian Wittgenstein, there thus remains a tension in both cases between context as particularizing and context as generalizing. If for the former pair that centred on a tension between particularizing content of context and homogenous form, we now have a morphology of context, but the problem has moved up a level: what Gildas Salmon calls 'system' in structuralism (2013), and what we have seen as 'grammatical rules' in Wittgenstein, are both types of generalizing metaphysics that govern this morphology. As Ardener puts it of French structuralism, 'Lévi-Strauss's system contains at its heart an outline of modes whereby individually arbitrary systems can be matched to each other. The data of a structuralist approach are in fact *all other systems*' (1971: 462; italics in original). Or, as Salmon characterizes Lévi-Strauss's views:

Only an arrangement meeting two conditions is a system: it is governed by internal cohesion; and this cohesion, inaccessible to the observation of an isolated system, is revealed in the study of transformations, thanks to which we find similar properties in systems that appear different. (2013: 7; my translation)

A Metaphysics of Magic

What Salmon calls structuralism's 'systematism' is quite explicit and worn on its sleeve, in other words. Where Wittgenstein's worries about the metaphysical weight he was attributing to the 'rules of grammar' will lead him away from such commitments, for structuralism, they are part and parcel of its theoretical apparatus, and abandoning its vision of a morphology of context will lead to anthropology largely abandoning structuralism itself.

The Rationality Debates

While structuralism maintained a clear morphology for context through linguistic models, the rationality debates of the 1960s and 1970s revealed the cracks in such formalist and morphological approaches. Where Needham and Leach preserved form through a reliance on relational concepts, the question of whether and how Western observers could comprehend radically different contextual frames like Zande witchcraft brought the very boundaries of contexts into question. These debates interrogated whether contexts could be discrete and complete systems, or indeed systems of any kind at all. In this sense, they anticipated the more radical dissolution of form that would characterize anthropology's later stance towards context. If structuralist contextualism looks like a near-perfect mirror for the contextualism of Wittgenstein's transitional period, the rationality debates – like the 'Remarks' on Frazer – show the influence of both transitional and later periods of Wittgenstein's work.

The rationality debates thus reveal both the further influence of Wittgenstein's ideas about language and context on anthropology beyond structuralism, and the complex ways these ideas were interpreted and deployed. They represent more than just theoretical disagreements – in many ways they mark a collision between different cultures of context. This clash reflected wider transitions in how mid-century social science conceived of context itself, and the ways in which that self-conception was influenced by Wittgenstein.

A Feeling for Form

At their heart was a tension embodied by Evans-Pritchard's work on the Azande, by Wittgenstein's worries over the persistence of metaphysics in his transitional scheme, and also by the push and pull between formalism and antiformalism that would come to define anthropology's approach to context. Evans-Pritchard tried simultaneously to demonstrate the internal coherence and logical interrelational of Zande beliefs – as if they formed a discrete and clear contextual structure – and to maintain the view from outside that structure that witches, 'as the Azande conceive them', cannot exist. That tension between internal contextual coherence and the insistence that such contexts are nonetheless not closed off from one another became the fulcrum around which the rationality debates turned. As a tension, it also replicates the problem that runs through Wittgenstein's career, from the *Tractatus* onwards, of how to speak about contextual frames without imagining oneself outside of them. This version of the problem will rear its head explicitly in anthropology in new iterations of arguments about cultural translation, pioneered by Asad among others, but which, like their forebears, draw on Wittgenstein too, as we'll see in Chapter 6.

A Feeling for Form

Wendy James quotes Evans-Pritchard as declaring that the anthropologist must have 'a feeling for form and pattern' (2007), but precisely what conceptualization of 'form and pattern' was at issue in his anthropology was not always straightforward, just as with Wittgenstein's philosophy. In his work on the Azande, the 'form and pattern' of their life with witchcraft and magic looks little like the tightly structured accounts of roles, political offices, and kinship statuses to be found in comparable anthropological work from the period. It is far more amorphous, far less tightly coherent, and far less bounded. *The Nuer*, on the other hand, whether read to epitomize structural-functionalism or as a forerunner of structuralism, certainly did not lack a clear sense of what 'form and

A Metaphysics of Magic

pattern' meant. Later again, in his Marett Lecture, Evans-Pritchard argued – in notably Wittgensteinian tone – that human societies be 'seen as systems only because social life must have a pattern of some kind, inasmuch as man, being a reasonable creature, has to live in a world in which his relations with those around him are ordered and intelligible' (1950: 123).

Evans-Pritchard's relationship to philosophy was complex despite Lienhardt's characterization of his attitude to 'philosophical bunkum'. Though the only contribution he himself seems to have made to the rationality debates in which his work was so much at issue was to point out that Winch and Macintyre confused Nuer and Zande's attitudes to cattle during an Oxford debate between the two of them (de Lara 2000: 120; Luhrmann 2013: 138); the simple notion of a coolly empiricist anthropologist interested only in counting Nuer cows being intruded on by rarefied philosophers who can't tell the difference between one set of people and another is far from the whole truth.

A series of three papers published whilst Evans-Pritchard was an assistant professor at the Egyptian University in Cairo, the first only a couple of years after Wittgenstein began dictating his 'Remarks' on Frazer, start to illustrate the possible lines of connection one might draw between the two men's thought. Whilst in large part targeted at Lucien Lévy-Bruhl, a French philosopher who had drawn on early anthropological accounts to argue that the character of 'primitive' thought was 'pre-logical', in qualitative contrast to the rationality of modern societies (e.g. 1926), in these papers and in later work (e.g. 1965), Evans-Pritchard also inveighed against Frazer and the British intellectualist tradition for precisely the reasons Wittgenstein was doing so at more or less the same time: their decontextualizing nature.

We have observed that selection on the level of bare observation had already produced an initial distortion. The scissors-and-paste method of compilation by the armchair scholars at home led to further distortion ...

A Feeling for Form

which was dignified by being labelled the 'comparative method'. This consisted, with respect to our subject, of taking from the first-hand records about primitive peoples, and willy-nilly from all over the world, wrenching the facts yet further from their contexts, only what referred to the strange, weird, mystical, superstitious – use which words we may – and piecing the bits together in a monstrous mosaic, which was supposed to portray the mind of primitive man. (1965: 10)

Evans-Pritchard also objects to the same intellectualizing approach to magical belief that we have seen Wittgenstein so concerned to attack in his 'Remarks': the idea – born from a lack of appropriate concern with social context – that belief in magic is merely faulty scientific reasoning, such as in the notion that ritually birthing an adopted child must involve failing to understand the difference between ritual birth and natural birth. As we have seen Wittgenstein noting, an Englishman such as Frazer might well kiss the picture of someone he loved without failing to understand that this is not the same as kissing the person themselves.[2]

But where Frazer saw magic as mistaken science, Lévy-Bruhl saw it as a different sort of reasoning altogether, one he called 'mystical' or 'pre-logical', whose preeminent character was affective rather than intellectual. As Philippe de Lara notes in a piece devoted to the overlap between Evans-Pritchard and Wittgenstein, 'He [Lévy-Bruhl] used to quote an Inuit shaman, who said of supernatural forces, "We do not believe, we fear"' (1936: 22; quoted in de Lara 2000: 120).

Witchcraft, Oracles and Magic is, in large part, a response to this qualitative distinction between magical and scientific reasoning. As Evans-Pritchard was already pointing out in 1934, 'Lévy-Bruhl has not paid sufficient regard to the fact that collective representations have an intellectual structure and indeed must have for mnemonic reasons. Unless there is a mutual dependence between ideas we cannot speak of thought at all' (1934: 55). And as he puts it in the book itself: 'My object in this book is ... to study the relations of [practices and beliefs related to witchcraft, oracles, and magic] to one another, to show how they

A Metaphysics of Magic

form an ideational system, and to enquire how this system is expressed in social behaviour' (1937: 2). He famously demonstrated that Zande ideas of witchcraft are not illogical but consistent with one another and with the institutions of Zande social life, once the initial premise of the existence of witches is accepted. The Azande do not mistake proximate natural causes of misfortune for witchcraft, in the same way in which people do not mistake ritual birth for natural birth; they posit witchcraft, when appropriate, as an ultimate cause of such misfortune, in a manner which gels with the moral universe in which they live, one of largely human responsibility for ills, and one in which witches are the embodiment of immoral emotions.

Michael Lambek puts this perfectly in relation to the argument here:

> To understand what [the Azande] are saying or doing, we need to understand the context in which they are doing it at that moment, under those circumstances, within particular forms of life. Thus Evans-Pritchard asserts that Zande ideas of witchcraft only become intelligible when they are not laid out like artifacts in a museum display case but understood as they follow one another in the practice of everyday life... In effect, he is pointing to a Wittgensteinian form of life. (2023: 8 and see de Lara 2000)

Lambek and de Lara are far from the only commentators to note the affinities between Wittgenstein's ideas and some of Evans-Pritchard's arguments about the Azande (see e.g. James 2003, 2007). Mary Douglas, in a book devoted to Evans-Pritchard's work, describes its central intention as 'relating moral philosophy and religion systematically with social behaviour' (1980: 11). Later, in the same book, she makes the following point:

> Looking back at his work as a whole and trying to trace the many influences on him, it seems extraordinary that he did not know what Wittgenstein was saying, or how closely they paralleled each other. But apparently the convergence results not from contact but from similar historical pressures.

A Feeling for Form

Once the trail is laid, anyone who reads the *Philosophical Investigations* will see even richer convergences, and further implications from Evans-Pritchard's scrupulous working out of a method and its philosophy. (Douglas 1980: 36)

Edmund Leach implies an even more direct connection in a short and autobiographical piece, in which he first remarks on the influence of Russell and the logical positivists on structural-functionalist anthropology (an influence we have noted in Chapter 2), before then going on to say,

It was not until the mid-1950s that, under the influence of the later Wittgenstein and Oxford linguistic philosophy, British social anthropologists began to show a serious interest in ideas rather than in behavior. This shift was initiated by Evans-Pritchard though the presence of Louis Dumont in Oxford for several years was also relevant, as was my own heretical idealism which had a variety of sources. It was certainly tied in with my early grounding in mathematics, though mathematicians are not necessarily of an idealist inclination. (1984: 17)

Similarly, though a direct connection with Austin and the other ordinary language philosophers of this period in Oxford is hard to establish, Evans-Pritchard was a fellow in the same college as – and firm friends with – Isaiah Berlin, who had studied with Austin and remained close to him throughout his life (James 2007: 107; see also Rowe 2023). James cites Berlin as likely a major influence on Evans-Pritchard's views as they emerged in the Marett Lecture, and it is impossible to believe that such influence would not have involved the linguistic philosophy that was taking Oxford by storm in this period. As James also notes, the institutional politics of Oxford at the time meant that as the chair of social anthropology, Evans-Pritchard was frequently in need of allies from other subjects, and these came from philosophy and from religion more often than they did from rivalrous cousins such as archaeology or sociology.[3]

A Metaphysics of Magic

Closed and Open Contexts

One obvious way to help resolve some of the paradoxes of Wittgenstein's relation to Evans-Pritchard, and to wider anthropology throughout the period we examine in this chapter, is to do what I've been aiming to do throughout this book: to bring Wittgenstein down to earth, and to put these various ideas into the context of his work as it developed and transformed over time. Rather than measure Evans-Pritchard against a singular 'Wittgenstein', we can see how Evans-Pritchard, some of his critics, and some inheritors of their arguments, all share aspects of Wittgenstein's approach at different points. Crucial in particular here is the conceptualization of context in the transitional period we met in the last chapter.

For example, we might note that whilst Lambek compares Evans-Pritchard's account of Zande society with Wittgenstein's later notion of 'form of life' (a far less bounded and completist notion of context than that of 'grammar', as we'll see in the next chapter), in fact Evans-Pritchard's emphasis on the 'ideational system' and 'intellectual structure' of ideas Zande ideas about witchcraft is in that sense of 'system' and 'structure' more akin to the systematically structured contextualism of Wittgenstein's transitional period.

We saw in the last chapter how Wittgenstein's understanding of context – conceptualized variously as 'logical space', 'calculus', or 'grammar' – became pluralized after his abandonment of the atomism of the *Tractatus*: ideas and propositions about colour make sense within the colour-system, not independently of it; likewise pitch, time, sensation, etc., and even pain:

'I have no stomach ache' is comparable to 'These apples cost *nothing*'. For they cost no *money*, but not no snow or no effort. The zero-point is a point on *one* scale. And as no point of a scale can exist without the scale, nor can the zero-point... I compare this state [i.e. not being in pain] to another state, hence it must be comparable. It must lie in pain-space as well, but in another place. – Otherwise my sentence would say that my current state had *nothing to do* with a painful one; as in: the colour of this rose has nothing to do with the conquest of Gaul by Julius Caesar. (MS 108)

As Pascal Zambito has recently made clear in a survey of Wittgenstein's changing views on the notion of logical space however, 'What stays the same [in the transitional view as in the *Tractatus*] ... is the idea of a logical or grammatical space which has to be *complete*' (2019: 79; italics in original). In other words, contexts, in Wittgenstein's middle period, are closed formal systems. Indeed, confusing such systems is what leads to philosophical error, as Russell described in an evaluation of Wittgenstein's work in this period written for Moore: 'Mistakes of grammar result from confusing "spaces"' (Quoted in Stern 2018: 29). Making this point around the same time in one of his lectures, Wittgenstein says:

The puzzles about time are due to the analogy between time and motion. There is an analogy, but we press it too far; we are tempted by it to talk nonsense. We say time 'flows', and the ask where to and where from, and so on. (AWL 60)

And this – together with the related idea of the autonomy of grammar from pragmatic use – is what will change in the shift to Wittgenstein's 'anthropological perspective', in which contexts lose their boundaries and sense of completeness, and the relation between grammar and use becomes more complex.

If we read back the arguments of Lévy-Bruhl and Evans-Pritchard – and, as we will see, a range of the rationality debates – we see how much they turn on this distinction of closed and open contexts, and on the relative primacy afforded to the 'rules' of a context versus their capacity to be bent in use in actual life. These debates turn, in other words, on the formalist (or otherwise) conceptualization of context at issue.

A Metaphysics of Magic

We see this, for example, in the 'expressivist' interpretations of both Lévy-Bruhl and indeed Wittgenstein himself in the 'Remarks' on Frazer. Both are sometimes taken to cleave to an affective, emotional, or 'expressive' interpretation of ritual action as opposed to the causal, intellectualist, or instrumental approach of Frazer (e.g. Cook 1983; Skorupski 1983). The implication of the expressivist interpretation is that the mistake of approaches like Frazer's is that of confusing two entirely separate and distinct contexts of action (such as time and motion in Wittgenstein's analogy above): 'the same savage who, apparently in order to kill his enemy, pierces an image of him, really builds his hut out of wood, and carves his arrow skilfully and not in effigy'.[4] In Lévy-Bruhl's case, we see the closed/open context distinction at work in the way he has been read to insist on a dualism of mystical and empirical thought, the major target of Evans-Pritchard's critique.

Similarly, it's clear that Evans-Pritchard's problem with Lévy-Bruhl was precisely the problem of context. That is, in failing to anchor so-called 'mystical thought' in the ethnographic details of its context – in the other ideas and beliefs that surround it, and in its institutional and sociological supports – Lévy-Bruhl failed to see the coherence and rationality of such thought, as determined by criteria perfectly recognizable in any so-called 'empiricist' context. Proper attention to contexts reveals *both* their internal coherence *and* their open nature. In other words, whilst Zande beliefs do form an 'ideational system', the system is not a closed one (*pace* some characterizations, e.g. Horton 1967). As Lambek puts it, '*once one accepts an initial premise* ... everything falls into place' (2023: 9, my italics; and see Palmié 2022). Thirty years after Evans-Pritchard began his work on the Azande, however, our capacity to accept the initial premise of the existence of witches is precisely what would become the central issue of the rationality debates, again with the question of open and closed contexts at its heart.

Winch's Wittgensteins

The initial salvo in these debates, Peter Winch's *The Idea of a Social Science*, makes no specific mention of Evans-Pritchard, but its whole ambition is to characterize what its author takes to be a properly Wittgensteinian approach in the social sciences, such as anthropology (1958). The thrust of the approach is that disciplines concerned with human understanding such as anthropology should not, in fact, conceive of themselves as 'sciences' at all, since what they ought to be in the business of is not 'causal explanation' but 'understanding', drawing at length on Wittgenstein to substantiate the argument.

As with other similar examples in this book, what I want to emphasize in explaining Winch's Wittgensteinianism are the various versions of Wittgenstein on offer in it, and indeed the variety in Winch's own positions. Again, as in the other cases, this is not in order to point which version is the 'correct' Wittgenstein, but to establish the different consequences of different kinds of Wittgensteinian contextualism. In some ways, Winch's trajectory through the rationality debates mirrors those of Wittgenstein and of anthropology at issue in this book.

In this first major salvo, Winch argues that the kind of knowledge provided of human practice by 'general laws' that offer predictions of behaviour based on past practice is not what we normally call 'understanding': 'To give an account of the meaning of a word is to describe how it is used; and to describe how it is used is to describe the social intercourse into which it enters' (1958: 123). This is not only true, as Winch goes on to argue, of words, but also of behaviour and action. But in this first version of Winch's Wittgensteins, 'social intercourse' turns out to have a strongly formalist flavour.

Winch views social life as governed by 'internal relations': that is, by meanings dependent upon their place in a wider system of meaning. Directly anticipating some of the points – and even the references – that we'll find Clifford Geertz making later, Winch gives an example from

A Metaphysics of Magic

the philosopher Gilbert Ryle, whose work evolved very much in dialogue with Wittgenstein:

> A sergeant calls 'Eyes right!' and his men all turn their eyes to the right. Now, in describing the men's act in terms of the notion of obedience to a command, one is of course committing oneself to saying that a command has been issued... It does not make sense to suppose that human beings might have been issuing commands and obeying them before they came to form the concept of command and obedience. For their performance of such acts is itself the chief manifestation of their possession of those concepts. An act of obedience itself contains, as an essential element, a recognition of what went before as an order. (1958: 124)

In other words, human ideas and practices – such as commanding and obeying commands – are intrinsically, essentially, and internally connected with one another, as in a coherent system. The picture of human social life as a system, though, is where things get controversial.[5]

As both a flood of subsequent criticism and Winch himself in later editions of the book, would note, other parts of his argument also lend themselves strongly to a vision of contexts as closed, formalist, and coherent systems, as well as to one in which rules always govern behaviour in the manner of transitional Wittgenstein's views on the 'autonomy of grammar'.

For example, pursuing the idea that 'criteria of logic are not a direct gift of God, but arise out of, and are only intelligible in the context of, ways of living or modes of social life', Winch goes on to argue that,

> It follows that one cannot apply criteria of logic to modes of social life as such. For instance, science is one such mode and religion is another; and each has criteria of intelligibility peculiar to itself. So *within* science or religion actions can be logical or illogical. (1958: 100; my italics)

As indicated by the word '*within*', Winch's conception here of the 'context of ways of living' is a closed and complete one. 'Religion' and 'science' are examples of such contexts, and it is a mistake to confuse the two, just as it is a mistake to confuse the 'logical space' of colour for that of time for Wittgenstein of the transitional period.

Similarly, on the question of rules, Winch argues that 'all behaviour which is meaningful (therefore all specifically human behaviour) is *ipso facto* rule-governed' (1958: 52). The importance attributed here to 'rules' echoes the anti-pragmatist reading of Wittgenstein's 'grammar' we met in the last chapter, in which this importance lies in the capacity of grammar to determine meaning and action, independently of human ends: 'Generally, both the ends sought and the means employed in human life, so far from generating forms of social activity, depend for their very being on those forms' (1958: 55).

To give Winch his due, he will go on to repudiate both of these specific claims in later editions of the book, and even elsewhere in the original text, there are contrasting traces of a less formalist conception of context and its structure: he speaks of the 'overlap' between ways of living (1958: 101), of the 'interwoven' nature of practice and the rules that govern it (1958: 63), and of the ways in which contexts change and develop, even if only in ways that must be grammatically coherent (1958: 63–64).

But in this first explicit entry of Wittgenstein into questions of social science, it is far from clear which Wittgenstein we meet: there is some of the formless 'anthropological perspective' we'll meet in the next chapter, but there is also a great deal of the transitional Wittgenstein, particularly in the formalist and closed conception of context Winch promotes, one obviously antithetical to Evans-Pritchard's account. This formalism is far from incidental to Winch's wider argument either, and it will form the linchpin of his next foray into questions of social science, one in which the Azande make their first appearance in his writing.

Both the Nuer and the Azande had already appeared in the pages of philosophy journals by this point.[6] They arise in Alasdair MacIntyre's 'Is Understanding Religion Compatible with Believing', in which MacIntyre

A Metaphysics of Magic

describes Evans-Pritchard's contextualist account of Nuer religion as an ethnographic parallel of Winch's Wittgensteinianism (1964: 66):

'When a cucumber is used as a sacrificial victim Nuer speak of it as an ox. In doing so they are asserting something rather more than that it takes the place of an ox'. When we have grasped the whole of Nuer practice have we grasped what more this could be? Or is there anything left over that we have not understood? Evans-Pritchard would have to answer this last question by 'No'. (1964: 65)

Here, in other words, we have Evans-Pritchard assimilated to Winch's position on closed contexts: there is such a thing as 'the whole of Nuer practice' and when we have grasped it we have grasped everything about its internal components. There is nothing to be added from outside of this whole.

MacIntyre himself thinks things are more complex than this apparent 'self-sufficiency' of contexts, pointing instead to the fact that, 'Criteria have a history. This emerges strikingly if we ask how we are to think of magic on Winch's view. Is magic a "mode of social life"? Or is it primitive religion? Or perhaps primitive science?' (1964: 67). Clearly, in other words, so MacIntyre assumes, magic is not a closed context: some might put it in the same category as religion; others might see it as mistaken science. MacIntyre argues it is only possible to evaluate Zande beliefs about magic as 'rational' in the light of scientific criteria they do not possess. It does not make sense to ask about 'rationality' without such criteria, so it cannot be the case that a discussion of such rationality is being conducted according to the Zande contextual norms.[7]

Having been attacked for being too Wittgensteinian by Macintyre, Evans-Pritchard is then attacked for not being Wittgensteinian enough in a response from Winch (1964). Winch argues that Evans-Pritchard's application of 'scientific' criteria of truth and falsity to Zande witchcraft beliefs leads him to the incorrect idea that such beliefs are equivalent to hypotheses about the world.

Winch's Wittgensteins

But by this point Winch has moved away from his earlier formalism:

Certainly we learn to think, speak, and act rationally *through* being trained to adhere to particular norms. But having learned to speak, etc. rationally does not *consist* in having been trained to follow those norms; to suppose that would be to overlook the importance of the phrase 'and so on' in any description of what someone who follows norms does. We must, if you like, be open to new possibilities of what could be invoked under the rubric of 'rationality' – possibilities which are perhaps suggested and limited by what we have hitherto so accepted, but not uniquely determined thereby. (1964: 318)

So where 'meaningful human behaviour' was entirely 'rule-governed' in *The Idea of a Social Science*, we now find the view, characteristic of later Wittgenstein, that understanding not only consists of more than obeying rules but that it must also be open to 'new possibilities'. He joins with MacIntyre – and the more pragmatist later Wittgenstein – in noting that to say 'that certain rules are followed is so far to say nothing about the *point* of the rules' (Winch 1964). Later, citing Rush Rhees, he argues that,

ways of speaking are not insulated from each other in mutually exclusive systems of rules. What can be said in one context by the use of a certain expression depends for its sense on the uses of that expression in other contexts (different language games). Language games are played by men who have lives to live – lives involving a wide variety of different interests, which have all kinds of different bearings on each other... (1964: 321)

The Wittgenstein Winch is invoking here is the 'anthropological' Wittgenstein, with language games 'played by men who have lives to live', rather than existing as isolated systems. It is possible, says Winch, for us to understand Zande beliefs about witchcraft, but not by evaluating them as pseudo-scientific propositions. They are instead ways of contemplating and reflecting on fundamental aspects of life (relations

A Metaphysics of Magic

with others, the existence of good and evil, etc). Thus to press witchcraft beliefs to the point at which they may yield contradiction, as if they were a theoretical system 'is in fact committing a category-mistake' (1964: 315). Yet the very notion of a 'category mistake' itself reveals ambiguity about whether contexts are 'closed' or 'open'.

Category Mistakes

The idea of the category mistake epitomizes much of the tension in the approaches to context we've met in this chapter, and it has a life far beyond the rationality debates, both in anthropology and philosophy.

Gilbert Ryle first introduced the idea in his critique of mind–body dualism in *The Concept of Mind* (1949). Summarizing it, he points to a number of exemplary errors in which the problem is an assumption about the status of an entity in relation to others: the classic example is the tourist visiting Oxford who, upon being taken to see a number of important locations ('Christ Church, the Bodleian Library, the Ashmolean museum') then asks to see 'the University'. The tourist assumes 'the University' is an entity in the same category as the others they have seen.

Ryle was considerably influenced by Wittgenstein (see e.g. Tanney 2009), as indeed was the wider school of 'ordinary language philosophy' of which he was an important if somewhat idiosyncratic member at Oxford. The Wittgensteinian undertones of the idea of the category mistake are obvious if we return to the idea of 'logical spaces' and the mistakes born of confusing them we met in the last chapter and earlier in this one, as well as to the Tractarian notion of nonsense. To assume that because we say that time 'flows' we should also say it flows 'from' somewhere or 'to' somewhere is to commit the category mistake of assuming time and motion are isomorphic. Yet the comparison also reveals that there are several different ways of imagining *why* a category mistake is a mistake in the first place.

Category Mistakes

By category mistake, we might mean a violation of established categorical boundaries, in the way that transitional Wittgenstein seems to mean the error involved in confusing systems of time and motion in his transitional period – the mistake is given by the presence of the closed logical systems and the rules that govern them. Or we might mean 'category mistake' in the way that Wittgenstein of the anthropological perspective might have meant it: as a practical failure of understanding identifiable only in the specifics of the situation. To this latter view, everything depends on context, and at the same time, the form of context is so unspecified and amorphous that there is nothing to provide us with a general rule for knowing what it will look like.

To make the distinction between these two senses of 'mistake' clearer, we might return to Ryle's example of the tourist in Oxford. Where, precisely, has the mistake taken place? The 'violation of rules' reading effectively treats a category mistake as the result of a previous failure – an incorrect understanding of the rules of grammar. There are categories – such as 'pieces of architecture' and 'institutions' – that do not intersect and confusing the two produces mistakes. But to separate out 'understanding' and 'application' in this way is distinctly foreign to both Ryle and later Wittgenstein. Just as the solider saluting his sergeant in the Rylean example given earlier is simultaneously 'obeying a command' and saluting – not doing two distinct things – so for Ryle and later Wittgenstein our understanding is given in our practice. The same is true of misunderstanding. The category mistake of the tourist is not a consequence of another, separate failure of understanding but a diagnosis of why a failure has taken place.

There is nothing absolute, in other words, about nonsense or mistakes in language, for this later version of Wittgenstein:

Again, you must not forget that 'A contradiction doesn't make sense' does not mean that the sense of a contradiction is nonsense. We exclude contradictions from our language; we have no clear-cut use for them, and we

A Metaphysics of Magic

don't want to use them. And if 'It's raining but I don't believe it' is senseless, then again that is because an extension along certain lines leads to this technique. But under unusual circumstances that sentence could be given a clear sense.' (RPP II 290)

But neither is there a rule to determine how to recognize the right 'unusual circumstances' that might give sense to an apparently nonsensical statement.

This ambiguity makes the category mistake a kind of transitional concept, an anthropological mirror for Wittgenstein's transitional views, a pivot between formalist and formless models of context. On the one hand, like the early Wittgenstein's insistence that logical form determines what can be sensibly said, or Radcliffe-Brown's vision of social structure as a coherent system of relations, it seems to maintain and indeed insist on the distinction between different formal categorical domains; yet it seems also to do so from a position, *sub specie aeternitatis*, that Wittgenstein, and later Winch and many anthropologists, will wish to argue is inaccessible.

Take Winch's accusation that Evans-Pritchard's analysis involves the category mistake of analogizing witchcraft and science.[8] Winch indicts Evans-Pritchard with his own words: 'Azande do not perceive the contradiction [involved in witchcraft accusations and the transmission of witchcraft substance] as we perceive it because they have no theoretical interest in the subject, and those situations in which they express their beliefs in witchcraft do not force the problem upon them' (1937: 25). Therefore, says Winch,

This suggests strongly that the context from which the suggestion about the contradiction is made, the context of our scientific culture, is not on the same levels as the context in which the beliefs about witchcraft operate... The European is in fact committing a category-mistake. (1964: 315)

Note Winch's reliance on the notion of 'context' and the idea that such contexts may exist at different 'levels'. In other words, despite the extent to which Winch has moved with this 1964 paper away from a transitional Wittgensteinian perspective, the introduction of the notion of the category mistake – which undergirds the paper's entire critique of Evans-Pritchard as not Wittgensteinian enough – returns us implicitly to the idea of closed and formalist notions of context, distinguishable from one another, the confusion of which causes error.

Yet Evans-Pritchard's actual point is *not* to say that witchcraft beliefs are like faulty scientific hypotheses – hence his critique of intellectualism exemplified in the quote about 'theoretical interests' – but to show the various practical considerations that render the idea of 'contradiction' meaningless in most situations in which witchcraft is under consideration. His point is not, in other words, to set up a 'context' of scientific hypotheses and another one of witchcraft beliefs, and say either that they are or are not the same. It is instead to make the eminently late Wittgensteinian claim that 'A Zande is interested in witchcraft only as an agent on definite occasions and in relation to his own interests, and not as a permanent condition of individuals' (1937: 26). If there is a 'metaphysics of magic' operative here, it is not that of the Azande or of Evans-Pritchard: it is Winch who turns 'magic' into a system, one which may or may not be like other such systems.[9] We'll have occasion to return to the problem of the category mistake and its ongoing life in contemporary anthropology later in the chapter.

The Persistence of Metaphysics

In this chapter so far, we've seen the ways in which a variety of developments in mid-century British anthropology both reflect elements of Wittgenstein's transitional views and were directly influenced by them.

What we've been especially concerned with are some of the consequences of implicitly or explicitly modelling context on language. In particular, we've seen how the rationality debates and structuralism

A Metaphysics of Magic

reflect two important aspects of such consequences. The first is the question of the closed or discrete nature of such contexts, which arises perhaps unsurprisingly from the linguistic model. Whether or not in reality languages are discrete entities – and much anthropological work on hybrid languages, for example, would suggest otherwise (e.g. Schieffelin & Doucet 1994) – it is easy to imagine them as such. One usually speaks Italian or Spanish, not Spitalian or Italish. Secondly, imagining context as like language can lead one to imagine that whilst such contexts may indeed be radically distinct from one another, they may yet also share a common morphology or 'grammar' and therefore lead one to invest such a grammar with a good deal of metaphysical weight.

One might imagine both these issues to be long resolved in anthropology, and certainly talk of relativism and structuralism might suggest that this is an exclusively historical set of debates. Indeed, to the extent that the problem of relativism and the model of 'translation' have the ring of historical objects to some contemporary ears, I suggest this is precisely because the formalist conceptions of context that undergirded them have become largely submerged beneath the dominant antiformalism we'll examine in Chapter 6.

Yet in closing this chapter, I want briefly to trace some of the afterlives of such formalist problems in recent anthropology. This afterlife of formalist notions of category mistakes and the problem of translation reveals some of the limits of antiformalism. Even in its most antiformalist moments, thinking about context seems to require some notion of boundary, distinction, and category – if only to mark what lies beyond formalism itself. This is the paradox Wittgenstein recognized in his concerns about the 'metaphysics of magic', and his anticipation that the rejection of metaphysics might itself take metaphysical form.

To get at some of this more contemporary relevance, it will help to start by returning to the rationality debates to highlight the contribution of a figure we've met in a previous chapter but not yet in this one.

The Persistence of Metaphysics

In the same year in which Winch published *The Idea of a Social Science*, Ernest Gellner gave a talk in Oxford that addressed Winch's arguments. Later published as 'Concepts and Society' (1962), it combined arguments in philosophy regarding the status of concepts and their meaning with readings of a range of ethnographic work. Gellner had achieved some public notoriety in the intervening years with *Words and Things*, a scathing attack on the linguistic philosophy of both Wittgenstein and the Oxford 'ordinary language' school (1959).

Words and Things is noteworthy for our concerns for several reasons. First, it and other parts of Gellner's work represent an unusual depth of engagement with Wittgenstein by an anthropologist. But despite this and its notoriety, it is rarely treated by anthropologists themselves. Its polemical tone stands in stark contrast to the deference typical of most anthropological engagements with Wittgenstein. It is therefore both singular as an in-depth analysis of Wittgenstein by an anthropologist and entirely uncharacteristic of anthropological views on Wittgenstein generally.

Gellner was in a unique position to address both Wittgenstein and anthropology, having trained in philosophy at Oxford before and after World War II, before going on to do a PhD in anthropology at the LSE under Raymond Firth, Malinowski's pupil, based on fieldwork in Morocco. He was at Oxford in the heyday of Austin's ordinary language philosophy, and so *Words and Things* was an attack on linguistic philosophy 'from the inside' (Rowe 2023: 596). The latter part of the book is in fact – appropriately, given Gellner's anthropological training – a sociological appraisal of why it should be that ordinary language philosophy had such appeal, concluding, as one reviewer put it, that its practitioners were simply 'smug, unintelligent, upper class, superciliously apolitical, unhistorical and anti-scientific' (quoted in Krishnan 2023: 226). In Gellner's own words, linguistic philosophers 'invented a philosophy fit for gentlemen and, *at the same time*, found a home for professional philosophy, sore pressed for a field by recession of faith in the transcendent realm and the conquest by science of the immanent world' (Gellner 1959: 328–329; italics in original). What he called 'this strange love-child of Wittgenstein's messianism and Oxonian complacency' (Gellner 1959: 339) could both provide philosophy with an elevated 'ivory tower pursuit' whilst at the same time denying it did so and insisting that it merely deferred to the common sense of the ordinary man on the Clapham omnibus.

This alleged hypocrisy is one of the book's philosophical targets, as is what Gellner regards as linguistic philosophy's inherent conservatism.[10] The substance of the claim rests on – among other things, including Wittgenstein's own famous definition of his philosophy as 'leaving everything as it is' – the idea that linguistic philosophy commits a 'systematic and dogmatic' version of the naturalistic fallacy: that is, of making a state of affairs the justification for its own validity (1959: 71).[11]

In later work, Gellner would put this more pithily by accusing Wittgenstein of holding the mirror image of the position he claimed to hold: the major implication of Wittgenstein's philosophy, Gellner argued, was not so much that 'meaning is use' as it is that 'use is meaning': it turns *de facto* matters of actual speech and language into *de jure* answers to philosophical questions. Worse, and to return to the issue of hypocrisy, when this is pointed out practitioners simply render the charge illegitimate by redefining 'philosophy' according to their own preferred criteria, such that one is not allowed to pose *de jure* philosophical questions in the first place.[12]

To return to the rationality debates, this claim is also crucial to Gellner's arguments in 'Concepts and Society'. Indeed, in some ways the paper aims to take the problem of contextualization as its object: 'there is nothing in the nature of societies to dictate visibly just how much context is relevant to any given utterance, or how that context should be described' (1962: 33).

Gellner's specific target is what he calls 'sympathetic', 'positive', or 'charitable' interpretations of apparently illogical assertions. Such interpretations are often founded on contextualism, as we have seen in Evans-Pritchard's case, and Gellner goes on to describe Evans-Pritchard's account of Nuer religion, which, like his work on the Azande, is framed in critique of Lévy-Bruhl's arguments about 'pre-logical mentalities'. The Nuer assertion that 'twins are birds' is, according to Evans-Pritchard, a prime example of the sort of claim that Lévy-Bruhl meant by pre-logical mentality since it appears to be a contradiction in terms. As in his other critiques of Lévy-Bruhl, Evans-Pritchard is at pains to show that there is in fact no contradiction involved, provided that such statements are interpreted in context rather than taken as isolated equivalents of logical propositions.

Gellner has no quibbles with Evans-Pritchard's particular interpretation, or enthusiasm for Lévy-Bruhl. His point instead, mirroring the one above about use-as-meaning, is that

> It may be that the sympathetic, positive interpretation of indigenous assertions are not the result of a sophisticated appreciation of context, but *the other way round*: that the manner in which the context is invoked, the amount and kind of context and the way the context itself is interpreted, depends on prior tacit determination concerning the kind of interpretation one wishes to find... (1962: 33; italics in original).

Or later,

> contextual interpretation, which offers an account of what assertions 'really mean' in opposition to what they seem to mean in isolation, does not by itself clinch matters. I cannot arrive at determinate answers (concerning 'what they mean') without doing a number of things which may in fact prejudge the question: without delimiting just which context is to be taken into consideration, without crediting the people concerned with consistency ... or without assumptions concerning what they can mean (which, again, is precisely what we do not know but are trying to find out). (1962: 38–39)

A Metaphysics of Magic

So, for example, interpreted in light of the context of 'action' – actual behaviour towards twins or birds, say – then *of course* no statement could look absurd or contradictory, Gellner says, because 'action' in what Gellner calls 'viable' societies is usually not absurd or contradictory (1962: 36). Behaving in practice towards twins and birds as if they were the same would be unsustainable, so it is circular to say that one has 'contextualized' a contradictory concept by framing it in a context in which contradiction is in practice impossible.

As in *Words and Things*, Gellner's argument is, in many ways, with one Wittgenstein rather than another. His problem is not with 'context' *per se* but with its reification in a particular form, in this case one that makes everything 'within' it look coherent. He makes a version of the 'use-as-meaning' critique, pointing out that contextualization has (can have, for our purposes) a naturalizing effect, such that it makes any instance of 'use' look like it must have a 'meaning'. Instead, as he points out, use

> may depend on [a concept's] lack of meaning, its ambiguity, its possession of wholly different and incompatible meanings in different contexts, *and* on the fact that, at the same time, it as it were emits the impression of possessing a consistent meaning throughout – on retaining, for instance, the aura of a justification valid only in one context when used in another. (1962: 45)

This is not, in fact, an anti-contextualist argument but an argument for 'better' contextualism, more sensitive to category mistake type errors that may arise from ignoring contextual boundaries we are not predisposed to see (those 'within' a culture, for example, rather than only between cultures).

Gellner's argument resembles in many ways one made seventy years later by David Graeber in critique of anthropology's ontological turn (2015), in which he perceives a tendency on its part to reify particular 'ontologies' in ways that obscure their internal incoherence, as well as –

The Persistence of Metaphysics

like Gellner – noting that such reification can naturalize the ideas of certain members of a society at the expense of those of others. And this isn't the only respect in which arguments from the rationality debates echo forward through the decades.

To return full circle to the start of this chapter, in the piece in which he highlights the predominance of the linguistic analogy in British anthropological models of culture, Talal Asad takes Gellner's essay as the central foil in his contribution to the seminal *Writing Culture* volume because, he argues, 'it represents a doctrinal position that is still popular today' (1986: 163–164). The position Asad has in mind is that it is possible and desirable for the anthropologist not only to 'translate' between cultures but also to critique them. Asad sees this position as only plausible in light of inequalities of power between the cultures in question, but none of this really leads him to doubt the model of 'cultural translation' in and of itself. Indeed, it is this model that gives his argument its power.

He directly addresses Gellner's point about the malleability of context in a manner that cannot have been formulated without the later Wittgenstein, whom he cites elsewhere in the essay, uppermost in mind: quoting the sentence we met above ('there is nothing in the nature of societies to dictate visibly just how much context is relevant to any given utterance, or how that context should be described'), Asad asks:

Yet can this last remark be meant seriously? *Nothing?!* How, then, is communication even between individuals in the same society ever possible? Why does one ever say to foreigners that they have misunderstood something they heard or saw? Does social learning produce no skills in the discrimination of relevant contexts? The answers to these questions should be obvious, and they are connected with the fact that the anthropologist's translation is not merely a matter of matching sentences in the abstract, *but of learning to live another form of life* and to speak another kind of language. (Asad 1986: 148–149; italics in original).

A Metaphysics of Magic

As with several of the contributions we've met in this chapter, what we have here is a mixture of Wittgensteins. On the one hand, with the introduction of the idea of 'form of life' – an idea we will meet in more detail in the next chapter – we seem to move beyond the 'grammatical' model of context, and instead into a way of thinking in which the parameters of context are not pre-given but themselves emerge precisely through life and social interaction. On the other hand, in the retention of the notion of 'translation', we find the idea that such 'forms of life' have specifiable boundaries, an idea reinforced in Asad's wider argument about the power relationship between 'Third World' societies, as he puts it, and the societies from which anthropologists tend to come.

In a famous passage from later in the essay, Asad argues that anthropological translation should consist in the deformation of the language of translation by the language to be translated. This passage – and the essay more broadly – will then go on after a further quarter century to form a key inspiration for several of the arguments of the ontological turn (e.g. Viveiros de Castro 2004), itself, of course, an enterprise premised on the problem of contextual discontinuities. Without straying too far into the details of such arguments, they are famously premised on the idea of 'radical alterity', contextual difference so great as to be incomprehensible without the conceptual realignment prescribed by advocates of the turn.

To take us back to Evans-Pritchard, for example, and to the problem of the category mistake, in one of the definitive ethnographic exemplifications of the ontological turn, Martin Holbraad takes Evans-Pritchard to task for what he sees as a contradiction in *Witchcraft, Oracles, and Magic*, one we met earlier in this chapter: on the one hand, Evans-Pritchard wants to say that Zande beliefs are not set apart from or closed off from 'commonsense' or 'scientific thought' in the way Lévy-Bruhl might have argued they were. On the other hand, he seems to rely on the idea of the 'closed' or 'circular' nature of Zande magical beliefs to explain why their 'commonsense' doesn't cause them to question the existence of witches (2012: 62–64; and see Horton 1967).

For Holbraad, it's clearly a category mistake to conflate the 'how' of causality (termites causing a granary roof to fall) with the 'why' of witchcraft (why it fell when people were sitting beneath it). He describes the relation of his own argument to Evans-Pritchard's problem thus:

What one would then need to do [to resolve the contradiction] is show that the two domains of interrogation are somehow insulated from each other, so that each domain corresponds to a distinct frame of belief (commonsense and mystical respectively) in such a way that the twain might never meet. Indeed, in a way this is just the kind of argument I shall be developing (2012: 63).

Holbraad aims to account for divination 'without recourse to other "beliefs" – viewing divination, in other words, as a sui generis source of truth, to be understood in terms of its own' (Holbraad 2012: 64). Thus Evans-Pritchard's error, according to Holbraad, consists of conflating distinct systems, in much the same way in which Wittgenstein diagnosed philosophical errors resulting from the confusion of logical spaces. As we've seen, this way of deploying the category-mistake argument rests implicitly on a formalist notion of the discrete nature of the categories or systems in question.

To identify a category mistake with the violation of a boundary between 'sui generis' types is to privilege a system of such types over the particulars of any given interaction in precisely the way in which Wittgenstein sought to avoid doing when he moved away from this view of language. Indeed, some have read – perhaps unfairly – the entire approach of the ontological turn in anthropology to be premised on some idea of 'closed contexts', so closed in fact that the boundaries between them are 'ontological' rather than merely epistemological (see e.g. Bessire & Bond 2014; Heywood 2020; Vigh & Sausdal 2014).

A Metaphysics of Magic

This is obviously not the only sort of way in which the idea of the category mistake gets invoked in anthropology.[13] But it is a good example of the ways in which the Wittgenstein-inspired problem of 'cultural translation' we have met in this chapter that began with the rationality debates did not end with them. It's also a good example of the ways in which formalist elements remain even in what are otherwise quite radically antiformalist approaches to anthropology – in the case of the ontological turn, for example, an approach premised on the dissolution of the formal distinction between concepts and objects (see conclusion below). As we'll see in Chapter 6, similarly antiformalist approaches focused on 'ordinary life' as an alternative to formal models of culture maintain implicit boundaries around what counts as 'ordinary'. The very act of identifying something as belonging to 'life' rather than 'system' or 'structure' performs the kind of formal boundary work that the notion of the 'category mistake' can be used to police.

As to problems of metaphysical commitments to a certain form of context, those too have been alive and kicking in anthropology long after the heyday of structuralism. Not only were such problems the key concern of a number of precursors to the 'ontological turn', who pointed to the latent and implicit commitments embedded in contextual notions of 'culture' and 'society' (see e.g. Strathern 1988; Viveiros de Castro 1998; Wagner 1975), but they also formed the linchpin of a range of critical interventions around the 'turn' itself, and the contrast between its rhetorical eschewal of metaphysics and the ideas about the relation between concepts and objects built into its theoretical scheme (see Heywood 2012; Laidlaw 2012; Laidlaw & Heywood 2013). The notion of 'ontology' as a way of describing contextual form certainly appeared to many to be a way of implicitly committing to the singularity of such a form (though cf. Holbraad 2017). The fact that the ontological turn may appear as already as much a historical object as structuralism is evidence of the fact that anthropology has still not resolved the problem of the metaphysics of magic.

Part III
Life: Contextual Aporetics

FIVE

Life without Form

One can say that the concept of a game is a concept with blurred edges. – 'But is a blurred concept a *concept* at all?' – Is a photograph that is not sharp a picture of a person at all? Is it even always an advantage to replace a picture that is not sharp by one that is? Isn't one that isn't sharp often just what we need?

– PI 71; italics in original

We last left Wittgenstein in the early 1930s, worrying, in the 'Remarks' on Frazer, about the 'metaphysics of magic', and about how to 'neither speak out for magic, nor ridicule it'. The point of noting those remarks was that they capture a clear sense of anxiety around the potential for performative contradiction involved in 'cancelling out magic[/metaphysics]', a manoeuvre that 'has the character of magic[/metaphysics] itself' (in da Col and Palmié 2018: 30). These remarks are significant because they spotlight two important aspects of Wittgenstein's later philosophy.

It should not come as much of a surprise by this point that Wittgenstein should be tempted to 'ridicule' or 'cancel out' metaphysics. Some of the readings of the *Tractatus* dealt with in the first chapter aside, Wittgenstein is usually read as the antifoundationalist philosopher *par excellence*, at least as far as the analytic tradition goes.[1] This 'anti-theoretical passion' (Monk 1991: 490) would become more and more pronounced in his later work, and it is in this later work that we find many of the kinds of antifoundationalist philosophical remarks for which he is famous in anthropology and beyond:

I want to say here that it can never be our job to reduce anything to anything, or to explain anything. Philosophy really is 'purely descriptive'. (BB, p18)

If anybody offers me a *theory*, I would say No, no, that doesn't interest me. Even if the theory is true it is not *what* I seek... (in Waismann 1965: 16; italics in original)

A theory is without value. A theory gives me nothing. (in Monk 1991: 304)

We never arrive at fundamental propositions in the course of our investigation; we get to the boundary of language which stops us from asking further questions. We don't get to the bottom of things, but reach a point where we can go no further, where we cannot ask further questions. (LWL 34)

Whilst this anti-metaphysical stance may constitute part of his attraction for anthropology, a discipline with a habitual suspicion of the a priori, it obviously did not appeal to everybody. It is what would lead Russell, his one-time mentor, to say of him,

The later Wittgenstein... seems to have grown tired of serious thinking and to have invented a doctrine which would make such an activity unnecessary. (1959: 193)

Just as in the case of anthropology, a corollary of Wittgenstein's antipathy for theory and abstraction was his particularism.[2] That is, as we saw towards the end of Chapter 3, Wittgenstein's 'anthropological perspective' would lead his philosophy to become increasingly about teasing apart an example (often but not always that of an imagined 'primitive tribe') to reveal its inherent specificity. As he famously puts it in the *Philosophical Investigations* when speaking of games, 'Don't say:

Life without Form

"There must be something in common ... but look and see'" (PI 66). In place of the philosophical sin of 'craving for generality' (BB, p17), in other words, this later Wittgenstein fills the *Philosophical Investigations* with an inordinate number of specific examples, which do not and are not intended together to add up to anything resembling a 'theory' (see Heywood 2023b). Hence the notion of 'family resemblance' – a connection between cases, but not one that comes in the form of a broader category within which they are subsumed, or a fundamental essence that underlies them.

The antifoundationalism and particularism of his later philosophy already go some way towards making clear why, in this guise, Wittgenstein might appear such a natural friend to anthropologists. As throughout this book, however, I want to try to avoid presentist assumptions that imply the naturalness of a given direction of the course of intellectual history. That is, rather than take Wittgenstein's genius for granted and pat ourselves on the back for having taken the right hints from him, I want to root this final set of ideas in the wider history of the cultures of context we have been examining in this book, in an attempt to bring them down to earth.

For that reason, this chapter will focus primarily on the idea of 'form of life' as a model of context in the later Wittgenstein. Despite only appearing a handful of times in Wittgenstein's writings, and never with clarity of meaning, this notion has spawned a huge secondary literature of commentaries, exegeses, and etymological analyses, as well as a range of anthropological work drawing on it.[3] The idea of 'form of life' is often taken to be a central one for Wittgenstein's later philosophy, and this, together with the absence of precise elucidation of what we should take it to mean from the man himself, has led to a range of debates over how it should be interpreted.

For our purposes too, the idea of 'form of life' is an absolutely central one for understanding this period of Wittgenstein's work and its influence on anthropology. It precisely captures the crucial shift in thinking

Life without Form

about models of context that defines his philosophy from the mid-1930s onwards, at least as far as relevance for anthropology goes. That shift consists of a move from language as the key analogy for contextual form – with the correlative implications of completeness and morphology we met in the last chapter – to the idea of 'life' as a model for context.

This leads me on to the second aspect of Wittgenstein's later philosophy I want to highlight here. Roughly speaking, what I want to suggest is that Wittgenstein's notorious lack of clarity about what he actually meant by 'form of life' is not an accident or an error. It may, instead, have been the way he chose to deal with his worries about neither 'speaking out' for metaphysics, nor 'ridiculing' it. 'Form of life' in this sense is an exercise in 'undefinition' as philosophical artifice – a deliberate blurriness about the form and boundaries of context, one which, as we'll see in the next chapter, will later be taken up in anthropology. Throughout this chapter, we'll see how what might appear as vagueness or imprecision in Wittgenstein's discussion of context may not have been a shortcoming but a philosophical strategy. Rather than offering another formal theory of context to replace those of his earlier work, he may have been aiming to show how to talk about context without getting trapped in theoretical commitments.

In each of the phases of his work we have examined so far, we have seen his allergies to metaphysical commitments grow ever stronger alongside his contextualism, and we've also seen the shapes and forms of his models for context grow looser and looser in tandem, to the point at which 'form' ceases to be an operative concept: first logic, in all its singularity; then language, in its multiplicity. But language as a form too, as we saw in Chapter 3, has a certain constancy to it, as revealed in the criticism that 'rules of grammar', even though their contents may vary, appear to be transcendental in their form.

We have seen Wittgenstein's anxiety about the performative contradiction involved in 'cancelling' metaphysics, and the fact that such a

Life without Form

manoeuvre has itself a metaphysical character. We have seen the remark from the *Philosophical Grammar* in which he declares the task of philosophy to be the destruction of (metaphysical) idols without the manufacture of new ones, and his concern in particular to avoid making an idol out of 'the absence of idols'.

What better antidote for these concerns than a model of context as apparently generic and formless as 'life' itself? And what better way to ensure it can only be read in this way than by eschewing any opportunity actually to give a form to 'form of life'?

That said, there isn't anything *necessarily* formless about 'life'. Anthropologists Stefan Helmreich and Sophia Roosth have traced some of the varied and complex genealogy of the term *lebensform* in its usage in the history of science, from Kant to the synthetic biology of the twenty-first century, with some of which Wittgenstein would undoubtedly have been familiar. One imagines that once again Wittgenstein's own context has some influence here on how life gets conceptualized in his thinking: '[real or ordinary] life' in his thinking ends up looking like the formless opposite of the highly formalized life of an academic philosopher and intellectual in a Cambridge college in the thirties and forties, a formless opposite Wittgenstein had himself often sought out, as we've seen several times.

While he taught at Cambridge, he was in the constant habit of urging his students to abandon the university and philosophy in favour of the 'healthier air' of 'real life' and become, for instance, a doctor, or a car mechanic (his own favoured choices of career, petrol fumes notwithstanding – Monk 1991: 360), and this notorious tic of his was obviously related to his antipathy for traditional (metaphysical) philosophy. One of his best known 'successes' in this endeavour was his favoured student Maurice Drury, who became a psychiatrist (having first attempted to become a clergyman, just as earlier Wittgenstein had tried being a monk). Whilst urging an escape from the lack of 'breathable air' in Cambridge on Drury, Wittgenstein said to him, 'It doesn't matter for me, I manufacture my own oxygen' (Rhees 1984: 121).

Life without Form

This casual egotism belies what we have seen in brief discussions of his biography: Wittgenstein was forever attempting to do exactly what he tried to foist on his students, or as his biographer Ray Monk puts it, to 'join the ranks', to abandon both the philosophy and the privilege with which he lived in favour of a more 'ordinary' life, whether as an 'ordinary' soldier at the front in World War I, an 'ordinary' schoolteacher in the most backwater posting he could find afterwards, or later, as when, in the 1930s, he tried unsuccessfully to persuade the Soviet government he should be allowed to immigrate in order to work on a collective farm. As Monk notes in casting this case as an instance of the more general issue in Wittgenstein's psyche,

> The Soviet authorities knew, just as the Austrian authorities had in 1915, that he would be more use to them as an officer than as a private; and Wittgenstein himself realized that he could not really tolerate life among the 'petty dishonesty' of the ordinary soldiers. Yet he continued to wish it could be otherwise. (1991: 354)

This passage captures precisely the anxiety that one imagines to be ever present in a man tortured by the simultaneity of what Monk calls 'the duty of genius' and the urge to 'join the ranks'; by the feeling that what was needed in philosophy was to 'cancel' metaphysics and the recognition that arguing for doing so was a contradiction in terms. It is not a stretch, I think, to imagine that such a man would find the wider 'contextual turn' of this period we met in this book's introduction congenial (Burke 2002), and that he would eventually light upon a model of context so loose, so non-specific, and so immune to criticism of metaphysical commitments, as 'form of life'.

A final reason to find this idea plausible is that it would fit with a trajectory of metaphilosophical worries in Wittgenstein's work over how exactly to present his thought. The quote from the 'Remarks' about 'preserving the depths' of metaphysics is itself metaphilosophical in that it was explicitly posed as a problem about how to write his book. As I noted at the end of Chapter 3, the deletion of those very passages also presumably had a metaphilosophical motivation, and we can guess at it involving the same worries present in the contents of the remarks themselves: that 'saying' anything about metaphysics is going to end up involving one in metaphysical commitments.

Framing the issue in terms of 'saying' should also remind us that this is far from the first time Wittgenstein has worried about the relation between the form and contents of his arguments. As we may recall from Chapter 1, that relation is crucial to the *Tractatus*, as well as to a variety of interpretive controversies over how it should be understood. Central to the question of this relation in the *Tractatus* is exactly the issue of a self-conscious holding back on Wittgenstein's part, of 'not saying', as in his famous remark to the effect that the *Tractatus* 'consists of two parts: the one presented here plus all that I have not written. And it is precisely this second part that is the important point'. There is good precedent, in other words, for Wittgenstein deliberately eschewing clarity and explicitness of argument where he thought they would be unhelpful or misleading, and that precedent concerns exactly the issue at hand here: form. As we will see, that tendency to worry about the form of philosophical argument persists in later work.

Again, however, my interest is less in this suggestion's plausibility as an explanation of Wittgenstein's shifting ideas and more in what its possibility reveals about the lessons anthropology should learn from him. The connections between this anxiety over performative contradiction and anthropology will be the subject of the next chapter.

From Rules to Life

We have seen that, around the time that he was reading Frazer, Wittgenstein's ideas were changing. This is visible in differences in his writing, between, for example, on the one hand the manuscript we know as *The Big Typescript*, composed around 1932–33, available today in its full form but parts of which were also published in a different form in 1969 in *Philosophical Grammar*; and on the other, work from 1933 onwards, such as the Blue and Brown Books. The notions of 'system' and 'calculus', in the very formalized senses in which we met them in Chapter 3, are replaced by far looser versions of themselves, useful perhaps in elucidating some aspect of the philosophy of mathematics, but no longer with the metaphysical weight that Sraffa had pointed out was attached to them in the transitional work (Engelmann 2013). 'Grammar' continues to be a crucial concept, not because it lays down transcendental and autonomous rules that determine meaning, but because it shows us what we do with language in specific and particular instances.

The Blue Book, dictated to a select group of students in place of lectures, was composed in 1933–34, and within a few years copies had made their way to Oxford.[4] This text already makes use of notions that will be vital to the ideas of the *Investigations*, such as 'family resemblance' and 'language game'; it deals with many of the same questions (meaning, understanding, rules) as the later book; and in its focus on the importance of the concrete and the specific – as opposed to the general – it already exemplifies Wittgenstein's 'anthropological perspective' in many ways:

> The idea that in order to get clear about the meaning of a general term one had to find the common element in all its applications has shackled philosophical investigation; for it has not only led to no result, but also made the philosopher dismiss as irrelevant the concrete cases, which alone could have helped him to understand the usage of the general term. When Socrates asks the question, 'What is knowledge?' he does not even regard it as a preliminary answer to enumerate cases of knowledge. (BB, p19–20)

It also already departs from the 'calculus conception' of language we met in Chapter 3 in explicit fashion:

From Rules to Life

In practice we very rarely use language as such as a calculus. For not only do we not think of the rules of usage – of definitions, etc – while using language, but when we are asked to give such rules, in most cases we aren't able to do so. (BB, p25)

The Brown Book was composed a year later and dictated directly to two friends. It begins, just as the *Investigations* do, with Augustine's account of how he acquired language, and goes on, as Monk describes (1991: 345), to do almost nothing but provide ever more intricate and detailed versions of examples of language games, with very little explicit signposting as to their broader relevance. One such instance of explicitness is worth noting for our purposes: having pointed out the 'grammar' of time and the ways in which words like 'now' do not in fact function like other specifications of time, he says,

This can easily be seen if we look at the role this word really plays in our usage of language, but it is obscured when instead of looking at the *whole language game*, we only look at the contexts, the phrases of language in which the word is used. (BB, p108; italics in original)

Clearly, the idea of a 'whole language game' signifies parameters of relevant context far beyond, say, the 'logical space' of colour, as we met it in Chapter 3. This is echoed in Oswald Hanfling's characterization of form of life as 'meant to convey the wholeness of system, and also the fact that it includes action ('life')' (Hanfling 1989: 162). On the other hand, the explicit holism here recalls the Tractarian problem of trying to see *sub specie aeternitatis*, as if one could step back and survey the entirety of life, and in later incarnations of the idea, it will fall away.

By 1937, Wittgenstein had a new typescript, which contained the first 188 or so of the 693 sections of what would become the first part of the *Investigations* (Hacker & Schulte 2009: xix; see also Venturinha 2013). He continued to add to, rework, and rearrange this material for the remainder of his life. Monk has the first part complete by around 1946.

Life without Form

He was still working on what would become the second part in 1951 and had intended to use the material to revise the first part, but death intervened. This material was added as 'Part II' of the *Investigations* by Elizabeth Anscombe and Rush Rhees when they published the manuscript in 1953, but in modern editions, it is often labelled 'Philosophy of Psychology – a Fragment', to make clearer its distinct status.

Form of Life in the Investigations

The problem with any attempt to summarize the *Investigations* is that they are clearly not intended to add up to anything like an 'argument', let alone a 'theory'. Running through them from the first to the last sections doesn't yield the arc of a set of claims, each building sequentially on those that came before (as in the structure of the *Tractatus*). For this and many other reasons, what follows in this chapter is not in any remote sense an attempt at a survey of the whole book, let alone of all of Wittgenstein's later work.[5] But what we'll see emerge from his discussions of form of life is not just a different content for context, but a deliberately formless way of discussing context itself. The very imprecision with which Wittgenstein deploys terms such as 'customs', 'practices', and 'form of life' will prove key to understanding his mature philosophical position.

'Form of life' (*lebensform*) only, in fact, appears five times across the totality of the *Investigations* as we have them from the Anscombe and Rhees version: three times in the first part (§19, §23, §241), and twice in the fragment on the philosophy of psychology (§1 and §345).[6] The first two occasions are early on in the text, during what has since become one of the most famous discussions of twentieth-century philosophy: that of a passage of the *Confessions* in which Augustine reflects on how he came to learn language. Augustine's picture of language-learning is essentially ostensive definition: 'When grown-ups named some object and at the

Form of Life in the Investigations

same time turned towards it, I perceived this, and I grasped that the thing was signified by the sound they uttered, since they meant to point *it* out' (PI 1; italics in original).

This appears a simple pastiche of mentalist or representationalist theories of meaning. But as several commentators have pointed out (e.g. Goldfarb 1983; c.f. Rhees 1960), the choice of Augustine as a foil with which to begin the *Investigations* is in lots of ways a curious one. The passage in question is not in fact an elaborate theory of the nature of meaning and nor is it intended to be. It is a picture of what it is to learn a language from the perspective of a child: words name objects. Clearly, Wittgenstein could have begun with Frege, Russell, or indeed perhaps his own work in the *Tractatus* if he'd wished to fill out a philosophical theory of meaning with which he was going to disagree. The choice of Augustine instead indicates that Wittgenstein's objection is not to a particular philosophical perspective on language – just as it is not his intention to offer such a thing himself – but to the ways in which any philosophical perspective tends implicitly to turn a description of a particular use of language like this into a general theory. No actual philosopher would ever be likely to sustain Augustine's brief description as a 'theory of language' – as Wittgenstein points out, 'this' and 'that' are not names and no-one could seriously think they were – but they might well use expressions like 'name some object' or 'signified' in ways that gave those expressions metaphysical weight (and perhaps indeed lead to representationalist or mentalist theories of meaning). There is nothing wrong, in other words, with Augustine's description as a description of a very specific sort of context – where things go wrong, for Wittgenstein, is when the ordinary notions involved in such descriptions become parts of general theoretical explanations (Cavell 1962).

This is illustrated by the long discussion in the *Investigations*, which follows the passage of Augustine, of what is often now called the 'Builders' Language': Builder A and Assistant B are building something with stones, and B passes A 'blocks', 'pillars', 'slabs', or 'beams' when asked. At first, we're told this 'primitive language' consists of nothing but these four words called out as commands. It is this discussion that will shortly lead to the passage in §19 in which Wittgenstein says, 'to imagine a language is to imagine a form of life', and later to the most famous section of the entire *Investigations*, in which he will assert that 'the meaning of a word is its use in the language' (§43). Understanding the work the concept of 'form of life' is doing here is thus crucial to both Wittgenstein's purposes and our own.

As soon as he gives us the builders' language, Wittgenstein tells us to 'conceive of this as a complete primitive language' (§2), and again later, in a more anthropological tone, he says 'we could imagine that the language of (§2) was the *whole* language of A and B, even the whole language of a tribe' (§6). Again, just before the first entry of 'form of life', Wittgenstein writes (in a passage Geertz will later make use of),

Don't let it bother you that languages (2) and (8) consist only of orders. If you want to say that they are therefore incomplete, ask yourself whether our own language is complete – whether it was so before the symbolism of chemistry and the notation of the infinitesimal; calculus were incorporated in to it; for these are, so to speak, suburbs of our language... Our language can be regarded as an ancient city: a maze of little streets and squares, of old and new houses, of houses with extensions from various periods, and all this surrounded by a multitude of new suburbs with straight and regular streets and uniform houses. (PI 18)

Immediately following this, we come to the first appearance of 'form of life':

It is easy to imagine a language consisting only of orders and reports in battle. – Or a language consisting only of questions and expressions for answering Yes and No – and countless other things. – And to imagine a language means to imagine a form of life. (PI 19)

Form of Life in the Investigations

Wittgenstein's repeated emphasis on the 'completeness' of the builders' language, together with the idea that imagining language is imagining a form of life, should strike us in light of our earlier discussions of Wittgenstein's different models of context. Is this another version of language as a model of context we met in Chapter 3, in which different such contexts are necessarily closed and complete and exist in their own logical space? Is the builders' language akin to the 'logical space' of colour or time?

Clearly not, if we are supposed to imagine it as 'complete' in the way in which we might imagine our own language as complete without features it may yet still acquire. In fact, the relation between the builders' language and 'our own language' is crucial to understanding Wittgenstein's wider point in invoking Augustine.

If the builders' language is 'complete' and 'whole' as Wittgenstein repeatedly insists we think of it as being, does that mean it is Augustine's picture of communication brought to life? It would seem so, since there's nothing in it beyond the four names of objects. But by insisting that we see it as 'whole' and 'complete', part of Wittgenstein's point is precisely to indicate how implausible it feels to refer to these words as 'names', or even to refer to the 'language' as a language, a point he will go on to extend. This is not to denigrate the builders' language – it is to point to the ways in which, when we use words like 'name' and 'signify', we cannot but conjure up the vast and varied universe of our own linguistic practices; we can't isolate them from that wider pattern.

In other words, the builders' language, as an instantiation of Augustine's picture, has 'a double edge' (Goldfarb 1983: 272). It reveals the legitimacy of the picture as a description of language in a certain specific form ('this narrowly described area' (§3)) – an activity of a certain type. But the very prospect of taking this activity seriously as exhausting the entirety of language shows how it is capable of misleading: our sense of notions such as 'naming', 'signifying', and indeed 'language' can't in fact be carved out from the enormously wide range of things we do with and mean by those words, and so they can neither be easily isolated from those surroundings nor made to stand for some basic, fundamental, or essential version of them. *If* we were like the builders, Augustine's picture might make sense. But we are not – and even though parts of our lives might look like the context of the builders, the fact that they are only parts means that it is a mistake to treat them separately from the rest of our linguistic existence. The builders' language, in other words, is 'primitive' in the same sense in which the gestural language we met Wittgenstein describing in relation to Sraffa is 'primitive', or indeed the child's language we also met him invoking then: not in a developmental or evolutionary sense, but in constituting a 'narrowly described area' (§3), a part of something more complex. Importantly, by this point in his thinking, Wittgenstein believes that describing such areas is all that can be done – as we shall see, the boundaries between them are not sharp or clearly defined, and they do not add up to a whole.

So this first appearance of 'form of life' already marks a distinct model of context, different from ones we have met previously. To say that the builders have a 'form of life' is not to say that their language has a 'grammar' in the technical sense in which it was meant by Wittgenstein in his transitional work – clearly it has no more of a grammar than Sraffa's Neapolitan gesture.[7] Hacker makes evident how different this idea is to the sense of context in Wittgenstein's earlier work:

A language is an open-ended series of language-games integrated into the actions and lives of its speakers. To learn a language is to learn how to do things with words. It is to learn how to act and respond to circumstances and to others, not how to calculate or compute the meaning (truth-conditions) of a sentence from the meaning of its constituents and their mode of combination. (2015: 6)

Nor is it to say their language conforms to rules of a general propositional logic – Wittgenstein refutes the whole idea of a 'general form of propositions' in this section:

Form of Life in the Investigations

But how many kinds of sentence are there? Say assertion, question and command? – There are countless kinds; countless different kinds of use of all the things we call 'signs', 'words', 'sentences'. And this diversity is not something fixed, given once and for all; but new types of language, new language-games, as we may say, come into existence, and others become obsolete and get forgotten. (We can get a rough picture of this from the changes in mathematics). (PI 23)

It is also not to say that the builders 'form of life' is closed off from or incomprehensible to others – Wittgenstein has much to say about the possibilities of translating from 'our language' to theirs, much of which comes down simply to the impossibility of taking either as more primary or essential than the other.

It is in fact to say little more than what Wittgenstein says himself on the second occasion he uses 'form of life':

The word 'language-*game*' is used here to emphasize the fact that the *speaking* of language is part of an activity, or of a form of life. (PI 23)

To say the builders have a form of life is not in fact then – at least so far – to add anything to what has already been said about them – that they are engaged in practical action, in a life of some sort. It sounds like saying that this is a form of life should pick out something special about that life (precisely a 'form') that it might share with other such lives beyond their existence as such. But, in fact, it does not.[8]

We can at least pick out some clear ideas of what form of life does not mean from other parts of the *Investigations*. In Chapter 3, we met Wittgenstein's transitional views on the 'autonomy of grammar', and the power he seemed to attribute to the rules governing the use of language in different logical spaces. The model of context at work in that period was akin to a 'calculus', or to a language with precise and exact grammatical specifications. Such 'rules of grammar' seemed to play a significant part in mapping out the contours and parameters of context.

Life without Form

In the *Investigations*, by contrast, rules famously do not exhaust the relevant descriptions of context:

For how is the concept of a game bounded? Can you say where the boundaries are? No. You can *draw* some, for there aren't any drawn yet. (But this has never bothered you before when you used the word 'game'.)

'But then the use of the word is unregulated – the "game" we play with it is unregulated' – It is not everywhere bounded by rules; but no more are there any rules for how high one may throw the ball in tennis, or how hard, yet tennis is a game for all that, and has rules too. (PI 68; italics in original)

And later, making a point we'll return to again,

One can say that the concept of a game is a concept with blurred edges. – 'But is a blurred concept a *concept* at all?' – Is a photograph that is not sharp a picture of a person at all? Is it even always an advantage to replace a picture that is not sharp by one that is? Isn't one that isn't sharp often just what we need? (PI 71; italics in original)

In a straightforward sense, Wittgenstein's point here is that no context is exhausted by its 'rules'. Later, he'll invoke the idea of a chair that vanishes as soon as one approaches it. Is it still a chair? No rules of grammar specify the answer to the question, for such rules only work within the wider – blurry and unbounded – context in which they are situated, a context in which disappearing chairs have no place. We'll return later to the possibility of taking this remark metaphilosophically too – that is, to the utility of blurred concepts in analysis, as well as in their form as descriptions of actual language use.

Neither is form of life governed by an essential logic, like that of the *Tractatus*:

Thinking is surrounded by a nimbus. – Its essence, logic, presents an order: namely, the a priori order of the world; this, the order of *possibilities*, which the world and thinking must have in common. But this order, it seems, must be *utterly simple*. It is *prior* to all experience, must run through all experience; no empirical cloudiness or uncertainty may attach to it. – It must rather be of the purest crystal. But this crystal does not appear as an abstraction, but as something concrete, indeed, as the most concrete, as it were the *hardest* thing there is (*TLP* 5.5563) [sic].

We are under the illusion that what is peculiar, profound and essential to us in our investigation resides in its trying to grasp the incomparable essence of language ... whereas, in fact, if the words 'language', 'experience', 'world' have a use, it must be as humble a one as that of the words 'table', 'lamp', 'door'. (PI 97; italics in original)

And later,

The more closely we examine actual language, the greater becomes the conflict between it and our requirement. (For the crystalline purity of logic was, of course, not something I had *discovered*: it was a requirement.) The conflict becomes intolerable; the requirement is now in danger of becoming vacuous. – We have got on to slippery ice where there is no friction, and so, in a certain sense, the conditions are ideal; but also, just because of that, we are unable to walk. We want to walk: so we need *friction*. Back to the rough ground! (PI 107; italics in original)

Just as it is not governed by a morphology of grammatical rules, so neither is form of life governed by an essential and irreducible logic. In fact, in the last passage and in the idea of the 'humble' role of words like 'language' and 'experience' in the first, we find the outline of a positive sense of form of life, albeit still one drawn in contrast: philosophy lifts concepts out of context, onto the 'slippery ice where there is no friction'. Wittgenstein wants to go 'back to the rough ground [of ordinary usage]'.

The contrast between philosophy and the forms of life Wittgenstein will be describing in the *Investigations* becomes still sharper in subsequent pages, and this picture expands the antifoundationalist metaphilosophical reflections we have already met, as he tells us that,

Life without Form

We may not advance any kind of theory. There must not be anything hypothetical in our considerations. All *explanation* must disappear, and description alone must take its place. (PI 109; italics in original)

He then goes on to say, in the passage with which we began this book, and with specific reference to the *Tractatus*:

A *picture* held us captive. And we couldn't get outside it, for it lay in our language, and language seemed only to repeat it to us inexorably.
 When philosophers use a word – 'knowledge', 'being', 'object', 'I', 'proposition/sentence', 'name' – and try to grasp the *essence* of the thing, one must always ask oneself: is the word ever actually used in this way in the language in which it is at home? –
 What *we* do is bring words back from their metaphysical to their everyday use. (PI 115–116)

This sense of form of life as a matter of everyday practice – like speaking a language – is reinforced when Wittgenstein returns to the question of rules. He has, as we have seen, abandoned any deterministic understanding of rules, as he makes clear in another famous passage:

This was our paradox: no course of action could be determined by a rule, because every course of action can be brought into accord with the rules. The answer was: if every course of action can be brought into accord with the rule, then it can also be brought into conflict with the it. And so there would be neither conflict nor accord here. (PI 201)

His point here is a continuation of the earlier ones regarding the finitude of rules: not only can they not exhaust the possibilities of action in any given context, but they can also lead one into infinite regress as regards their interpretation. How do we know how to follow rules about the mathematical series of even numbers, for example, without also knowing an unspecifiable number of rules about how to interpret the first-order set of rules?

Form of Life in the Investigations

Wittgenstein's resolution of this question, which will lead him onto the final invocation of form of life in the first part of the *Investigations*, is to set aside the issue of interpretation altogether. Earlier, for example, he imagines the possibility of 'private rule-following':

It is not possible that there should have been only one occasion on which only one person followed a rule. It is not possible that there should have been only one occasion on which a report was made, an order given, or understood, and so on. – To follow a rule, to make a report, to give an order, to play a game of chess, are *customs* (usages, institutions).

To understand a sentence means to understand a language. To understand a language means to have mastered a technique. (PI 199; italics in original)

In other words, following a rule is not an interpretation, but a practice (PI 202). It needs no further justification. This conjures up the spectre of Moore's objections to some of Wittgenstein's transitional arguments, in which Moore points to the fact that there seems something non-arbitrary about the fact that 'red' means the colour red. If there is no justification for rules about colour terminology, then calling the colour red by any name would be legitimate.

The absence of justification by formal rule though is not the same as arbitrariness and it does not lead to 'choice':

When I follow the rule, I do not choose.
I follow the rule *blindly*.
  (PI 219; italics in original)

The connection to form of life here is Wittgenstein's point that there is no question of choice, legitimacy, or interpretation in such matters (and the boundaries of such matters are, again, left unspecified). Because they are matters of 'practice', 'customs', 'usages', 'institutions', etc., they are prior to any question of legitimacy.

Life without Form

Versions of the same point are made in later and famous discussions of phenomena such as pain and the giving of orders. Our understanding of the word 'pain' and other such sensations functions against the background of a form of life. They do not simply 'name' inner things in the way that words in Augustine's picture 'name' outer things, because if such things only existed for us their names would have no sense at all – hence, in the analogy of the 'beetle in the box', if everybody had such a box but couldn't see into anyone else's, the word 'beetle' wouldn't function as a name because its object could have no linguistic relevance. A name, in most language games, picks out the same object; but in the language game of the beetle, *anything* could be in the box. The point here again is that our use of words is always accompanied by an unspoken and unquantifiable set of associated notions – we don't learn what it is to be 'in pain' by suffering and naming the inner sensation, but by sharing in the form of life of other people who seem to feel similarly and can talk about such feelings.

This is not a behaviourist argument about the nature of reality but a 'grammatical' argument about the way we use language. Wittgenstein's point is not meant to be about the metaphysical priority of the external world over internal experience, but about the impossibility of isolating concepts from practical context. The same point applies in the discussion of giving orders (a point we met Gilbert Ryle making in the last chapter): the idea that an order is to be followed is embedded in the concept of an order. Without the accompanying set of human practices (of obeying orders), the concept of 'an order' makes no sense. A world in which orders were never obeyed would not be a world of disobedient people but a world without the concepts of orders and obedience.

Hence the final invocation of form of life:

Disputes do not break out (among mathematicians, say) over the question of whether or not a rule has been followed. People don't come to blows over it, for example. This belongs to the scaffolding from which our language operates (for example, yields descriptions).

'So you are saying that human agreement decides what is true and what is false?' – What is true and what is false is what human beings *say*; and it is in their *language* that human beings agree. This is agreement not in opinions, but rather in form of life. (PI 240–241; italics in original)

The contents of these arguments will be familiar to many anthropological readers, and for many others, it will no doubt confirm the received view that Wittgenstein's later philosophy takes an admirably 'anthropological perspective'. It is one of the most compelling and esoteric portrayals of the contextualist viewpoint one could imagine: 'red' means red because a certain set of human beings agree that it does, and moreover to even ask why it does so, or whether it should, is to attempt to put oneself outside of that agreement (for better but more likely for worse). So, the whole question of the arbitrariness of any particular facet of customary rule-following is a more or less misguided one, at least from the point of view of anyone doing the rule-following.

Again, however, what I want to highlight here is the formlessness of the language around form: how exactly are we to define the parameters of this contextualism? Are they 'customs'? 'Usages'? 'Institutions'? 'Languages'? 'Practices'? The final invocation of form of life in the *Investigations* makes very clear that it is a matter of form: it is not that people agree in what they say, or their opinions – in the contents or substance of anything, in other words – it is that they agree in the form of (their) life. But, once more, the nature of that form remains blurry, indistinct, and unspecified.

Form of life recurs twice more in the second part of the *Investigations*. The first occurrence again suggests the possibility of narrowing down its sense by contrast:

One can imagine an animal angry, fearful, sad, joyful, startled. But hopeful? And why not?

Life without Form

A dog believes his master is at the door. But can he also believe that his master will come the day after tomorrow? – And *what* can he not do here? – How do I do it? – What answer am I supposed to give to this?

Can only those hope who can talk? Only those who have mastered the use of a language. That is to say, the manifestations of hope are modifications of this complicated form of life. (If a concept points to a characteristic of human handwriting, it has no application to beings that do not write.) (PI II 1; italics in original)

Wittgenstein's point here is again not an empirical point about the mental abilities of dogs. It is about the forms of life against the background of which the use of words like 'anger', 'fear', and 'hope' make sense. The first two we use in a way that indicates that they may appear and disappear in a moment. Whereas the contexts in which we invoke 'hope' are more temporally complex and demand that we treat someone as capable of anticipation of a longer-term future. Such capacities are usually indexed for us by language – we usually don't treat a dog as capable of thinking about what will happen the day after tomorrow because the dog doesn't tell us of such thoughts. Its behaviour may indicate reactions to proximate surroundings or desire for immediate gratification, but behaviour alone doesn't usually communicate what we need to be able to use the word 'hope' of somebody.

The reference to non-human forms of life calls to mind the famous assertion, occurring later in Part II, that 'If a lion could talk, we wouldn't be able to understand it' (PI II 327). Is there, then, a sense in which we might distinguish a human from a non-human form of life, and thus at least the possibility of criteria by which we might define such forms? As we'll see below, some interpreters of Wittgenstein have stressed a kind of natural, or species-like, dimension in their understandings of the term. We'll discuss such readings in more depth in a moment; for now, I think it's hard to claim this passage alone helps us narrow down a meaning for the 'form of life'. All Wittgenstein really seems to be saying here is that it is true (contingently, one assumes) that hope and other

Form of Life in the Investigations

concepts are 'manifested' only in 'complicated' (linguistic) forms of life; not that a dog has no form of life, or that there is always an absolute and hard boundary between linguistic and non-linguistic forms of life.

The final explicit occurrence of the term is at §345 of Part II and runs simply:

What has to be accepted, the given, is – one might say – *forms of life*. (PI II 345; italics in original)

This occurs in the context of a discussion akin to that of PI §240–241 about mathematical certainty and is clearly connected to the wider set of discussions about 'certainty' that Wittgenstein has in the notes later published as *On Certainty*. In the remarks here, Wittgenstein reminds us that mathematicians don't usually dispute the results of calculations – that is, we don't need to go back over and check that $2 \times 2 = 4$ each time we write the calculation down, as if the value of the numbers may have altered since the last time we carried it out. There is clearly a sense in which – as in the application of colour names – we simply agree that it is the case. On the other hand,

'But mathematical truth is independent of whether human beings know it or not!' – Certainly, the propositions 'Human beings believe that $2 \times 2 = 4$' and '$2 \times 2 = 4$' do not have the same sense. The latter is a mathematical proposition; the other, if it makes sense at all, may perhaps mean: human beings have *arrived* at the mathematical proposition. The two propositions have entirely different *uses*. – But what would *this* mean: 'Even though everybody believed that $2 \times 2 = 5$, it would still be 4'? – For what would it be like for everybody to believe that? – Well, I could imagine, for instance, that people had a different calculus, or a technique which we wouldn't call 'calculating'. But would it be *wrong*? (Is a coronation *wrong*? To beings different from ourselves it might look extremely odd.)

Of course, in one sense mathematics is a body of knowledge, but still it is also an *activity*. And 'false moves' can exist only as the exception. For if

Life without Form

what we now call by that name became the rule, the game in which they were false moves would have been abrogated. (PI II 348–349; italics in original)

As noted, here we seem to be in the territory of certainty. That is, form of life in this context seems to denote that which cannot be questioned or which goes without saying – 'the given', as Wittgenstein puts it. This reinforces the point above about 'agreement' from PI §241 – form of life is not 'agreement' in the sense of choice, or a social contract. It is rather simply *the fact that* what we do is patterned somehow (that we have 'regular ways of acting', as he puts it in another manuscript – CE 397 – though again, the form taken by the pattern is left unstated).

This point is echoed in an earlier version of the passage above, published in *Remarks on the Philosophy of Psychology*, in which it is put like this:

Instead of the unanalysable, specific, indefinable: the fact that we act in such-and-such ways, e.g. *punish* certain actions, *establish* the state of affairs thus-and-so, *give orders*, render accounts, describe colours, take an interest in others' feelings. What has to be accepted, the given – it might be said – are facts of living [*Tatsachen des Lebens*]. (RPP I 630)[9]

It's interesting to note here that the choice Wittgenstein offers is between the 'unanalysable, specific, indefinable' and 'facts'. It is hard not to hear this as another metaphilosophical aside, that is, as asking how to pose the issue of 'form of life': one might describe it as being all the things a philosopher would think a concept should *not* be ('unanalysable, specific, indefinable'); or one might describe it as simply the way things are ('facts of living').

Indeed, this is not really a choice but two alternative descriptions of the same thing, as implied by the version of these remarks in which 'facts of living' and 'form of life' are offered with a dash between them. We should note how both of these alternative visions of 'life' are *the opposite of philosophy and of contemplation*, in what is surely not a coincidence. Again, Wittgenstein's vision of 'life' is surely constructed in part by contrast to his own existence, one from which he regularly sought escape.

The idea of 'facts of living', and of 'the given' also returns us to the question of whether there is some natural quality to forms of life, a question reinforced by comparable remarks in *On Certainty* in which Wittgenstein speaks of form of life as 'something animal' (OC 359). The question of whether to interpret form of life as a natural or cultural model of context has gone on to dominate a great deal of the exegetical literature, including some anthropological contributions.

The Collapse of Form

Helmreich and Roosth argue persuasively that the multiple meaning of *lebensform* 'are fundamental to its prevalence in the life sciences: the term's elasticity, its capacity to gesture toward senses and doctrines beyond itself, allows it to operate as a frame through which biological thinking can be worked out' (2010: 29). More specifically, they point to the arguments of isomorphism enabled by conceptions of shared form and ask what sorts of visions of isomorphism are conjured up in usages of 'life form': 'The primary operation, of course, is generalization – that disparate living things share form as such. More grandly, the claim of isomorphism across diverse biological entities authorizes the attempt to craft an encompassing *theory* of the biological' (2010: 43).

Although we'll come to the question of the 'natural' dimension of form of life in Wittgenstein's work, it should be clear by now that he is not in the business of offering 'theories' – or perhaps better, he is in the business of going to lengths to try to avoid doing so. So, the precise extent to which we should hear echoes of *lebensform* in its natural scientific usage in Wittgenstein's work is hard to assess, but we should not hear in it an attempt at a 'theory of the biological', or a return to an equivalent of Radcliffe-Brown's 'structural form'. Indeed, part of the point made thus far in this chapter is that any isomorphism invoked by form of life is, in fact, pretty hard to pin down since the form in question is left unspecified.

Helmreich and Roosth don't discuss Wittgenstein, but a number of Wittgenstein scholars have made use of their work and that of others in various attempts to construct a genealogy of the term that would reveal something about its invocation in Wittgenstein's philosophy (see e.g. Abreu e Silva Neto 2011; Gaffal 2011; Padilla Gálvez 2011). As Hacker puts it, 'there is no question that the expressions 'Lebensform' and 'Form des Lebens' and their cognates were in the air in Austria and elsewhere in the first decades of the twentieth century' (2015: 3). A few specific sources are mentioned by Hacker and others as potential places from which Wittgenstein may have derived the term: the German journalist Alfred Wechsler, who wrote a book, titled *Lebensformen*, about social manners and mores (see Gaffal 2011; Haller 1988); the psychologist Eduard Spranger, who wrote a book with same title about different types of psychological temperament (see Janik & Toulmin 1973); and finally Oswald Spengler, whom we have already met as a definite influence on Wittgenstein, and who is the only one of these authors we know for certain Wittgenstein read (see Baker & Hacker 1980). Spengler, as we saw briefly in Chapter 3, saw human societies as 'forms of life' in the biological sense, complete with a life cycle of their own (1965 [1918]).

The idea of a form of life as equivalent to a society or a culture is an unsurprising one, and indeed a large number of Wittgenstein's interpreters have subscribed to some version or another of the view that this is what he himself meant. As we examine these interpretations and others though, what becomes clear is how the very act of interpreting Wittgenstein's notion of form of life tends to introduce precisely the kind of formal specificity he worked to avoid. This is not a criticism of these interpretations but rather reveals something important about

The Collapse of Form

Wittgenstein's strategy and its relation to later anthropological invocations.

Gordon Baker and Peter Hacker are often taken as exemplary of the culturalist or linguistic reading of forms of life. As they put it, writing together,

A form of life is a way of living, a pattern of activities, actions, interactions and feelings which are inextricably interwoven with, and partly constituted by, uses of language. (1985: 74)

Elsewhere, Hacker alone characterizes things as follows:

In short, human beings in different epochs, in different cultures, have different forms of life. Different educations, interests and concerns, languages, different human relations and relations to nature and the world constitute distinct forms of life. For different cultures form different conceptual structures, adopt distinctive forms and norms of representation, limited only by the vague boundaries of the concept of a form of representation or a language. (2015: 11)

And taking specific issue with 'naturalist' readings of form of life, he adds later,

although it is correct that Wittgenstein contrasts the form of life of language-users with the ways in which other creatures that do not speak a language live, that does not mean that he thinks that there is only one human form of life. On the contrary, he is inclined to think of different languages as integrated into different ways of living, and to link the notion of a form of life to a culture. So the notion of a form of life is patently not predominantly a biological one... Wittgenstein's concept of the 'natural history of man' is predominantly anthropological. What interests him will hardly be found, as it were, in the Natural History Museum (Department of Human Biology), but in the Ethnological Museum of Mankind. (2015: 16–17)

Life without Form

Many anthropological references to the concept also clearly have something like culture or society in mind in their invocation of it. In such invocations, Wittgenstein is being read in the most literal possible sense as taking an 'anthropological perspective': when he says forms of life, what he means is (something like) what anthropologists mean when they say 'culture'; anthropologists too similarly can say 'form of life' in place of 'culture' without pausing for long.

Before assuming any kind of exact equivalence however, it is worth noting that Wittgenstein could quite easily have said 'culture' if that is what he had intended. Indeed, in passages from the Blue Book that directly anticipate some of the sections of the *Investigations* we've just seen quoted, that is exactly the word he uses:

> Imagine a use of language (a culture)...
> We could also easily imagine a language (and that means again a culture)...
>
> (BB, p 134)

Hacker uses these passages to justify his culturalist reading of form of life, but we might just as well ask why Wittgenstein stopped using the word 'culture' between the *Blue Book* version of the argument and the PI version we have. He uses more or less the same formulation as above in a draft of the Brown Book (see MS 115, 237), but throughout the manuscripts that will become the *Investigations*, 'culture' only appears on a single occasion, in a Spenglerian reference to 'cultural decline' (MS 152, 16). All of which at least hints at the possibility of a deliberate decision *not* to invoke culture and to use form of life in its place.

Then there are the occasions we have met in which form of life appears to refer not to a culturally particular way of thinking or acting but to a distinctively human context. Some interpreters of Wittgenstein have laid the stress entirely on this side of the matter, suggesting that form of life refers to 'the common behaviour of mankind' (PI 206; Garver 1994: 258). In Newton Garver's words, 'the identification of forms of life with life-style or cultures has no basis whatsoever in the

The Collapse of Form

text, and is particularly antithetical to Wittgenstein's thought' (1994: 266).

So there is quite a lot of room for dispute over what model of context form of life is supposed to constitute, as prefigured at the opening of this chapter. On one side are those in no doubt that it is a more or less straightforward synonym for culture and any hint of the biological or natural should be excluded from our understanding of it; on the other side are those who take exactly the reverse position.

A third school of interpretation takes what it sees as a much more nuanced view and is premised on the idea that Wittgenstein intended form of life to capture both cultural and biological dimensions of context, in some fashion or another. A number of these interpretations derive from a 1988 paper by the American Wittgensteinian Stanley Cavell, about whom we'll hear more in the next chapter.

Cavell suggests that the idea that Wittgenstein meant to specify something social when he wrote of form of life is a reasonable one, but he also suggests that this emphasis on form of life as social context by commentators 'eclipses' what he calls 'the natural', as in Wittgenstein's references to 'natural reactions' (PI 185), 'the common behaviour of mankind' (PI 206), and to his project in the *Investigations* as one of 'fictitious natural history' (PI II 335). Cavell calls the 'social' sense of form of life 'anthropological', or 'horizontal', and the 'natural' sense biological, or 'vertical' (1988: 255). According to this view, there is a sense in which form of life refers to the particular differences between different kinds of human collectives and a sense in which it refers to human life more generally.

Cavell is making more than just a banal point about the importance of taking into account both natural and social contexts here. Cavell sees Wittgenstein as using the term form of life, with its roots in the biological sciences, and in particular in Spengler's and Goethe's vitalist organicism, quite deliberately in order to stress that the 'form' in question is that of *life*, that is, that the form of human conventionality

Life without Form

and sociality is itself somehow a natural form, though this is, as Spengler puts it, 'the living Nature of Goethe, and not ... the dead Nature of Newton' (Spengler 1965 [1918]: 17):

Spengler's vision of Culture as a kind of [vitalist, organic] Nature (as opposed, let us say, to a set of [exclusively social] conventions) seems to me shared, if modified, in the *Investigations*. (Cavell 1988: 256)

In some ways then, this returns us to the concern for morphology we met in Chapter 3: the 'form' of 'form of life' is variable insofar as it clearly is to some extent intended to capture the variety of cultural and social contexts in which human beings live; but the character, as it were, of that form is always that of 'life', of human life specifically.

Rooted as it is in Wittgenstein's connection with Spengler and his interest in morphology, this argument feels plausible, at least more so than ones that aim at excluding either the 'human' or the 'social' dimension of form of life. It also reveals some important implications of this final shift in Wittgenstein's contextualism, implications revealed more clearly in some examples of readings of form of life that draw partly or directly on Cavell.

In a range of important and influential work, the anthropologist Veena Das and philosopher Sandra Laugier have drawn on Cavell's understanding of form of life to argue for 'the mutual implication of the natural and the social' (Cavell 1991: 44). Echoing Cavell, Laugier argues,

What discussions of [Wittgenstein's conventionalism] have obscured is the strength in Wittgenstein of the natural and biological sense of form of life, which Wittgenstein picks out in evoking 'natural reactions' and 'the natural history of humanity.' What is given in forms of life is not only social structures and various cultural habits, but everything that can be seen in 'the specific strength and dimensions of the human body, the senses, the human voice' and everything that makes it the case that, just as doves, in

The Collapse of Form

Kant's phrase, need air to fly, so we, in Wittgenstein's phrase, need friction to walk (PI §107) (Laugier 2018b: 208)

Das articulates these distinct dimensions as 'the horizontal or ethnological sense of *form* and the vertical dimension of *life*':

In the former case, we might think of the difference between, say, coronation and inauguration, or different societal arrangements for the devolution of property. In the latter case, the differences alluded to are those of being human, being animal or being bird – thus eating, pawing or pecking – each act meeting a biological need but only in ways that humans, animals or birds do. (Das 2016: 171; and see Han and Das 2015: 24)

Drawing directly on Das, Laugier interprets her as follows:

Das's point is that the idea of life form involves not a banal distinction between natural and conventional but a naturalness of the acts of eating, pawing or pecking as belonging to our lives as humans, as distinct from what is natural for other animals or birds, and as distinct from mere [sic] ethnological variation. (Laugier 2018b: 208)

And she goes on to quote Cavell articulating the distinction along similar lines:

In being asked to accept this [natural sense of form of life], or suffer it, as given for ourselves, we are not asked to accept, let us say, private property, but separateness; not a particular fact of power, but the fact that I am a man, therefore of this (range or scale of) capacity for work, for pleasure, for endurance, for appeal, for command, for understanding, for wish, for will, for teaching, for suffering. (1989: 44)

These interpretations, like Cavell's, are persuasive and plausible. Though, as elsewhere in this book, my interest is not in adjudicating

Life without Form

the merits of different exegeses of Wittgenstein's work, for what it's worth I find these versions compelling.

But precisely insofar as they are compelling, they are also distinct from Wittgenstein's own arguments. What I mean by that is that they make clearer and more explicit several aspects of Wittgenstein's invocations of form of life; but *precisely in doing so*, they distinguish themselves from those invocations, and they do so in ways that I think are significant: not because such distinctions render these interpretations problematic or incorrect as readings of Wittgenstein – but because of what these distinctions reveal about the value of Wittgenstein's arguments for anthropology.

The key distinction I have in mind is that what these interpretations do is make explicit what remains only implied – and, I think, deliberately only implied – in Wittgenstein's own words: the collapse of form.

To illustrate, let's go back to that remark from an earlier draft of work that was intended to go into later parts of the *Investigations*:

Instead of the unanalysable, specific, indefinable: the fact that we act in such-and-such ways, e.g. *punish* certain actions, *establish* the state of affairs thus-and-so, *give orders*, render accounts, describe colours, take an interest in others' feelings. What has to be accepted, the given – it might be said – are facts of living [*Tatsachen des Lebens*]. (RPP I 630)

In a still earlier version, 'facts of living' and 'form of life' are presented next to one another with a dash between them, as if they are alternative and equally legitimate descriptions (see MS 133, 28r).

What this nicely captures – though only for Wittgenstein, as these remarks were not intended for publication – is the ambiguity that is made completely explicit in the idea that form of life has two 'dimensions': on the one hand, it tells us that life *has a (singular, natural, human, biological, etc) form*; on the other hand, it tells us that that form in question consists in the 'unanalysable, specific, indefinable', or better

The Collapse of Form

yet, simply the 'facts of living' in all of their variety. As Das quotes Wittgenstein as putting it in the remarks we now have as *On Certainty*:

You must bear in mind that the language-game is so to say something unpredictable. I mean it is not based on grounds. It is not reasonable (or unreasonable).
It is there – like our life. (OC 559)

Form of life, to put it more simply, refers to both life ('facts of living' in all their particularity, which are just 'there') and to a singular form such life takes.

What remains almost entirely latent in Wittgenstein though is anything that will give specificity to that singular form. That should not surprise us – we've already met the problems he encountered in trying to give a shape to 'rules of grammar' that would be singular and transcend any particular logical space. And we've met his characteristic and increasing allergy to metaphysics. Giving specificity to form of life would surely have seemed like another route to a 'metaphysical' cancellation of metaphysics. It would also have led to paradoxes with which anthropologists are more than familiar: saying that one thing as opposed to another is an essential feature of the form of human life seems to deny or at least blunt the sense of form of life as variety and particularity.

Yet such specificity does appear sometimes in his writing, and it is this that his interpreters pick up and run with. It is there, for example, in the reference to the 'common behaviour of mankind' – although it's worth noting that the only thing acknowledged here is the existence of such common behaviour, rather than any particular form it takes. It is there in a reference we have already seen to 'regular ways of acting', though again it is notable that nothing beyond their regularity is indicated about such ways.

Occasionally Wittgenstein is more specific though. Danièle Moyal-Sharrock, for example, who draws on both Cavell and Gertrude Conway

Life without Form

in making an argument comparable to Das's and Laugier's, quotes this passage, from Wittgenstein's lectures on mathematics in 1939:

You say to someone 'This is red' (pointing); then you tell him 'Fetch me a red book' – and he will behave in a particular way. This is an immensely important fact about us human beings. And it goes together with all sorts of other facts of equal importance, like the fact that in all the languages we know, the meanings of words don't change with the days of the week.
   Another such fact is that pointing is used and understood in a particular way – that people react to it in a particular way. (LFM 182; quoted in Moyal-Sharrock 2015: 34)

Likewise, she later quotes from the *Zettel* and expands:

Were we to meet a tribe of people brought up from early youth to give no expression of feeling of any kind, we could not see these people as human beings: 'These men would have nothing human about them' (Z 390). The human form of life would by definition include behaviours such as these, as well as breathing, eating, walking, hoping, dying but also speaking, thinking, giving orders, asking questions, telling stories, having a chat. (2015: 34)

Her expansion of Wittgenstein's passing reference to a thought experiment about people who don't give expression to emotion to include other, apparently similar, criteria for a human form of life ('breathing, eating, walking, hoping, dying but also speaking, thinking, giving orders, asking questions, telling stories, having a chat') is characteristic of these interpretations. Later in the same piece, she writes,

There is then a basic as well as a more sophisticated – or modified – notion of culture, and the former characterises the human form of life. Basic sociocultural activities such as playing, helping, fighting, dancing; and sociocultural relations, such as parenthood, community, leadership are shared by humans universally; but as we evolved from proto-linguistic into linguistic forms of communication, different languages embedded in specific cultural norms and values emerged. (2015: 33–34)

So we may now add 'playing, helping, fighting, dancing; and sociocultural relations, such as parenthood, community, leadership', as well as 'giving expression to emotion', to our list of substantives ('basic sociocultural activities') that characterize a human form of life.

Or we could return to Das and Laugier, who are somewhat more circumspect in their explicit commitments but still give, I think, far more of a distinct shape to form of life than Wittgenstein does. We have already met 'the specific strength and dimensions of the human body, the senses, the human voice' (Laugier 2018b: 208) as well as 'eating, pawing or pecking' as distinguishing human from animal and bird forms of life. In Laugier we also meet 'What we may call general traits of human nature such as birth, death and sexuality' (2018b: 215), and Das's ethnographic descriptions of people engaged in 'ordinary life' by eating, walking, having domestic disputes, offering one another glasses of water, etc. are well known.

Again, my intention here is not critical, either of the arguments themselves or of the propriety of their interpretation of Wittgenstein. It is to highlight the fact that attempting to clarify Wittgenstein or even only to interpret him is liable to lead one into commitments that he seems to have taken pains to avoid. In this case, those commitments regard how exactly to characterize the 'form' of form of life.

One assumes that Wittgenstein could have quite easily stated himself that he wished to designate a distinct natural set of capacities of human beings. It would hardly have been beyond him to do so. Or he could have been more specific – as we have seen his interpreters having been – about what sorts of features of this form he had in mind in giving examples.

But what happens in the process of interpretation of him is a slip from the language of form to the language of content: that is, from the claim that there is a form – 'unanalysable, specific, indefinable, etc.' – to the claim that the form is substantiated in certain activities. Wittgenstein tends to leave these activities unspecified, or at least rarely ever to specify them in a way that elevates them to the level of essential characteristic. But in interpretations of him, eating, sex, birth, death, walking, domestic disputes, violence, language, giving expressions to feelings, etc., come to stand for the form. This fact of substantives coming to characterize a form slips past one quickly without care because it is so tempting to read these activities as basic universals and accept them as characteristic of humanity for that reason. But to substantiate form of life in this way – to make such features into essential characteristics of humanity – is surely to risk slipping back into the magic of metaphysics, not to mention activating anthropological allergies to universalizations about humans and their behaviour.

There is also a second and more complex layer to the rendering explicit of the substantive content of form of life: the idea that what gives human life its form is precisely its taste for the 'conventional', or the culturally and socially particular:

Here the array of 'conventions' are not patterns of life which differentiate human beings from one another, but those exigencies of conduct and feeling which all humans share. Wittgenstein's discovery, or rediscovery, is of the depth of convention in human life; a discovery which insists not only on the conventionality of human society but, we could say, on the conventionality of human nature itself. (Cavell 1979: 110–111)

This is even clearer in Moyal-Sharrock, who quotes John Canfield and Pascal to the effect that 'Custom is our nature':

If language is a set of customs in which words play a role, and if language develops out of an earlier set of proto-customs, then it seems plausible to suppose that certain customs are to be found in every human society. The hypothesis is, in particular, that every extant or historically known human

The Collapse of Form

culture has language-games of greeting, requesting, responding to requests, refusing, responding to prohibitions, make-believe, intention-utterance, responding to intention-utterance, and possession-claiming. Across the vast differences between the various human cultures, one finds those customs, and others, as a common factor. (Canfield 2007: 73; quoted in Moyal-Sharrock 2015: 33)

Or later, in her own words, defending Wittgenstein from the charge of relativism:

Whereas there can be countless forms of human life, there can only be one human form of life, a form of life which collectively characterizes all of 'mankind'. Wittgenstein makes clear he has this understanding of form of life in mind when he writes that '[t]he common behaviour of mankind is the system of reference by means of which we interpret an unknown language' (PI 206, Anscombe translation). By this, he means that it is this universally-shared human behaviour, to which patterns of life and language-games belong, that constitutes the bedrock from which any human being can begin to understand another human being, and from which any human being must begin to make sense. This precludes a thoroughgoing relativism. There is multiplicity, yes, but within a fundamental unity. (2015: 39)

Here again, the basic idea should be familiar to anthropologists from similar suggestions about the notion of 'culture': that it is both universal and particular, universal in its form and particular in its contents (Geertz 1973; Strathern 1995: 159). 'The nice thing about culture is that everyone has it', as the title of a piece by Marilyn Strathern goes.

It is notable though that often – at least in recent decades – where anthropologists have raised this fact about the concept of culture they have done so in order to highlight a problem, not a virtue. Transcendentalizing particularity may feel like a happy way out of the problem of relativism, but as Strathern and others point out, it's a mistake to imagine that doing so comes without a certain set of

Life without Form

metaphysical commitments – for instance, to the view that particularity is a property of social conventions, or to the idea that such conventions are the defining and exclusive property of human beings. The same work that has pointed out such commitments – alongside the fact that they are not shared by all the people we may work with – has led anthropologists, if not to abandon concepts of culture and society entirely, at least to be extremely wary of the commitments such concepts may imply.

One imagines Wittgenstein knew little or nothing about Amazonian shamans or Melanesian perspectives on gender. But his capacity for imagining difference was extensive, and it is not hard to believe that he might have imagined differences over difference of the sort anthropologists such as Strathern, Roy Wagner, and Eduardo Viveiros de Castro have highlighted in recent decades.

Speculation aside, we don't lack evidence of the fact that Wittgenstein had a track record of worrying about the form of his arguments, as noted at the outset of this chapter. He also had a track record of worrying about what the *Tractatus* might refer to as the 'ineffability' of form; that is, of taking the view that form – logical or representational form in the *Tractatus*, for example – serves not to 'depict' or itself to 'represent' but to stipulate or to instruct. What this implies, as Chon Tejedor argues, is that

Sentences can be used to express form, but, when they do, they are expressing instructions. The role of expressing instructions is different from the role of expressing pictures (i.e. of representing possible states). The two roles have to be distinct and mutually exclusive, insofar as all there is to the distinction between pictures and instructions is precisely such a difference in roles: the same sign can be used to express a picture or to express an instruction, and the difference lies precisely – and exclusively – in this use: in the role that the sign is being made to play... If a sentence is used to express an instruction, it is not simultaneously used to depict or say. It is in this deflated respect that all forms, including (optional) representational

The Collapse of Form

and scientific forms, are ineffable (i.e. cannot be said) for Wittgenstein. (2015: 101–102)

Tejedor argues that this insistence on the ineffability of form persists through to the discussions of form of life in the *Investigations*, and this is, I suggest, one more reason why Wittgenstein may have chosen to leave unsaid the range of commitments implied by form of life made explicit by some of his interpreters. He may not have been using form of life as a depiction of or representation of a certain context or set of contexts, but as a suggestion or indication of how to talk about context: in the blurriest, loosest, and least formally committed way possible.

To reiterate a point made at the outset of this chapter, my interest here is not in uncovering Wittgenstein's 'real' intentions or meanings in speaking – or avoiding doing so – about form of life. What, instead, I'm trying to make clear are some consequences of being explicit about the nature of 'life' as a form or model of context, and of the fact that form of life in fact has no form. The key among such consequences is the fact that 'life' comes to stand for both the general and the particular, as exemplified in the way in which the social scientific use of the Wittgensteinian notion of 'ordinary life' attempts to make the idea stand for both concreteness and portability at the same time: everybody has an 'ordinary life' ('form of life'), but when such 'ordinary life' is invoked, it is in order to point to specificity and uniqueness ('the facts of living') (Clarke 2014; Fadil & Fernando 2015; Heywood 2023c, 2024; Lempert 2013). Form collapses into contents. In the next and final chapter, we'll look at the history of this collapse in anthropology and some of its consequences.

SIX

Anthropology after Wittgenstein

> I am by no means sure that I should prefer a continuation of my work by others to a change in the way people live which would make all these questions superfluous. (For this reason I could never found a school).
>
> – CV 61

This chapter in some ways sets itself a more ambitious task than the others of this book. Where thus far our narrative has been more or less chronological and historical, and chapters have dealt with recognizable 'periods' of the history of anthropology – even if they may have done so idiosyncratically in some ways – this final part of the story traces parts of an impossibly broad swathe of time, from the 1960s to the present day, and moves from the rarefied air of the British academy that Wittgenstein loved to hate to its American cousin, in which he spent a very little time towards the end of his life, but which felt his influence long after his death.

It's hard to imagine what might unite scholarship from such disparate times and places beyond the fact of their being, as the subtitle of a recent book has it, 'Anthropology after Wittgenstein' (Das 2020). I'm going to take the liberty of putting a small sample of this wide variety of scholarship under the heading of one chapter because I'm interested in painting it with the broadest of brushes. The broad brush picture I'll try to paint is of the collapse of form over the last half century of anthropology: the disappearance of (false) clarity about the models of context described in earlier chapters. Alongside the disappearance of those models comes their slow and almost imperceptible replacement by ways of speaking about contextual difference that often still insist upon the facts of difference, and on the cardinal importance of context in understanding it. But these new ways of talking about context can rarely tell us (and sometimes make a virtue of not telling us) exactly how we should understand the shape or form of such context beyond a blurry sense that it is 'life' itself.

The antiformalist turn in anthropology manifested across a range of theoretical trajectories, of which I'll highlight only a small sample, though I'll try to suggest it's an exemplary one. The transformation visible in these theoretical trajectories reflects a broader disciplinary pattern: from early and tentative rejections of systematic frameworks in interpretive anthropology, through more radical dismantling of contextual forms in *Writing Culture*, to the elevation of 'ordinary life' as a category that is both transcendent and immanent. What unites these otherwise distinct approaches is a progressive intensification of antiformalism, as well as, I'll argue, a debt to a particular reading of Wittgenstein.

Of course, these intellectual developments didn't occur in isolation. The spread and uptake of Wittgensteinian ideas in American universities over the latter half of the twentieth century, the institutional pressures shaping anthropology departments following the 'crisis of representation', and the broader cultural turn away from grand narratives in the humanities all contributed to shaping environments in which the antiformalist approaches I describe here found receptive audiences. In this sense, the thinkers who exemplify them were as much responding to these conditions as they were shaping them. Engagements with Wittgenstein offered resources for addressing challenges that were already confronting anthropology. In the

Anthropology after Wittgenstein

Wittgensteinian vocabulary of one subject of this chapter, Clifford Geertz:

The surge of interest in 'myth,' 'fiction,' 'archetype,' 'semantics,' 'systems of relevance,' 'language games,' and so on is but the symptom that [a] transformation in viewpoint [across the social sciences] has in fact taken place, and – from the very multiplicity of the terms – that it has taken place in intellectual contexts much more isolated from one another than the commonality of their concerns would warrant. (1971: x–xi)

Similarly, my claims here are about disciplinary trends rather than about particular theories or theorists. Figures like Geertz, for example, as he implies above, didn't simply initiate trends that others passively adopted. Instead, just as I have been suggesting about Wittgenstein throughout this book, they articulated emerging possibilities and gave specific form to otherwise intangible tendencies, tendencies that others could then transform and develop. The elevation of antiformalism I describe here, from methodological preference to ontological commitment occurred through countless small transformations in the ways in which anthropologists conceptualized their projects, transformations visible in, but not caused by, the ideas I explore here. These ideas are windows onto a wider current, not origins of them.

So as elsewhere in this book, the claims in this chapter are partly intended to be heard as historical, in the sense that – as I will try to show – there are clear points of crossover and connection between the vitalist antiformalism of anthropology as it develops and the influence of Wittgenstein's philosophy. But, again as elsewhere in this book, as well as the possibilities of causal and biographical influence, I hope the connections themselves are elucidatory for what they show about the wider cultures of context in which Wittgenstein and anthropology were and are imbricated. Whichever direction of 'influence' is primary, putting anthropological and Wittgensteinian models of context themselves in context reveals their fragility and the ways in which they may be just as symptomatic of broader ways of thinking as the models they replace.

The Turn Against Form

Matei Candea captures the multivalent but incredibly powerful nature of the transformations at issue in this chapter perfectly:

The past half-century, in sum, has seen multiple interwoven attacks on form and formalism. Postmodern anthropology was wary of form as order and power. Later developments retained this insight even as they pushed away from the perceived literary abstractions and epistemological neuroses of the 1980s in favor of a concern with substance – thereby adding another kind of anti-formalism to the mix. While they came from different angles, and were otherwise in tension, these critiques of form as order and of form as abstraction met in the middle. In its valuation of life, transformation, flow, and mutability, as against the vague sense that 'form, to recall Klee's words, is death' (Ingold 2010: 92), the material turn echoed and amplified post-structuralist anxieties about form as power. (Candea 2025: 51)

The antiformalism of contemporary anthropology becomes even more striking when viewed from the perspective of context more specifically. Ladislav Holy once argued that 'in spite of all the changing fashions or epistemological shifts, context is and always has been the key anthropological concept' (1999: 48). As he later also puts it, 'the whole intellectual history of anthropology bears witness to this. However else the conceptual shifts in anthropology might be envisaged, they can be seen as shifts in the conceptualisation of what constitutes the relevant context of the phenomena which anthropologists try to explain' (1999: 50).

Yet when seen in terms of context, the shift – slow and hard to isolate as it has been – that Candea characterizes as one to antiformalism marks a break of a different kind to those we have been examining thus far in this book. Whether we conceive of those earlier moves as ones from the logical models of context to the linguistic models of context, as I have here, or from the context of social structure to the context of symbolic systems, or in any other way, what should be clear is that they are moves from one form to another, from one model with clear(ish) and sharp(ish) shape to another of the same kind. Whereas antiformalist contextualism is, in some important ways, of a very different species to its predecessors, as captured for example in Marilyn Strathern's characterization of postmodern contextualism as involved in 'play with contexts' (1987a). Michael Degani similarly describes the ways in which what Miyazaki characterizes as anthropology's antiformalist 'aesthetic of emergence' (2004: 137) 'refuses a contextualising depth-surface hermeneutics for a flat ontology of pastiche, heterogeneity, and assemblage ... anthropologists in this mode are sensors recording events in high fidelity, whether that be the event of some global assemblage or the singular event of the life of a suffering subject' (2025: 66).

As suggested in the quote above, Candea perceptively roots the collapse of form in anthropology in what are often otherwise seen as two distinct theoretical 'turns':

> The first ... sought freedom from form, structure, and grand narratives in the pursuit of formlessness, open-endedness, and play. This is the moment often glossed as the 'crisis of representation', that is, the rise of poststructuralism ... [the second displayed a] multifaceted concern with substance, with reaching the reality behind or beneath the abstractions and supposed epistemological navel-gazing of the literary turn. Retrospective accounts of anthropology since the 1980s have tended to emphasize the break between the literary turn and these later developments, as well as the internecine struggles of twenty-first-century anthropology, between politics and ontology, for instance, or between anthropologies of darkness and of the good. (Candea 2025: 48)

The Turn Against Form

As he goes on to point out, 'those periodizations, perspicuous in some respects, also obscure what those consecutive and opposed waves of theory shared – namely, a joint, pincer-like, rejection of earlier anthropological formalisms' (2025: 48).

What I want to point to in this chapter are the ways in which this rejection of form in favour of 'life' – whether understood as the formlessness of processual heterogeneity and emergence, or the reality of embodiment or life – mirrors so closely the final trajectory of Wittgenstein's contextualism we met in the last chapter: 'the unanalysable, specific, indefinable' or the 'facts of living' come, as two versions of the same argument, to take the place of the formal 'picture' that held us captive.

This characterization of anthropology's antiformalist trajectory necessarily simplifies a complex disciplinary landscape. Several substantial traditions maintained commitments to formalist elements of analysis throughout this period, including – to name only a few – parts of linguistic anthropology, some approaches to the study of kinship, Marxist anthropology's models of political economy, and cognitive anthropology's visions of knowledge transmission. Yet the fact that such traditions often appear as distinct from the mainstream of anthropology in many ways is telling – their persistence alongside, rather than counter to, the trends I point to here suggest the latter's dominance rather than challenging them.

The trends in question, I'll suggest, represent more than just a theoretical preference – they mark the emergence of a distinctive culture of context in late twentieth-century anthropology. Where earlier cultures of context had sought formal patterns or linguistic structures, new approaches elevated formlessness itself to a principle. The very indeterminacy and openness of context in some ways becomes seen in some cases, paradoxically, as the only legitimate way to frame anthropological understanding.

Anthropology after Wittgenstein

Wittgenstein's Anthropological Reincarnation

Clifford Geertz's student Richard Shweder wrote of him shortly after his death that,

> He would probably not have accepted the label 'Wittgensteinian', at least not without qualification, but, in some sense or another, I do think he may have viewed himself as Wittgenstein's reincarnation as an anthropologist. For in some of Wittgenstein's writings, Geertz apparently discovered a philosophy – one opposed to big-systems thinking and ideas about universally fixed essences – that suited his temperamental disclination to be pinned down... In accord with Wittgenstein, Geertz saw reality as an almost unthinkably complex continuum of overlapping likeness and differences that it was a bad job or a kind of violence to try filing into neat boxes... 'I don't do systems,' he would say. (2007: 201–202)

Why begin our discussions with Geertz? For reasons that this characterization neatly epitomizes. Firstly, and most obviously, because no history of the influence of Wittgenstein on anthropology would be complete without some discussion of a man whose debt to Wittgenstein Shweder makes clear here and who himself described Wittgenstein as his 'master' (Geertz 2000: xi; and see e.g. Inglis 2000); but secondly also because of the form that debt and influence took: the respect in which Geertz might have liked to see himself as Wittgenstein's anthropological reincarnation, Shweder suggests here, the parts of Geertz that came most clearly and self-consciously from Wittgenstein, are precisely the most antisystematic and antiformalist parts of him. This is obviously a very different 'Wittgenstein' to the one we met Needham drawing on in earlier parts of this book.

In focussing on Geertz's engagement with Wittgenstein and antiformalism, I necessarily highlight only one dimension of his rich and multifaceted intellectual project. His work encompasses numerous other concerns and contributions that can't be reduced to the trajectory I trace here. The tensions within his work – such as those I highlight below, between systems theory and Wittgensteinian scepticism – mirror wider contradictions and aporia embedded in the wider disciplinary currents in which he was moving. My aim isn't to offer anything like a comprehensive account of Geertz's anthropology but to identify a certain direction in it that resonates with later disciplinary developments.

There is a great deal more that could be said even of Wittgenstein's influence on Geertz than regards only their shared antiformalism. Geertz's early essays were among the first to import ideas from Wittgenstein's work into anthropology (e.g. 1973), perhaps the most famous of which is 'thick description', which may come directly from Ryle but whose indirect debt to Wittgenstein is clear. In a survey of Geertz's intellectual influences, Fred Inglis notes that Geertz's teacher at Antioch, George Geiger, a student of Dewey's, introduced Geertz both to American pragmatism and to the ordinary language philosophy of Austin and Ryle, as well as to their Cambridge cousin, Wittgenstein, with the latter – alongside literary theorist Kenneth Burke - as the key figure:

Wittgenstein taught [Geertz] to abandon the long-lived psychology of Romanticism, whereby human beings are divided into inner states and outer appearances, and in which the key to understanding other people is to discover how they think and feel about the world. We do this by way of our imaginative sympathy (sometimes 'empathy') with those thoughts and feelings, helped by the capacity of other people so to able to describe to us their feelings that they make us feel the same. (Inglis 2000: 45)

Inglis notes, as we might, the obvious connections between Wittgenstein's views of language and meaning as fundamentally public, social matters and Geertz's vision of cultural symbols, before concluding,

[Geertz] not only seizes the Wittgensteinian contention about ideas, passions and beliefs as not being 'unobservable mental stuff' but as made manifest in signs and symbols, he also catches up gratefully the attendant figure of a 'form of life'. The usefulness of such a term would have been quickly apparent to someone raised on Sapir's and Whorf's hypothesis derived from the multifariousness of syntactic and grammatic forms in the six thousand languages of the world. There is no call to raise the cry of 'relativist' simply because of what anthropology has taught us about the singularities of conception that come from thinking and perceiving in one language rather than another; translation is always possible, always inexact, always leads to misunderstandings, always holds out the hope of feeling at home in Babel. 'Forms of life' captures the object of anthropological enquiry, and enjoins us to respect it. (Inglis 2000: 48)

Here again it's notable that beyond the very clear parallels about the public nature of meaning, Inglis also makes much of the utility of Wittgenstein's conception of form of life for Geertz, and specifically its amorphous and blurry quality.

In one of his last collections of essays, Geertz himself made his debts to Wittgenstein eminently clear:

The main figure making [a positive shift in the nature of philosophy] possible, if not causing it, is, again in my view, that posthumous and mind-clearing insurrectionist, 'The Later Wittgenstein'. The appearance in 1953, two years after his death, of *Philosophical Investigations*, and the transformation of what had been but rumors out of Oxbridge into an apparently endlessly generative text, had an enormous impact upon my sense of what I was about, and what I hoped to accomplish, as did the flow of 'Remarks,' 'Occasions,' 'Notebooks,' and '*Zettel*' that followed it out of the *Nachlass* over the next decades... I was surely one of the more thoroughly preadapted to receive the message. If it is true, as has been argued, that the writers we are willing to call master are those who seem to us finally to be saying what we feel we have long had on the tip of our tongue but have been ourselves quite unable to express, those who put into words what are for us only inchoate motions, tendencies, and impulses of mind, then I am more than happy to acknowledge Wittgenstein as my master. (2000: xi)

Wittgenstein's Anthropological Reincarnation

Geertz goes on to list a selection of some of Wittgenstein's most well-known utterances as influences on him, but interestingly picks from amongst these as the most 'inviting' for an anthropologist the following, which we met in the last chapter:

'Back to the rough ground!' 'We have got,' Wittgenstein wrote, 'on to slippery ice where there is no friction and so in a certain sense conditions are ideal, but also, just because of that, we are unable to walk. We want to walk: so we need *friction*. Back to the rough ground!' (*PI*, 107). The notion that anthropology (though, of course, not only anthropology) is exploring the rough ground on which it is possible for thought, Wittgenstein's or anyone else's, to gain traction is for me not only a compelling idea in itself: it is the idea, unfocused and unformulated, that led me to migrate into the field, in both senses of 'field', in the first place... I wanted to walk. Or walkabout. In moving across places and peoples, restlessly seeking out contrasts and constancies for whatever insight they might provide into any enigma that might appear, one produces less a position, a steady, accumulating view on a fixed budget of issues, than a series of positionings – assorted arguments to assorted ends. This leaves a great deal of blur and uncertainty in place; perhaps most of it. But in this, too, we are following Wittgenstein: One might ask, he writes, '"is a blurred concept a *concept* at all?" – Is an indistinct photograph a picture of a person at all? Is it even always an advantage to replace an indistinct picture by a sharp one? Isn't the indistinct one exactly what we need?' [sic] (*PI,* 71). (2000: xii–xiii)

One thing immediately worth highlighting here is the primacy Geertz affords to Wittgenstein's idea of the 'rough ground' of everyday life. As I've described elsewhere, Geertz's invocations of 'the ordinary', 'the everyday' and 'ordinary' or 'everyday life' are among the first in anthropology to be explicitly Wittgensteinian in tone, adding the definite article, and gesturing simultaneously to both particularity and transcendence, and in this way they also prefigure later anthropological invocations of these ideas, as we'll see below (Heywood 2023c and see Heywood 2024).

Even more importantly for our purposes, the second thing worth highlighting from this passage is the celebration of antiformalism: 'Is it even always an advantage to replace an indistinct picture by a sharp one? Isn't the indistinct one exactly what we need?'.

This is in fact a misquotation of Wittgenstein. The phrase from the *Investigations* that Geertz cites actually runs 'Isn't [a concept] that isn't sharp *often* just what we need?' (PI 71; my italics).[1] In Geertz's quotation of this passage above, the word 'often' ('oft' in the German original) has completely disappeared, rendering a characteristically subjunctive claim from Wittgenstein into an absolute version in Geertz.

Geertz makes a very similar claim in much earlier work: 'An accurate picture of a vague object does not consist of a clear picture but a vague one' (Geertz et al. 1979: 199). But here again, as in the case above, what sounds like the Wittgensteinian point about the contingency of criteria of exactitude is actually a claim about the quite singular criterion of 'accuracy'.[2]

These are of course two minor examples, but they are examples of something significant: of the transformation of Wittgenstein's particularistic and pragmatic antiformalism into a much more transcendental, absolutist version of itself (whether or not Geertz himself consciously intended this).

We'll return to repeated iterations of this idea several times throughout the chapter as it recurs in anthropology's recent history, for example in the 'aesthetics of emergence' Candea describes as valuing 'analyses which are provisional and indeterminate, in order to match the perceived provisionality and indeterminacy of the world itself' (2018: 351).

The wider point I'm aiming to make with these illustrations is the point prefigured in Shweder's characterization: it is clear that Geertz took a great many insights indeed from Wittgenstein, and important histories might be recounted about the influence of any number of such insights on him (the most obvious perhaps being the public nature of meaning, an idea without which it is hard to imagine a Geertzian

Wittgenstein's Anthropological Reincarnation

anthropology, or the notion that 'we must pay attention to that which gives symbols their life: their use' – Geertz 1973: 405; see also Laidlaw 2018). Yet for Geertz himself, and for some of those close to him, what seems to have constituted the major influence of Wittgenstein is precisely the antiformalism that Shweder highlights: the idea that a 'blurry' or 'indistinct' concept might sometimes – or in practice, perhaps always – be exactly what we need. The difference between 'sometimes' and 'always' in that idea is significant.

Yet Geertz is hardly a thoroughgoing paragon of antiformalism. The idea that he didn't 'do systems' might come as a surprise to some, since he was trained in systems theory by Talcott Parsons, a background which has been wielded in critiques of some of his ideas (e.g. Asad 1993). And among the variety of notions, he is justly renowned for is that of 'cultural systems', such as religion, domains that share qualities across any given specific instantiations (1973). Yet, as James Laidlaw notes, 'that idea never received more than impressionistic expression and it was unclear what Geertz thought followed from it' (2018: 155). Likewise, he is sometimes said to have developed an essentialist and homogenizing conception of culture that made 'the Balinese', say, appear united in their difference from anybody else, near or far (e.g. Crapanzano 1986). Yet pressed to defend the relativizing vision of homogenous and discrete cultural contexts such a conception would seem to lead to, the best he could famously do was to attack its opponents (1984).

There is in other words something complex and a little paradoxical about Geertz's contextualism: on the one hand, it is clear he took inspiration from his 'master', Wittgenstein's antiformalist 'form of life' approach to context; on the other hand, he is most renowned for introducing into anthropology the idea that cultures are like 'texts', which surely suggests a degree of clarity about their form and shape. And the deployment of the notion of 'culture' itself delineates a frame for context: 'culture is not a power, something to which social events,

Anthropology after Wittgenstein

behaviors, institutions, or processes can be causally attributed; *it is a context*, something within which they can be intelligibly – that is, thickly – described' (1973: 14; my italics).³

The famous notion of 'thick description', gestured to above, in some ways embodies the tensions I've been describing. Borrowed from Ryle (himself, as we've seen, influenced by Wittgenstein), thick description seems to promise a solution to the push and pull of form and antiformalism in Geertz: a way to capture context – 'culture is context', Geertz tells us (1973: 14) – without reducing it to formal properties. It acknowledges the need for contextual framing but resists any reductive models. Yet in its applications it too, in some ways, contains the seeds of anthropology's later antiformalist commitments – Geertz himself pointed to its lack of evaluative standards in introducing it, and others have famously suggested that his own versions of thick description 'blur the boundaries' between the perspective of the anthropologist and that of the 'native' (e.g. Crapanzano 1986: 72–73; see also Shankman 1984; Zeitlyn n.d.). The journey from thick description to some of the later ideas we'll meet in this chapter is not direct, but some of the continuities are revealing. As Shankman points out of thick description, in the years after Geertz's coinage it would come to take 'the path that [Geertz] anticipated for it: finer and more elaborate descriptions of culturally situated phenomena with less emphasis on theoretical or methodological rigor' (1984: 269). Shankman was writing in the 1980s and his charge itself feels dated; later versions of anthropology will mirror this privileging of the granular texture of the everyday, but will feel less of a need to defend themselves against calls for more 'theoretical or methodological rigor'.

I don't think we should find the tensions in Geertz's work altogether surprising: as already noted, Wittgenstein wasn't the only influence on him, and it's easy to imagine how both his training under Parsons and his penchant for the literary might make him undesirous of dispensing altogether with a formalist disposition. It's also worth bearing in mind that when Geertz would have first encountered him, Wittgenstein was himself being read and interpreted in a variety of different ways, not all of which emphasized his antiformalism, and indeed some of which leant more on some of the ideas we have here characterized as 'transitional', for example a more or less transcendental or conventionalist approach to the idea of 'rules of grammar'.

So my suggestion is not that Geertz is Wittgenstein's anthropological Moses, leading the discipline successfully out to the promised land of vague pictures of vague objects. He is though, in some senses at least, his anthropological John the Baptist, a precursor of the dominant antiformalism to come, and come soon it would.

Beyond Systems

Ernest Gellner is, perhaps unsurprisingly, one of the commentators most forthright in blaming Geertz – and Wittgenstein, along the way – for the emergence of the *Writing Culture* movement in anthropology in the 1980s (it is, of course, a matter of blame in Gellner's view):

We have seen that the mild dose of ['epistemological hypochondria'] contracted by Geertz is surpassed by far by his defiant intellectual progeny, who now disavow him as not nearly sceptical, Hamlet-like, self-bound, postmodernist enough. Whatever Geertz's achievements in anthropology, his pro-relativism endorses and underwrites the excess of those who would go 'beyond him' along the path he has indicated. (1992: 44)

Elsewhere in the same text, Gellner names 'Wittgenstein, Heidegger, and Rorty' as philosophers responsible for the 'epistemological hypochondria' he identifies with *Writing Culture*, presumably in part because they are listed in the *Writing Culture* volume itself, alongside Dewey, as inspirations for the turn against epistemology: 'Their aim was not to improve epistemology but to play a different game ... knowledge without foundations.' (Rabinow 1986: 236). In Chapter 4 too, we have already met some of what we assume to be a Wittgensteinian inspiration behind Talal Asad's contribution to the volume, itself a critique of Gellner, an inspiration even more obviously on show in some of Asad's other writing (e.g. 2020). In a later piece, clearly inspired by Gellner, Richard A. Wilson makes this connection very explicit, building a case for blaming anthropology's disregard for epistemology entirely on the later Wittgenstein (2004; and see Myhre 2006; Wilson 2006).

I think it would be a hard sell to make Wittgenstein solely or even largely responsible for the post-structuralist turn in anthropology, and Gellner doesn't attempt this (though Wilson very much does). But it is much less difficult, I think, to point to the fact that the Wittgensteinian antiformalist contextualism that is vitally important, as we have seen, but still incipient in Geertz, is what gets radically intensified in *Writing Culture* and some of its adherents. As James Clifford argued in a later work,

The old conception of context as a fixed framework within which social activities take place becomes stretched and even shattered by means of movements of people between 'intersecting contexts'. (1997: 81)

Michael Taussig, meanwhile, is even more contemptuous of 'context', writing of an Igbo representation of a white man:

I know next to nothing of the 'context' of ritual, belief, or of social practice in which an older anthropology, eager for the 'native's point of view', would enmesh this [image], 'explain' him (away), 'Africanize' him (as opposed to 'whitenize' him). All I have is the image and its brief caption, and I am my own gaping subject of analysis. (1993: 238; cited in Dilley 1999)

And later, somewhat more circumspectly:

Context [is] not ... a secure epistemic nest in which our knowledge-eggs are to be safely hatched, but context is this other sort of connectedness incongruously spanning times and juxtaposing spaces so far apart and so different to each other. (1992: 46; cited in Daniel & Peck 1996)

In some of its more extreme variants, the antiformalist contextualism of post-structural anthropology may have fallen all the way over into outright anticontextualism, in which Self and Other are the only entities that remain. This is itself a form of radically intensified contextualism, as the philosopher Ben-Ami Scharfstein makes clear: 'the emphasis on context tends to make every event and individual essentially different from ever other... [This] leads to the essentially beguiling notion that everyone and everything is an absolute individual' (1989: xiii; cited in Dilley 1999). Coupled with its dominant concern for reflexivity and insistence on the impossibility of standing outside of epistemological frameworks, this solipsistic reading of post-structural anthropology makes it an odd descendant of the *Tractatus* in some ways.

As Marilyn Strathern notes, however, writing about the history of context in anthropology and noting the Frazerian echoes of post-structuralism, a more common result is exactly the collapse of form and content we saw in interpretations of Wittgenstein's form of life at the end of the last chapter:

This is a world 'with too many voices speaking all at once, a world where syncretism and parodic invention are becoming the rule, not the exception, an urban, multinational world of institutionalized transience' (Clifford 1986: 147) – one that treats differences like consumer choice, multicultural events as international food, that sees distinctions in the end as cultural creations and not also the workings of social interests against one another – in short, where *all contexts are alike*. All contexts are alike insofar as they give rise to the situated statement, are the frames for people's performances – every reason to adduce example after example simply to show that people's beliefs and practices are all equally bizarre. (1987a: 268–269; italics in original; and see 1995).

Anthropology after Wittgenstein

In *Writing Culture* and related work, what began in Geertz as a methodological preference for blurred descriptions becomes an ontological claim about the nature of reality itself. As Strathern notes, this leads to a collapse in which 'all contexts are alike' in their fundamental indeterminacy.

In this sense, again, the dimensions of Geertzian anthropology that get radically intensified by *Writing Culture* are precisely those that he himself and others around him thought most Wittgensteinian. Fewer anthropologists writing in the wake of *Writing Culture* than before it would feel the need to say out loud, as Geertz did, 'I don't do systems'.

Pain and the Real

In a volume published a decade after *Writing Culture*, one which called amongst other things for context to be 'contextured', anthropologist E. Valentine Daniel followed Geertz in giving Wittgenstein pride of place (shared with structuralism) in inaugurating anthropology's linguistic turn and what followed: '[he] provided a means for the narrowly linguistic to expand into a broader interest in discourse in general and counterdiscourses in particular' (Daniel & Peck 1996: 9).

In Valentine's well-known contribution to that volume, subtitled, 'Is There a Counterpoint to Culture?' he traces some of the history we have briefly covered here. While in his chapter he doesn't invoke Wittgenstein explicitly, the latter's shadow is omnipresent. For example, in tracing a shift in the social sciences and humanities from a focus on 'the bearers of Culture (with a capital "C")' to one on 'those who found themselves embedded in culture (with a small "c")', he quotes the title of a well-known essay by Raymond Williams ('Culture Is Ordinary' 1989 [1958]), but in many ways he'd have been better off citing Wittgenstein, since Williams's affinity with Marx made him somewhat suspicious rather than wholly celebratory of the turn to ordinary life and language (Daniel 1996: 359; and see Ware 2011).

Pain and the Real

Later, turning to Geertzian conceptions of culture, Daniel highlights, as we've seen here, the way Geertz 'played down the *systematicity* of culture' and 'was committed to taking "culture" from out of the private, especially from within people's minds or heads, and recognising it as public' (Daniel 1996: 360; italics in original).

The main reason, though, for discussing Daniel's essay is that it will be invoked seventeen years later by Joel Robbins as exemplary of a wider turn in anthropology in the 1990s towards what Robbins calls 'the suffering slot' (2013).

Robbins's argument has since been lauded and critiqued both for its diagnosis of this turn and its advocacy of an anthropology of the good. My interest here is in the diagnostic aspect of Robbins's claims. In these claims, his central point is that through the nineties, in the wake of the anxieties induced in the discipline by *Writing Culture* and related work, anthropology shifted its relation to its subjects 'from one of analytic distance and critical comparison focused on difference to one of empathic connection and moral witnessing based on human unity' (2013: 453). In place of the 'savage slot' of an otherness contextualizable through culture, anthropologists found the suffering subject, 'without borders', which 'knows no cultural barriers', and which is 'the very embodiment of our common humanity' (Fassin & Rechtman 2009; cited in Robbins 2013: 453).

Robbins invokes Fassin and Rechtman's work on trauma to point to a wider Western loss of interest in difference, accompanied by the rise of humanitarianism and human rights discourse, as well as the shadow of the Holocaust and emergence of diagnostic categories such as post-traumatic stress disorder (see also Antze and Lambek 1996). This is eminently plausible as a description of that wider cultural shift in the West, and in connecting it specifically to developments in anthropology Robbins notes that the universalization of trauma in the West gave anthropologists the means to re-found their discipline without need for recourse to otherness and to the contextual frames it implies.

Anthropology after Wittgenstein

Here though I want to add to this diagnosis by pointing firstly to the ways in which this collapse of contextual form in 'suffering slot' anthropology continues the wider trajectory we have been noting here from Geertz's Wittgensteinism onwards, and secondly to the coincidence – or not – of the fact that the subject anthropologists chose to use to exemplify common and shared humanity was also the later Wittgenstein's most famous and favoured topic too: pain and suffering.

Later we'll see this connection made manifest explicitly in the work of Veena Das, but already in what Robbins describes as Daniel's 'raw, still relatively unformed statement of the status of violence and suffering as realities beyond culture' (2013: 454) we can continue to find the echoes of the Wittgenstein we have been tracing through Geertz and *Writing Culture*.

In introducing the idea that violence and suffering may be 'beyond culture', Daniel points to what he thinks of as a key distinction between 'those who privilege the word – a group to which most academic scholars belong – and those who privilege the deed... Deeds, even when culturally centred... threaten to push against culture's limits' (1996: 362). Daniel goes on to develop the claim, specifically with reference to violence and suffering, that the problem with 'culture' in the contextual sense in which anthropologists use it is that it is 'supposed to end up, in anthropological analysis, to have a certain harmony... In our monographs, how much time do we spend "rounding it all up," especially through the crafting of a closing statement or conclusion?'. As he himself will go on to conclude, 'The culture concept, even in its processual mode, relies on a unifying metaphysical process ... culture totalizes' (1996: 364).

Note here that, despite the earlier recognition of the antiformalist, antimetaphysical, antisystematic 'progress' anthropology has made since the inauguration of the linguistic turn, it is these same impulses – alongside others too, of course – that inspire Daniel to push, as he sees it, yet further in the same direction. Moreover, it isn't only the

Pain and the Real

antiformalism that harks back to Wittgenstein, nor even the preference for deeds over words (or theories, or conclusions, or 'roundings up') – we may recall from Chapter 3 that Wittgenstein suggested Goethe's reframing of the gospel as a motto for his later philosophy: 'In the beginning was the deed.' It's also both the form of the path taken in this direction and the destination it leads to.

'The only way' Daniel says he knows how to convey the deeds that lie beyond culture is 'by intimation, by example', and to 'plunge into ethnography'. This form of intimation is, as Robbins suggests,

a new way of writing ethnography, in which *we do not primarily provide cultural context* so as to offer lessons in how lives are lived differently elsewhere, but in which we offer accounts of trauma that make us and our readers feel in our bones the vulnerability we as human beings all share. (2013: 455; my italics)

The form in which anthropological knowledge is expressed here is not through analysis or contextualization within a frame but through a withdrawal from or withholding of such analysis (again echoing Wittgenstein in his antifoundationalism and opposition to explanation). One is 'plunged' into the real, the ethnographic, often, as in Daniel's case, through the device of direct transcriptions of testimony to violence and suffering. The point is not, in other words, anti-contextualist; it is antiformalist – context remains in the dimension of description (we learn a great deal about the where, the when, the who, the how, etc. from Daniel's depiction), but its form has collapsed so as to be unassimilable to 'culture' or anything resembling it. In yet another passage that gestures to Wittgenstein, Daniel recognizes the potential for paradox in his attempt to 'say' the reality of life and violence:

Violence is an event in which there is a certain excess: an excess of passion, an excess of evil. The very attempt to label this excess (as indeed I have done) is condemned to fail... Everything can be narrated, but what is narrated is no longer what happened. (1996: 370)

At the heart of this very early manifestation of the trend Robbins rightly identifies as later dominant in turn-of-the-century anthropology, in other words, we meet a radical extension of the Wittgensteinianism in Geertz (and one centred, unlike in Geertz's own case, on a topic – pain and suffering – on which Wittgenstein wrote often and famously in his later work), an extension that unites both of the elements Candea highlights as fundamental to the disappearance of form in anthropology: the freedom of provisionality, of openendedness, and of indeterminacy as against 'totalization', 'conclusions', and 'systems', and the avowal of 'life' and of the reality to be found in it.

The Philosophy of Ordinary Life

In order to understand the direction this new version of Wittgensteinian antiformalism took in anthropology, and the even closer connections back to Wittgenstein this reveals, it's first necessary to take a short detour through late twentieth-century American Wittgensteinian philosophy.

Stanley Cavell, whom we've met briefly already, was studying graduate philosophy at Harvard when he first encountered the *Investigations* upon its publication in 1953. In memoirs and in the foreword to his *The Claim of Reason*, he tells us that, at first, he found it a 'less trustworthy and less orderly' version of Dewey's pragmatism (1979: xvii; see also 2010: 312). What seems to have prepared the ground for his conversion was the arrival of J. L. Austin at Harvard for six months in 1955. Harvard philosophy at the time was largely dominated by Russellian Logical Empiricism, as were most large American philosophy departments, though Wittgenstein had spent a brief period at Cornell with his former pupil Norman Malcolm in 1949 (Rowe 2023: 516). Cavell

The Philosophy of Ordinary Life

describes what he elsewhere calls 'the shock' of Austin's procedures as follows:

> Rarely in a lifetime can one know intellectual gratitude of the kind I felt toward Austin after his first seminar meeting on the subject of excuses. I felt elated ... as if I were tasting intellectual liberty, my own intelligence, for the first time ... the questions raised here are to be decided by us, here and now. No one knows more about what mistakes and accidents are, or heedlessness, or lack of thought, than we do, whatever we think we do or do not know. It was a frightening, exhilarating prospect. (1987: 315–316; cited in Rowe 2023: 515).

'[Austin] knocked me off my horse', as he puts it on the opening page of *The Claim of Reason*. As well as attending Austin's seminar on excuses, Cavell was present for his William James Lectures, later published As *How to Do Things with Words* (1962).

I regret I lack the space for a more extensive discussion of the relation between Austin and Wittgenstein (or 'Witters', as Austin referred to him). That both an intellectual and a historical relation existed is clear, and Cavell is far from the only philosopher to have been influenced by both. Excellent historical material on their connections is be found in the only extant biography of Austin (Rowe 2023), and recent fascinating work in the history of philosophy has made impressive advances in specifying their intellectual relationship, including Wittgenstein's influence on *How to Do Things with Words* (Harris & Unnsteinsson 2017). Contemporaries noted such influence at the time: Elizabeth Anscombe deeply disliked Austin for a number of reasons, foremost amongst which was her belief that 'everything of value in Austin's philosophy ... had been stolen from his great contemporary' (Rowe 2023: 556).

Cavell would cite both Wittgenstein and Austin in the same breath as his formative influences for the remainder of his career, but his first major essay, which gave its title to his first published collection, *Must*

Anthropology after Wittgenstein

We Mean What We Say? (1969) was written in 1957 and focussed on Austin. Cavell had 'thrown away' his PhD dissertation after encountering Austin and begun anew, and the essay is a defence of ordinary language philosophy in the face of some American critics.

At more or less the same time though, Cavell was asked to review one of the first monographs devoted entirely to Wittgenstein's philosophy, as well as the newly published joint version of the Blue and Brown Books. The monograph in question, David Pole's *The Later Philosophy of Wittgenstein*, is now famous largely only as the target of Cavell's corrosive and scathing review, which was published in 1962 and republished in a number of later collections as 'The Availability of Wittgenstein's Later Philosophy'.[4]

As we saw briefly in Chapter 3, one of Cavell's major disagreements was with Pole's overly conventionalist or deterministic reading of the *Investigations*. Pole – and in his defence, he was far from alone in this reading at the time – interpreted the *Investigations* in the same way in which we have seen others, with more plausibility, interpret the transitional work like the Big Typescript: as claiming that in some sense 'rules of grammar' determine the correctness or incorrectness of use of language in the straightforward sense in which rules determine the correctness of (some) moves in (some) games, or in, say, mathematical calculation. We have seen enough of the later philosophy by now to imagine why one might disagree with this interpretation, but a famous passage of Cavell's describing his own version of Wittgenstein is worth quoting in full:

We learn and teach words in certain contexts, and then we are expected, and expect others, to be able to project them into further contexts. Nothing insures that this projection will take place (in particular, not the grasping of universals nor the grasping of books of rules), just as nothing insures that we will make, and understand, the same projections. That on the whole we do is a matter of our sharing routes of interest and feeling, modes of response, senses of humor and of significance and of fulfilment, of what

The Philosophy of Ordinary Life

is outrageous, of what is similar to what else, what a rebuke, what forgiveness, of when an utterance is an assertion, when an appeal, when an explanation – all the whirl of organism Wittgenstein calls 'forms of life'. Human speech and activity, sanity and community, rest upon nothing more, but nothing less, than this. It is a vision as simple as it is difficult, and as difficult as it is (and because it is) terrifying. (1962: 74)

Already, in other words, in 1962, not only is Cavell comfortably demolishing the conventionalist reading of the *Investigations* in which some semblance of form ('rules of grammar') remains, but he is also offering up in its place a powerfully articulate combination of the antiformalist impulses we've been tracing in this chapter – indeed, his 'nothing more, but nothing less, than this' framing perfectly encapsulates the twin dimensions of both the ethereal groundlessness of freedom from form ('nothing more'; 'the unanalysable, specific, indefinable'), and the immense weight of granular reality constituted by the endless and infinite list of things shared by people within a form of life ('nothing less'; 'the facts of living').

A related and also significant discussion of Wittgenstein that is worth mentioning briefly forms a part of the book that eventually developed – with many twists and turns – out of Cavell's doctoral dissertation, *The Claim of Reason*. It's relevant partly because it helps us to fill out some of the discussion in Chapter 1 about divergent interpretations of Wittgenstein's philosophy and partly for its reiteration of the themes we're treating here.

In Chapter 1, we met the so-called 'resolute reading' of the *Tractatus*, which – unlike more conventional readings such as, most paradigmatically, those of Peter Hacker – draws a strong connection between the *Tractatus* and Wittgenstein's later work such as the *Investigations*. One of the most significant ways in which it does so, a way that ties it into a broader movement, sometimes called, after a prominent collection of essays, 'the new Wittgenstein' (Crary & Read 2000), is by arguing that the aim of Wittgenstein's philosophy as a whole – early and late – is therapeutic. Put very simply, the claim is that Wittgenstein is aiming at a 'psychological effect', rather than at any claims or arguments.

Cavell was an important influence on this later set of ideas, and his 'Excursus on Wittgenstein's vision of language' is exemplary of why that's so. It begins with almost exactly the formula of the quote above (itself from the Blue Book (BBB, p9) regarding the fact that we learn words 'in *certain* contexts' but are then expected to know when and how to project them appropriately into others, before taking the reader through problems with various commonsensical 'pictures' we might have of how a child learns language – such as Augustine's picture of ostensive definition. His point, as we have seen Wittgenstein's was in treating Augustine in the *Investigations*, is that such pictures never quite do the job they are supposed to when elevated to general explanations:

That the justifications and explanations we give of our language and conduct, that our ways of trying to intellectualize our lives, do not really satisfy us, is what, as I read him, Wittgenstein wishes us above all to grasp. This is what his 'methods' are designed to get us to see. (1979: 175)

This is 'therapeutic' in the sense that it leads not to new arguments or claims but (ideally) to the recognition that using language as if it could get so free from its moorings as to turn back on them is never going to succeed.

Once more, too, the image of Wittgenstein's alternative 'vision of language' is called up as 'terrifying': 'a thin net over an abyss' (1979: 178), but as above Cavell's claim is that it only appears so if one begins from the premise that the 'facts of life' are, as it were, not enough; that if we don't find an absolute purchase somewhere beyond life and language then we'll be constantly vulnerable to the possibility that the 'agreement' we find in our shared form of life will collapse, as if such an agreement were a kind of 'social contract' from which we might be withdrawn or withdraw ourselves (and see Laugier 2018b).

Anthropology After Form

The issue of vulnerability, as well as Cavell's particular interpretation of Wittgenstein, returns us to the path we were tracing through anthropology and to the next and final step in it. Of any living anthropologist, Veena Das is probably the one most associated with Wittgenstein. Her published engagement with him spans nearly three decades, and Cavell himself wrote the foreword to her 2007 *Life and Words*. In what follows, I focus only on a narrow selection of her early writing on violence in order to situate her within the genealogy traced here, but the trajectory begun in that early work continues.

Das's explicit engagement with Wittgenstein dates back to the 1990s, at a time in which her writing also exemplified the kinds of currents we met Joel Robbins diagnosing earlier. As the foreword to a recent re-issue of Veena Das's *Critical Events* (1995) notes,

Even though [Joel] Robbins does not explicitly name Veena [Das] as an expression of the tendency that he wants to arrest and redirect, in the picture of the intellectual landscape that he offers, *Critical Events*, first published in 1995, would be a 'typical' example of the 'suffering slot' and a skilled, albeit dated example of 'its time.' (Singh 2018: xv)

The author also notes – because it will perhaps surprise readers familiar only with Das's later work – that Wittgenstein makes only two appearances in the book, 'although the second appearance presages a much deeper entanglement to come.' (2018: xvi).

Critical Events, together with an essay on Wittgenstein that followed shortly after (1997), are in some ways paradigmatic cases for the argument of this chapter, since firstly they do indeed resemble, as one might imagine, other work in anthropology from this period, including Daniel's essay, published at the same time, and which the latter piece discusses; and secondly they also presage and manifest a development of this kind of work in which Wittgenstein has a crucial and explicit role to play.

Anthropology after Wittgenstein

The resemblances between *Critical Events* and other anthropological work of this period are neatly summarized in Das's original introduction to the book, in which she makes pain a central focus. Drawing on Nietzsche, she argues that society is always in the business of inscribing pain on the bodies of its members. The connection to Daniel's arguments, and the wider set of arguments we've met above, is clear in what follows:

> For such victims of terror, who cannot rely on articulate and literate accounts but who must live through terror with other kinds of languages, what can anthropology offer? If it is the recovery of 'voice', it cannot be a disembodied voice, just as a lament or dream or a nightmare cannot be a disembodied narration. To recover such embodied narrations seems to me the only way in which one can resist the totalizing discourses that become evident not only in narratives of the state and narratives embedded in the professional organization of knowledge, but also in the discourses of resistance that use the very logic of the state which they seek to resist.
>
> What follows in this book are faltering attempts to arrive at the truth of the victim, a truth which is made up not of the abstract iniquities of a system but of the daily suffering, the daily humiliation, and the everyday experience of being violated. I hope it will be read not for any sophistication of abstract arguments – there are too many gaps in my thinking here – but by the concreteness of events which make up the lived solipsism of the victim. (2018: 23)

Here we meet, in a manner clearer perhaps even than with Daniel, the basic opposition between 'totalizing discourses' (including those of anthropology in the form of 'abstract arguments') and 'embodied', 'everyday experience', and the 'concreteness of events'. Form is the enemy, and life (even 'lived solipsism') is the discipline's proper subject. Whilst there is a distinctly un-Wittgensteinian ring to the idea of 'arriving at the truth' – though note its resemblance to Geertz's remark about 'accuracy' – the notion that it is the depiction of concreteness and the reality of everyday experience that yields 'the truth of the victim' in

Anthropology After Form

some ways makes explicit some of the problems of performative contradiction we've already encountered: the reliance on truth recalls the Geertzian critique of *Writing Culture*, namely that its endless pursuit of intersubjectivity often sounded as if it were aimed at the same ideal of transparency that it objected to in the work of others (e.g. Geertz 1988), as well as Wittgenstein's worries about the 'metaphysical' character of trying to 'cancel' metaphysics.

Wittgenstein himself appears in substance only towards the very end of the book. This occurs across just two pages, in one of its final discussions of pain. Although brief, the purpose of this invocation of Wittgenstein is to legitimate the concluding argument: firstly, the view that pain is a public, intersubjective matter, and secondly, and crucially for Das's vision across the book as a whole, that it may be shared. One may feel the pain of others, no matter the contextual differences involved.

The healing force of social anthropology can come if the experiences of suffering we have encountered in these chapters do not become cause for consolidating the authority of the discipline, but rather an occasion for forming one body, providing voice, and touching victims, so that their pain may be experienced in other bodies as well... I hope this book as a whole has shown that constructing memory through the common sharing of pain is quite a different activity from constructing it through collections in museums. (1995: 196)

Here, in other words, we find precisely the tendencies of antiformalism in their manifestation through a focus on suffering appearing directly out of engagement with Wittgenstein and his engagement with pain. Wittgenstein gives Das the philosophical language with which to articulate pain and suffering as key objects of the discipline, not because they imbue it with authority in the way the culture concept did, and not because they allow us to construct the differential taxonomies (cultures) of museum collections based on such authority, but because they are 'common' and 'shared'. Anthropology's 'healing force' is in establishing this commonality through the articulation of real experience – allowing us to 'feel pain in other bodies'.

Das pursues these themes a couple of years later in a review article devoted to Wittgenstein and anthropology, also drawing directly on Daniel:

In his recent, passionate work on the 'anthropography' of violence, Daniel (1997) is moved to say, 'Anthropology has had an answer to the question, What is a human being? An answer that has, on the whole, served us well, with or without borrowings from philosophers. The answer keeps returning to one form or another of the concept of culture: humans have it; other living beings do not' (p. 194). (1997: 172)

Das traces a range of ways in which to think about culture and practices of socialization, emphasizing repeatedly that the lesson Wittgenstein's work offers us is that it is a mistake to model culture on any putatively simple forms (texts or sets of rules, for example). This complexity should be reflected in anthropological accounts:

Most ethnographies provide more than the theoretical scaffolding requires. It has been argued by some that this excess is embedded in the emplotment of ethnography as a performance (Clifford 1990). Others have spoken of the difficulty of portraying ways of life that are 'experience distant' to their readers (Scheper-Hughes 1992). I suggest that this excess or this surplus expresses equally the distrust of formal rules and obligations as sources of social order or moral judgment. If culture is a matter of shared ways of life as well as of bequeathing and inheriting capabilities and habits as members of society, then clearly it is participation in forms of sociability (Wittgenstein's forms of life) that define simultaneously the inner and the outer, that allow a person to speak both within language and outside it. Agreement in forms of life, in Wittgenstein, is never a matter of shared opinions. It thus requires an excess of description to capture the entanglements of customs, habits, rules, and examples. It provides the context in

Anthropology After Form

which we could see how we are to trace words back to their original homes when we do not know our way about. (1997: 179–180).

This passage encapsulates the afterlife of the aphorism that itself captured Geertz's Wittgensteinian anitiformalism: 'An accurate picture of a vague object does not consist of a clear picture but a vague one' (1979: 199). To repeat, this is the spirit that persists in what Miyazaki (2004) and later Candea describe as the matching of 'provisional and indeterminate' analyses with a provisional and indeterminate world (2018: 351).

Pain and suffering appear again here too, this time with significantly more engagement with Wittgenstein than in *Critical Events*. The connection between Wittgenstein's and Das's version of 'suffering slot' anthropology though is here even clearer:

As in the case of belief, I cannot locate your pain in the same way as I locate mine. The best I can do is to let it happen to me. Now it seems to me that anthropological knowledge is precisely about letting the knowledge of the other happen to me... In Wittgenstein's remarks on pain, to find my way is similar to letting the pain of the other happen to me. My own fantasy of anthropology as a body of writing is that which is able to receive this pain. Thus while I may never claim the pain of the other, nor appropriate it for some other purpose (nation building, revolution, scientific experiment), that I can lend my body (of writing) to this pain is what a grammatical investigation reveals. (1997: 192).

A final point worth drawing out of this piece is the inauguration of the theme of 'everyday' or 'ordinary life' as a kind of synonym for form of life, or, as she puts it in the quote above, 'the context in which we could see how we are to trace words back to their original homes'. The idea of 'tracing back' noted here gestures to the idea of depth that often appears in her writing on the subject. Discussing the possibilities of 'recovery' from the kind of pain and violence Daniel's work describes, she writes,

Anthropology after Wittgenstein

From a Wittgensteinian perspective, these seem to be only possibilities of recovery through a descent into the ordinariness of everyday life, of domesticity, through which alone the words that have been exiled may be brought back. This everydayness is then in the nature of a return – one that has been recovered in the face of madness. (1997: 184)

'Violence and the descent into the ordinary' is the subtitle of Das's next book, *Life and Words* (2007), in which Wittgenstein, Cavell, and the idea of ordinary or everyday life will have extensive roles to play, as they will go on to do in much of the remainder of her work to date (e.g. 2020, 2023). In characterizing her understanding of these concepts in more recent work, she writes,

I am interested in the everyday as the site on which the life of the other is engaged but this other is not the radical Other of either philosophy or anthropology. As an anthropologist I am attuned to concrete others, even daring to suggest that it is in following concrete relations, quotidian turns of events, the waxing and waning of intensities, that we learn to be in the world. I have taken inspiration from Wittgenstein's idea that the task is to lead words back from the metaphysical to the ordinary and to make do with what words we have in hand. (2020: 10)

This appeal to concreteness is also, in line with the wider trends we have been noting, tied up with an appeal to contingency and incompleteness. Earlier in the same work, she writes, again in reference to Wittgenstein, of the 'open texture of concepts' and cites a passage from Sandra Laugier that neatly encapsulates this duality:

The question of realism is deeply transformed by attention to the particular and by the sensitivity of our concept to experience... The radical transformation of concepts is what I call our life with concepts: the fact that they are in this world and even often (for ordinary concepts) in or of the *ordinary world*. As Cavell says of the ordinary world, that may not be all there is but it is important enough! (2017; cited in Das 2020: 9)

The idea of everyday or ordinary life here, in other words, is simultaneously both 'realist', 'concrete', and 'at hand', whilst also 'experience-sensitive' and 'open textured'. As an analytic, it both travels and yet also denotes a given and immediate reality. I've written elsewhere of the ways in which this duality allows the anthropologist to talk about context – everyday life sounding like the most 'textured' of all contexts, in some ways – without actually giving them form; hence one can both find 'everyday life' everywhere, and yet what one finds in any given instance is supposed to be by definition specific, particular, and concrete (Heywood 2024).

The Ubiquity of the Ordinary

Readers interested in the content of Das's engagement with Wittgenstein as such will find much that is rewarding in the rest of her work. My interest is more in the fact of her engagement in the first place. Das's work represents the final step in the trajectory I've been tracing not because it culminates anthropology's engagement with Wittgenstein, but because it makes explicit what has become implicit throughout much of the discipline. While her direct engagement with Wittgenstein distinguishes her approach, the antiformalist commitments she articulates have become so naturalized in contemporary anthropology that they often go unmarked and unexamined. Das's philosophical justification for an anthropology of 'ordinary life' provides a rare and conceptually sophisticated window into assumptions that typically operate as disciplinary common sense. What sets her apart is not her antiformalism itself, but her willingness to theorize what many others practice unreflectively.

Her focus on 'everyday life' reflects what has become a dominant conceptual framework across contemporary anthropology. The last three decades have witnessed an extraordinary proliferation of 'the ordinary' and 'the everyday' as organizing categories throughout the discipline. This trend extends far beyond Das's specific intellectual genealogy through Cavell and Wittgenstein.

The ubiquity of such categories is striking. From to a turn to 'ordinary ethics' of which Das has been a part (Lambek 2010), and to related arguments in the anthropology of religion (e.g. Schielke 2009), we also have 'everyday' resistance (e.g., Scott 1985) 'everyday' utopias (Cooper 2014); 'everyday' religion (e.g., Ammerman 2007); 'everyday' politics (e.g., Boyte 2004); 'everyday' shame (Probyn 2004); and 'everyday' violence (e.g., Bourgois 1998), to give just a few examples of titles from anthropology and the wider social sciences in the last two decades (see Heywood 2022).

In some ways, this ubiquity of the ordinary is unsurprising, at least as far as anthropology goes. As Morgan Clarke has pointed out, 'Sociocultural anthropology, with its characteristic emphasis on participant observation and hence lived practice, could be seen as having the complex skein of "everyday life" as its normal subject matter' (2016: 798), though it has not been without its critics (e.g. Clarke 2014; Fadil & Fernando 2015; Heywood 2023c, 2024; Lempert 2013).

But as I've pointed out elsewhere (2023c, 2024), anthropology's 'generic preference for the specific' (Candea et al. 2025; Yarrow 2011) – one that Wittgenstein saw already in speaking of his 'anthropological perspective' – has radically intensified in the wake of the collapse of form in the discipline. This is not only an intensification of quantity – though it is that too – but also a qualitative intensification: when earlier generations of anthropologists spoke about ordinariness they did so against the backdrop of wider contextual frames. Certain sorts of Trobriand decorations or magical practices or occupations were ordinary or everyday, for Malinowski, in the context of Trobriand culture. 'Ordinary' or 'everyday' didn't appear as adjectives with the definite article. Their appearance as such makes them into a context themselves, albeit one without any clear shape or form. Marilyn Strathern made a similar point in the midst of the period

The Ubiquity of the Ordinary

with which we're concerned in relation to comparable analytical perspectives on 'society' and 'social life':

To present society as though it were composed of categories and groups is to falsify the reality of human social life [such perspectives inform us]: we should study human actions as processes in time. (Everyone has had experience of 'social life'!). A feature of this argument is the assumption that a proper subject for study is what individuals experience. All the variability of family forms are thus flattened out in the assertion that everyone has some sort of family life. (1992: 145).

This disciplinary shift transcends individual intellectual traditions or theoretical commitments. Whether coming from phenomenological, post-structural, practice-oriented, or actor-network approaches, much contemporary anthropology increasingly converges on a focus on granular descriptions of 'ordinary life' as both object and methodological framework. What Das makes explicit through her philosophical engagements operates implicitly across much of the discipline: a conviction that only through attention to the formless flow of the everyday can anthropology access truth.

So what makes Das's case particularly revealing for our analysis is that she explicitly articulates what has become, for much of the discipline, taken-for-granted background knowledge. She has found in Wittgenstein a philosophical language with which to justify an approach that many others adopt without feeling any need for justification. Indeed, for many, the value of focussing anthropological attention on 'ordinary life' appears so self-evidently correct that philosophical justification would seem not just unnecessary but potentially counterproductive – a retrogressive return to the very kind of systematic theorizing that the approach implicitly rejects.

The fact that Das stands out precisely because she theorizes what others simply practice reveals how thoroughly naturalized the antiformalist turn has become. When anthropologists across diverse subfields can invoke 'ordinary life' or 'the everyday' without feeling any need to

Anthropology after Wittgenstein

justify these as analytical frames, we witness not the absence of a shared picture but rather the triumph of a particular one: a picture whose power lies partly in its apparent transparency, its seeming to be no picture at all but simply life itself.

The Form of Formlessness

As I noted at the outset of this chapter, its aim has been to highlight a dominant disciplinary current, rather than document a history. Even though that dominant current is itself multifaceted, I want to call its antiformalism a picture, blurred though it may be. Wittgenstein once asked whether an indistinct picture was still a picture. It's hard to believe that he thought the question had a definite answer. But what this chapter has sought to do is to give some form to the blurred picture of 'anthropology after Wittgenstein'; to show, indeed, that it *is a picture:* that it does have shape and form, even though the edges might be blurred, and that the dimensions of that shape and form consist in what is at least in some ways an eminently Wittgensteinian refusal of form itself: a form of formlessness.

The picture is perhaps best encapsulated in the Geertzian version of Wittgenstein's discussion of blurriness and vagueness, a version we've seen recur in several guises throughout the chapter: that an 'accurate' picture of a vague object is not a clear picture but a vague one. We've seen some version or other of that idea return repeatedly through *Writing Culture,* 'suffering slot' anthropology, the 'aesthetics of emergence' identified by Miyazaki, and come home to Wittgenstein again in the work of Veena Das. Writing of this attitude in relation to 'postmodern anthropology' in 1991, Marilyn Strathern once noted 'Of course, [textual] anguish can never be adequate to the power relations involved [in life], any more than a confused text is equal to the confusions of life.' (1991: 10). Yet in a sense it is exactly this idea of 'accuracy' through mirrored blurriness and confusion that emerges as anthropology's dominant contemporary culture of context.

The Form of Formlessness

One thing worth noting about this picture is its singularity - the fact that it is *a* picture, and in many ways an exclusivist picture, as suggested by the implication of 'accuracy', and 'arriving at the truth'. If we recall Wittgenstein's discussions of the builders' language, his point there was not that there was something 'wrong' with that language, or with the picture underlying it. Nor was it that there was something 'wrong' with Augustine's picture of ostensive definition. It was only that as pictures of language they had their limits - they weren't the only such ways in which language operated. In the same way, his point about the utility of blurred concepts was a pragmatic and subjunctive one - they may be sometimes, or even often of use. This is quite different to the elevation of antiformalism to the level of absolute principle, epitomized in Geertz's re-writing of Wittgenstein's original language.

Because, even granted the partial and limited nature of the account here, I think the reason the antiformalism narrated here seems barely to require such narration is that it has become part of our disciplinary set of certainties, a point at which our spades are turned and we can go no further.

Arguably at least, what began as a liberation from overly rigid models became, paradoxically, its own form of rigidity. In freeing itself from one form of captivity, anthropology may have entered another - one perhaps more constraining because its bars remain largely invisible, rendered as they are in the seemingly obvious and natural language of 'life'. A consensus that the only accurate representation of a vague object is a vague representation reveals not the absence of a picture but the dominance of a specific one.

Here we have exemplified precisely the magical/metaphysical character of cancelling magic/metaphysics that Wittgenstein worried about in his 'Remarks on Frazer' - the performative contradiction of elevating formlessness to the one and only truly 'accurate' anthropological form. This picture, blurred though it may be, has shaped anthropological practice as powerfully as any of the formal models it replaced.

Conclusion: The Unanalysable Facts of Life

Then more time passed, and it seemed to everyone that the carpentry game and the science game were not games at all, but vitally necessary tasks, which had to be performed in order for mankind to survive. Thus, although all of the apparently productive activities of man were games, they were not believed to be games. Games were once again relegated to the role of mere pastimes useful for bridging the gaps in our serious endeavours. And if it had been possible to convince these people that they were in fact playing games, they would have felt that their whole lives had been as nothing – a mere stage play or empty dream.

– Suits (1978: 177)

One cannot recapture the point before explicitness. Hence . . . new ideas always come before old – but this is accomplished simply through putting current ideas into perspective, acting on and finding contexts or reasons for them.

– Strathern (1992: 44)

This book has sought to put the radically antiformalist contextualism of much contemporary anthropology in its own sort of context. In that aim, it is far from alone. Take, for example, the following recent characterization of the discipline in relation to formalist ideas about computing and automation from Paul Kockelman, in which Wittgenstein features:

Forty years of anthropology has spent its time trying to show that each and every social form (such as a practice, sign, identity, behavior, movement,

The Unanalysable Facts of Life

value, institution, or belief) is 'emergent', 'contested', 'fluid', 'embodied', 'non-deterministic', 'dialogic', 'constructed', 'distributed', 'context-bound', 'reflexive', 'mediated', and so forth. In some sense, computers (or rather a widespread folk-theory of computers), have been the favorite bogeyman of anthropology (and social scientists more generally). The mantra goes something like this: where there are rules, give us practices; where there are symbols, give us indices; where there is truth-conditioning, give us poetry and performance; where there is mind, give us body; where there is abstraction give us interaction; where there is form or content, give us context; where there are ideal languages, give us forms of life. (2017: 146–147)[1]

Despite such moments of recognition, however, the acontextual, progressivist, and whiggish picture of anthropological theory as leading inevitably and happily to the realization that blurred concepts are not 'sometimes' or 'often' but *always* the only ones we need is a picture we do seem to continue to repeat to ourselves, inexorably, over and over.

Ironically, this is somewhat in contrast to Wittgenstein. Consider how alert we have seen him be to the possibilities of performative contradiction inherent in aspects of his project, forever worrying not only about what he was saying but about how he was saying it, and what he was not saying: the *Tractatus* is 81 pages long, and according to Wittgenstein the most important part of it is the part that isn't in it. Recall the crossed-out sections of the 'Remarks on Frazer' in which he worries about the metaphysical character of cancelling metaphysics, or his remark about turning the 'absence of idols' into a kind of idol-worship of its own. Or witness the subjunctive qualifications in his remarks about blurred concepts ('often', 'sometimes', 'what we need') that sometimes disappear in some of their anthropological equivalents.

Wittgenstein was very often not certain about things despite his capacity for brazen arrogance. At its best, anthropology is also not certain about things, hence that cardinal capacity to change one's mind I noted in this book's introduction. But this book is about how

The Unanalysable Facts of Life

anthropology has in some respects become very certain of some things, and in ways that are not always productive.

At the end of the last chapter, I suggested that Wittgenstein provides some anthropologists with a philosophical justification for an approach that many others take without recourse to philosophical justification at all. So, one of the things I want to do by way of conclusion to this book is briefly to try to fill out the picture of that wider and often implicit conceptual aesthetic, an aesthetic that I think is Wittgensteinian in spirit, even when not in name.

The Hegemony of Antiformalism

To begin at the end: as I write these words the ink is barely dry on a sharp exchange in a prominent journal in part over the concept of 'culture'. On one side is Joel Robbins, who has long advanced and defended a complex and carefully argued vision of anthropology informed by an unabashedly formalist commitment to the utility of, amongst other things, a Weberian/Dumontian approach to values and indeed to culture (e.g. 2004, 2007, 2013, 2024). On the other side, a critic attacks Robbins for this formalism on the basis that it fails to capture the world as it truly is: 'social relations regularly defy this degree of formalisation... as [Emir Mahieddin] puts it, social relations in a globalized world defined by rapid change and worldviews are better characterised as "relational, partial, fragmentary flows, to which actors adhere unevenly or variably over the course of their lives"' (Lockwood 2025: 89). Projects like that of Robbins, this critic suggests, 'emerge out of a distinctly anthropological hubris – that cultural differences can be observed and qualified, that epistemic murk can be conveniently dispensed with' (Lockwood 2025: 92). In place of such hubris, the critic commends 'tak[ing] seriously the historical and material reality of political economy' (Lockwood 2025: 93).

Note the ways in which this argument mirrors precisely the twin pincers of both the late Wittgensteinian attack on form, as well as the

The Hegemony of Antiformalism

two approaches which Candea points to as characterizing antiformalist anthropology more broadly from the 1990s onwards (2025): on the one hand, the idea that because the world is made up of blurry 'relational, partial, fragmentary flows' then our analysis should reflect this blurriness in the form of 'epistemic murk'; on the other hand a commitment to concreteness and tangibility in the guise, in this case, of the 'reality of political economy'. Again, in other words, we meet the 'unanalysable, specific, indefinable', coupled with 'the facts of life'.

I raise this as only the most recent example of a longstanding tendency in anthropology to reiterate some version or other of the picture we've encountered in the final chapters of this book, with or without Wittgenstein as philosophical accompaniment. I continue to refer to it as a 'picture', in Wittgenstein's own sense, both because often it is less explicit than either this recent example or Das's highly philosophized version, and also because it is not necessarily the obviously defining feature of any particular instance. Yet when seen across a wide swathe of otherwise quite distinct and diverse visions of anthropology, it adds up to more than a family resemblance, and leaves those visions that are underlain by a slightly different picture – such as that of Robbins' (and see below) – looking unusual, and thus perhaps as prime targets for knee-jerk antipathy.

For example, we have seen the ways in which we can pick out the genealogical influence of Wittgenstein on the 'play with context' formlessness of some variants of American post-structural anthropology (Strathern 1987a). But as Candea points out, even far more formalist versions of post-structuralism live on in anthropology precisely for their antiformalist features: Bourdieu, for example – another devotee of Wittgenstein (Bouveresse 1977; Salgues 2008) – is not primarily identified with writings 'on fields, doxa, or taste, but [with] the much vaguer, processual-relational notion of practice. Under the guise of hyperformalism, [habitus] worked to dissolve structure into process, stability into change, rules into strategies, and analytical binaries into the polysemy of practice' (2025: 49). Likewise, Foucault's work has endured in significance in anthropology not, for the most part, through the notions of episteme, archive, or even discourse, but through an understanding of power as so dispersed, relational, and unspecifiable that it is ubiquitous.

The legacy of Deleuze for anthropology is even more characteristic in this regard, as is talk of 'becoming' more generally, and it is sometimes envisioned precisely as an 'out-processualising' of Foucault:

> In emphasizing the powers and potentials of desire ... the ways in which social fields ceaselessly leak and transform (power and knowledge notwithstanding), and the in-between, plastic, and ever-unfinished nature of *a* life, Deleuze lends himself to inspiring ethnographic efforts to illuminate the dynamism of the everyday and the literality and singularity of human becomings... 'To write is certainly not to impose a form (of expression) on the matter of lived experience,' says Deleuze. 'Literature rather moves in the direction of the ill-formed or the incomplete' (Deleuze 1997: 1). (Biehl & Locke 2010: 318–320; italics in original).

Note again the conjunction of the indefinable with the real: 'lived experience' is ever-unfinished and incomplete and thus 'Ethnographic realities are never fully reducible to the books and theories we bring to the field' (Biehl & Locke 2010: 320: 320), or indeed to 'a form (of expression)'; yet thanks to Deleuze we know that they are 'realities', and that any instance of them merits the italicized indefinite article (*a* life) because of its 'literality and singularity'.

Of course, this lumping together of three enormously complex thinkers elides a vast array of differences between them and ignores the lengths anthropologists have gone to in order to tease them apart from one another as more or less useful for the discipline. My point though, again, is not that this rough sense of a shared picture makes them the same – it is that seen from the vantage point of the dominant antiformalist picture or aesthetic of anthropological approaches of the last few decades, they are or have been taken as grist to that dominant

Concrete Processualism and the Reality of Flow

picture's mill, not challenges to it. Likewise, not all post-structuralist French philosophy is so amenable to this picture – some anthropologists have made productive use of various formal devices of, for example, Luc Boltanski and Laurent Thévenot (2006), as well as of Alain Badiou (see e.g. Jansen 2019). Yet it is the antiformalist interpretation of the most antiformalist versions of post-structuralism that have most shaped our discipline, in ways that replicate the twin desire both to escape from the abstract and the systematic and to somehow arrive at the literal, the singular, and the concrete.

Concrete Processualism and the Reality of Flow

Speaking of the concrete, the 1990s also saw a retreat from the antiformalist textualism of post-structuralism, but one to an equally antiformalist materialism. Indeed, as we have seen Candea pointing out in the last chapter, whilst post-structuralism and materialism are often imagined as both historically and conceptually distinct, they are in fact a perfect echo of one another in respect of form, differing only in emphasis (2025). The contextual play of *Writing Culture* and the 'becomings' of Deleuzian anthropology may have emphasized leakiness, dynamism, 'the ill-formed or the incomplete', but the illuminating 'literality and singularity' of '*a* life' in all its concreteness remained the motivating spirit. Likewise, anthropology's material turn put 'literality and singularity' at its heart, but, as I'll try to show, it did so often by opposing such concrete realities to the abstractions of form in exactly the way prefigured by post-structuralism. Again, in other words, 'the unanalysable, the specific, indefinable', and 'the facts of life'.

One of the most characteristic ways in which this duality emerges is in the manner in which various iterations of anthropology's turn to the 'real' involved a kind of two-step dance: first a new and defining interest in an aspect of 'reality' – bodies, matter, objects, things – was confidently asserted, and then any defining sense that 'reality' possesses was undermined by dissolving it back into one version or another of a 'processual-relational haze' (Humphrey 2008: 358).

To take embodiment as an initial exemplary paradigm: a part of its powerful driving impetus emerged from a feeling of dissatisfaction with structuralism and symbolic anthropology's concerns with ideas, myths, and the mind; this was all 'culture from the neck up' (Csordas 1994: 2). Attending to the concrete reality of bodies would get our feet back on the ground. Unsurprisingly though, this ground turns out to be far from stable. Take Emily Martin's formative investigation of immunity in 1990s American culture and science: titled 'flexible bodies', and citing Wittgenstein via Geertz within the first few pages of its introduction (1994: 7–8), it aims to capture 'the complex of immune system concepts and practices that ... is *emergent*' (1994: 16). Where this emergent character of systems is in any way stabilized it is so in the form of what Martin calls 'configurations', a term meant to refer to 'a pattern or shape (*more or less fuzzy*) that is simultaneously how we see the world and a result of how the social world is ordered' (1994: 15; my italics).

As we saw above with invocations of Deleuze in relation to Foucault, the new paradigm also both drew on earlier iterations of a concern with the body, such as those of Bourdieu, whilst simultaneously aiming to 'out-processualise' them, despite its focus on the 'reality' of bodies: thus Martin coins the term 'practicum' in place of habitus, to denote 'less formally structured' modes of learning how to be in one's body (1994: 15), and Christina Toren points with others to the absence of a sense of historicity and change in habitus in her work on children's bodily dispositions (e.g. 2012). Much other groundbreaking work on embodiment drew on phenomenology to aim, in a similar fashion, at collapsing the subject/object dualism by showing that the body is both 'real' and also particular, partial, and situated (Csordas 1994).

This perspective, of course, throws up some tensions with ideas about context, as Maryon McDonald (2018) points out. Citing Setha Low's essay from Thomas Csordas's seminal *Embodiment and Experience*

Concrete Processualism and the Reality of Flow

(1994), McDonald notes that Low wants to argue both for the 'reality' of 'nerves' as an embodied condition and response to poverty, alienation, and social and familial disruption, and yet also for the claim that such contextual conditions are in fact what is being 'embodied' – hence the ease with which the language of 'metaphor' and 'symbol' slip in to such accounts, and the 'reality' of the body disappears in a wider (and processual-relational) context (2018: 188).

Tim Ingold's distinct language of 'flow', 'pathways', 'lines of becoming', 'dwelling', 'walking', etc. perhaps carries this tension and its underlying antiformalism to its furthest extent, as it imagines 'form ... is death' (2010: 92). In his appropriately titled *Imagining for Real*, Ingold cites Wittgenstein's injunction to silence from the *Tractatus* in an attack on explicit, propositional knowledge and in celebration instead of 'bodily know-how' that is 'restless, fluid, and dynamic. Above all, it is not deposited as a stable substrate, housed in lower levels of consciousness, but is fundamentally animate – immanent in the sensuousness of a body that is mobile, alive, and open to the world.' (2021: 230–232; and cf. Cook 2016).

Many readers will also be familiar with a version of the tensions of 'concrete processualism' from the work of Bruno Latour and the ideas of actor network theory (ANT). Hopefully, it is unnecessary to reiterate the engaging and often persuasive conceptual and terminological acrobatics by means of which ANT both insisted on its intensification of this trend towards an attention to the 'real', whilst also refiguring the meaning of such a 'reality' by conjuring networks of 'flat ontologies', undifferentiated by anything more substantial than the artifice of analysis (2005). As we saw in the case of Bourdieu and Foucault, it is this antiformalist universe that captured anthropological attention far more than the more systematic aspects of Latour's work, such as distinctions between 'actors' and 'actants', and definitions of 'associations' and 'articulations'. The tensions we saw above between the 'concrete processualism' of embodiment and anthropological reliance on some notion of context

The Unanalysable Facts of Life

are confronted head on here, with Latour echoing the architect Rem Koolhaas: 'context stinks' (2005: 148). The formal and explanatory models anthropologists were used to deploying were merely 'ways of stopping the description when you're too tired or lazy to go on' (2005).

Perhaps the epitome of the two-step dance of 'concrete processualism' is an approach we met earlier in this book and whose relation to questions raised by earlier and explicitly Wittgensteinian currents in anthropology we have already seen: the ontological turn. Here the 'facts of life', in all their 'literality and singularity', receive their most emblematic airing in the word 'ontology', designed to signal anthropology's furthest yet intensification of interest in the 'real' and the concrete, and cast iconoclastically in opposition to classical anthropological concerns with culture and epistemology (e.g. Henare et al. 2007). Partly perhaps though because of the intensity of its iconoclastic language, almost as soon as the ontological turn appeared, critics were wondering whether 'ontology is just another word for culture' (Venkatesan et al. 2010) and pointing out that the ethnographic particularism promised by its emphasis on concrete singularity was somewhat belied in analyses that resembled one another in finding Deleuzian becomings wherever they went (e.g. Heywood 2012; Laidlaw 2012; Laidlaw & Heywood 2013). As some critics noted, such repetition should not have been too surprising given that the ontological turn, despite its iconoclasm, was underwritten by precisely the same processual-relational understanding of reality as were previous versions of materialism, hence the (re)discovery of a nondualism of concepts and reality, symbols and matter, ideas and things.

The same tensions with regard to context appeared: 'ontological' accounts of peoples and places in the world were brilliantly, evocatively, and anthropologically contextual in their portrayals of such different lives, despite the claim that such difference, or alterity, was always and everywhere a conceptual question ('literal and singular', harking back to Deleuze), as liable to be found between two individuals as between two

Concrete Processualism and the Reality of Flow

geographical territories (Venkatesan et al. 2010: 185). To make matters worse, because their accounts were so contextually rich and persuasive, they were read by some to be equating context and 'real' ontology in the worst possible sense, and thus essentializing the differences between the peoples and places they described: cultures were in fact worlds, and thus also worlds apart (e.g. Bessire & Bond 2014; c.f. Heywood 2020).

The two-step dance of 'concrete processualism' is not limited to these acute examples but extends through other visions of contemporary anthropology. Consider the recent turn to infrastructure, in which scholars such as Brian Larkin, Nikhil Anand, and Hannah Appel examine the physical materiality of roads, water systems, and oil platforms while simultaneously arguing that these seemingly solid structures are actually fluid, relational, and emergent processes. Larkin's (2013) formulation of infrastructure as both material substrate and cultural phantasmagoria exemplifies this duality – infrastructure is concrete yet perpetually unfinished, both 'things and also the relation between things' (Larkin 2013: 329). Similarly, Anand's (2017) study of Mumbai's water system presents pipes and pumps as both physical engineering networks and shifting sets of social and political relations that can never be fully formalized (and see Appel 2019).

The 'affective turn' repeats this pattern as the most obvious heir to post-structuralist approaches. Works like Kathleen Stewart's (2007) *Ordinary Affects* attend to the concrete reality of everyday bodily experience while deliberately refusing to formalize these experiences into analytical categories. Drawing partly on post-structuralist philosophers such as Roland Barthes, Stewart argues that ordinary affects are 'at once abstract and concrete, more compelling than ideologies, as well as more fractious, multiplicitous, and unpredictable than symbolic meanings. They are not the kind of analytic object that can be laid out on a single, static plane of analysis' (2007: 3). This perfect echo of the twin poles of our antiformalist picture – appeals to the concreteness of reality and resistance to systematic formalization – continues in a focus on moods and sensations that exceed capture in formal systems.

'Assemblage' is another concept that exemplifies this dual appeal, deployed by both Deleuze and Latour but also widely adopted in anthropology. Anna Tsing's famous *Mushroom at the End of the World* (2015) uses assemblage thinking to describe concrete ecological and economic relations while insisting on their fundamentally emergent, contingent nature. Matsutake mushrooms are emphatically real, yet their significance emerges through what Tsing calls 'indeterminacy and the conditions of precarity, that is, life without the promise of stability ... the uncontrolled lives of mushrooms are a gift – and a guide – when the controlled world we thought we had fails' (2015: 2). Tsing's book traces connections too messy and too heterogeneous to be reduced to formal models. Like the equally influential 'global assemblages' of Aihwa Ong and Stephen Collier (2005), Tsing's work appeals simultaneously to material facts and to their essential unanalysability.

Form and Formalism

I raise all these approaches in a necessarily brief and cursory fashion. What I want to point to is the recurrent and reiterated nature of the underlying picture, and the way in which it passes through and reproduces itself in what are otherwise – and in important respects – very distinct and diverse visions of anthropology.[2]

Some readers will be thinking of the formal elements that many of the approaches I've mentioned contain. Many, if not all, of these approaches do contain such elements, including those of Foucault and Bourdieu I've noted, or the interest in variations of aesthetic form (such as collage) present in elements of post-structuralist anthropology.

More recently and more clearly, the turn to ontology in all of its various manifestations contains a range of formal elements, particularly insofar as it draws on structuralist ideas, and some of its manifestations

Form and Formalism

are even overtly formalist, as most obviously in the work of Philippe Descola (e.g. 2005). Similarly, Brian Larkin has recently written explicitly and persuasively of infrastructure as a 'form', rejecting the antiformalism of anthropology's turn to materiality in favour of a nondualist understanding of 'form' as part of the material world (2017).[3]

To put my own positional cards more clearly on the table, and to emphasize that in identifying an antiformalist consensus underlying a range of views of anthropology, I'm not also trying to suggest that such a consensus invalidates all of those views: the theoretical background from which a range of my work emerges is the anthropology of ethics, which has its own internally diverse attitudes to form. At one end of the spectrum, approaches grounded in ordinary language philosophy and indeed, as we have seen, in Wittgenstein, are predominantly antiformalist in conception, often understanding ethics to be capillary, relational, and ubiquitous in a manner not dissimilar to Foucault's understanding of power (see e.g. Das 2020; Lambek 2010). At the opposite end of the spectrum, as we've also seen, Joel Robbins's and others' understandings of the good, of value, of hierarchy, and indeed of culture promise a return of sorts to a more unashamedly formalist vision of anthropology (e.g. Haynes 2017; Robbins 2004; Robbins and Sommerschuh 2016). Meanwhile, the works of pioneers in the field such as James Laidlaw, James Faubion, and Michael Lambek exhibit – like many of the approaches described above – both formal and antiformalist characteristics: the use of Foucault's quadripartite schema for understanding projects of self-cultivation, for example, alongside other similar devices, has been hugely productive for a range of scholars (e.g. Cook 2010; Laidlaw 2013; Mahmood 2004); yet so has the insistent rejection of Durkheimian models of culture and society, together with mechanistic understandings of the relationship between people and the norms and contexts with which they live (e.g. Faubion 2001; Laidlaw 2002). I myself have found an array of different works within the field of ethics to be helpful in my own thinking, formalism and antiformalism notwithstanding.

The Unanalysable Facts of Life

So my point is not that anthropology of the last three decades or so contains no formal elements whatsoever. Indeed, beyond the examples above, there has long been a powerful undercurrent of ethnographic interest in form. For instance, Larkin's interest in material form (2017) echoes both older and other contemporary work concerned with the aesthetics or materiality of form, from Alfred Gell's writing on art and agency (1998) through Annelise Riles's groundbreaking work on documents, legal knowledge, and networks (2000, 2006), Joanna Cook's demonstrations of how mindfulness practitioners cultivate and learn forms of bureaucratic advocacy and thus turn their practice into a political object (2023), Thomas Yarrow's meticulous studies of architects (2019) and development experts (2011; and see also Mosse 2005, 2013), and Boyer's and Yurchak's analysis of the aesthetics of 'empty' political forms (2010).

Likewise, other work has explored the relevance of form to questions of ethical and social life: formal concepts such as those of 'character' open out the possibilities of thinking with literary formalism as a way of imagining 'the convergence of aesthetic and ethical forms of practice, technique, and judgement' (Bialecki & Reed 2018: 160); value and values have emerged as productive formal operators in a number of different anthropological projects (e.g. Graeber 2001; Kockelman 2020; Robbins 2007), including that of Robbins's powerful revival and defence of the culture concept, and Naomi Haynes's work on hierarchy (e.g. 2017); the figure of the 'knot' is, for Sarah Green and others, a critical device for interrogating social and conceptual entanglements beyond notions of relation and connection alone (2014), as is that of the 'container' for Andrew Shryock and Daniel Lord Smail (2017). Morgan Clarke's work on the Wittgensteinian topic of 'rules' demonstrates both the ethnographic importance rules can assume and that anthropologists can engage with such formal devices in ways that go beyond scepticism about their power or existence (See e.g. 2018; Clarke & Corran 2021; see also Dresch & Scheele 2015; Shryock and Scheele 2019). Similarly,

Form and Formalism

Webb Keane's (2018) work on ethical life, while attentive to context, offers formal analytical frameworks – such as that of 'affordance' – for understanding moral experience across cultures.

On the other hand, where form does appear in contemporary anthropology, it often does so as a tacit or subordinate element within a larger antiformalist framework. To give just one example, even Larkin's recent explicit call for attention to 'infrastructures of form' is still premised on the dominant picture we've been examining, as indicated by its non-dualist (antiformalist) rejection of the form/matter distinction:

One of the most exciting sides of new materialism is its emphasis on emergence and the becoming of matter rather than its fixed ontology (Barad 2007; Coole and Frost 2010). I see the dynamics of encounter as formed through the constant evolution of objects in relation to discrete environments ... the relationship between the material and the figural – particularly in the case of infrastructures – is reciprocal and entangled rather than causal and successive. (2017: 197–198).

So, the various anthropological engagements with form one might pick out rarely add up to a coherent 'formalism' to challenge antiformalist orthodoxy.

Where ethnographic interest in form does begin to turn into formalism, on the other hand, such approaches can appear for that very reason as distinctive counterpoints to the dominant consensus, attractive therefore to some but also unusual and easily singled out for critique. We've seen this already in the accusation of 'hubris' levelled at Robbins (and see Venkatesan et al. 2015), and we might similarly note Bruno Latour's description of Descola's version of Amerindian animism as a mere (formal) 'type', in comparison to the antiformalist 'bomb' it becomes in the hands of others such as Eduardo Viveiros de Castro.[4]

Again, my point here is to highlight the widespread nature of the picture we saw emerging through the last chapter of this book. Whilst I hope to have made a case for the fact that this picture resembles

The Unanalysable Facts of Life

Wittgenstein's late philosophy in many important ways, and for the direct influence of that late philosophy on some versions of this picture, the picture itself lives on far beyond those versions that invoke Wittgenstein explicitly. They are, as I suggested in that chapter, simply the ones that say it the loudest and the clearest, and with the most explicit attempt at justification. With or without Wittgenstein as backing, the approaches I've discussed here share a claim of access to the ethnographic 'facts of life' *as against analytical abstraction* and a claim to reject the formalization of such 'facts of life' *by means of analytical abstraction.*[5] It is to the facts of life that anthropology has become used to appealing, and we always find such facts to be, at bottom, unanalysable, specific, and indefinable. We reach for the real, and yet we also repeat to ourselves that we will in some sense fail to make sense of it unless our devices for doing so are self-consciously blurry and indistinct. Perhaps then, we should not wonder at the fact, noted in the Introduction, that we seem less interesting to others as a discipline than we have done in the past – a lot of what we say seems to come down to the fact that life is real, messy, and complex, and that as a consequence nothing explanatory can be said about it (Heywood & Candea 2023).

The Point Before Explicitness

In one of the epigraphs with which this book begins, Bernard Suits's character of the Grasshopper describes his nightmare vision of a Utopia in which he has succeeded in convincing everybody that everything they work and labour at is really just a game.[6] Without faith in some instrumental, ends-based, 'striving' activities, Suits worried, it would be impossible to lead a meaningful and worthwhile existence: 'Life for most people will not be worth living if they cannot believe that they are doing *something* useful, whether it is providing for their families or formulating a theory of relativity' (1978: 128). So, in the 'vision' outlined

The Point Before Explicitness

in the first epigraph to this chapter, the Grasshopper imagines people recapturing 'the point before explicitness', as Strathern puts it in the second epigraph, before his compulsive missionizing of the lusory attitude to life had ruined them by forcing them to become conscious of the games they were really playing.

The parallel with Wittgenstein – and with this book's argument – is striking. Just as the Grasshopper feared the consequences of explicitly recognizing the game-like nature of human endeavours, this book has examined what happens when anthropology becomes self-conscious about its own pictures of context. What I've attempted to demonstrate is not simply the existence of a historical trajectory from formalism to antiformalism as a consequence of that self-consciousness, but also how any picture – even one designed to celebrate openness, indeterminacy, and formlessness – can ossify into dogma. I've tried to point to the ways in which aspects of an antiformalist consensus in contemporary anthropology have, in some respects, taken on some of the rigid characteristics it originally opposed in earlier formalist approaches.

Wittgenstein's most anthropological characteristic was his constant resistance to dogmatism and generalization: to turning a particular answer into one valid everywhere and for all time. This characteristic is, in lots of ways, at the heart of the connections this book has traced between anthropology and his ideas. The idea that one should not assume but 'look and see' is the epitome of the core anthropological virtue of openness to changing one's mind that I set out in this book's introduction. Equally though, in some ways the story of this book is the story of the transcendentalization of this stance: of how 'looking and seeing' went from being the business of anthropology to being its philosophy, and at the cost of alternatives.

In this sense, we might say this stance underwent a kind of reverse version of the transformation Pierre Hadot advocated for certain philosophical perspectives.[7] Hadot famously argued that we should see such perspectives not as philosophy but as ways of life, exercises for living;

The Unanalysable Facts of Life

not as systems or principles but as practices (1995). In naming his later philosophy his 'anthropological perspective', perhaps Wittgenstein inadvertently began the process by which anthropology has risked ceasing to be a practice and a way of life – albeit one for a professionalized discipline – and becoming instead a system and a philosophy. In making it thus philosophically explicit, even naming it after our discipline, he made it into an 'idol', in his own words, the allure of which has sometimes proven impossible to resist.

Surely though – since Wittgenstein may have learnt this trait in part from Myers's and other Torres Straits alumni back in 1912, from Malinowski's writings on primitive language in 1923, and even some version of it from his readings of Frazer in the 1930s – there is a way for us to inhabit the stance of 'looking and seeing' without needing to say it explicitly to ourselves over and over and over again until it itself becomes the one and only general and transcendental truth we know?

Marilyn Strathern's claim that 'new ideas always come before old – but this is accomplished simply through putting current ideas into perspective' captures what I've tried to argue in relation to this possibility: by contextualizing some of anthropology's current antiformalist commitments – tracing their emergence through Wittgenstein's philosophical trajectory and its uptake in anthropology – I hope to have shown their contingency. Not in order to dismiss them, but to allow them to be held a little more lightly.

So this is not a call to 'recapture the point before explicitness' and to return to earlier anthropological formalism. As Strathern also notes, such nostalgic returns are both impossible and misguided, and it is far from clear in any case that such formalism was always as dogmatic as it is often taken to be: 'anthropology's past seems littered with texts that do not fit into the realist/representational mode', as she puts it, asking 'Did we not always know that descriptions of the Tallensi and the Nuer were mediated by anthropological schools of thought and the writings of predecessors and colleagues?' (1991: 19).[8]

The Point Before Explicitness

My point, again, is less about the formalism/antiformalism binary either analytically or historically than it is about the fact that either type of approach can become ossified, reductive, or dogmatic, but equally neither type need do so. For example, readers may well take issue with specific examples I've discussed in this book – I tried to make clear that my characterization of Geertz, for example, was self-consciously far from complete. But whatever one's view on particular instances, the central argument remains: antiformalism can become just as dogmatic as formalism when it ceases to be a methodological approach, deployed in specific contexts, and becomes instead an unexamined article of faith. The important question is not whether any specific thinker has fallen prey to this ossification, but whether the disciplinary current as a whole has developed unquestioned commitments that limit rather than enable our understanding.

So the problem is not with form or its absence, but with the insistence that either approach represents the only legitimate path to anthropological knowledge. If this book has succeeded at all, it has been by showing how, to the extent to which anthropology is captive to a picture of formlessness as the only accurate representation of a formless reality, that captivity is just as constraining as earlier captivity to pictures of determinate form.

I hope that seeing the picture of formlessness more clearly than we always have done helps to recover some of the explanatory and comparative power that has sometimes seemed at risk in contemporary anthropology, without at the same time sacrificing its hard-won reflexivity and sensitivity to difference. If there is a lesson worth learning from Wittgenstein, perhaps it is not how to choose between form and formlessness, but how to escape the tyranny of having to choose at all.

Notes

Introduction

1 Life is not of course necessarily formless, as evidenced by the history of biological interest in form (see e.g. Helmreich and Roosth 2010).
2 The partial connections Strathern describes as 'merography'; and see also Candea et al. (2015).
3 Vincenzo Latronico's novel about creative professionals in Berlin, *Perfection* (2025), is a brilliant literary representation of 'life without dimension' or life as décor, 'with diversity and multiplicity contained within'.

Chapter 1

1 Translations of the *Tractatus* are also subject to disputation and controversy. I use the Pears and McGuinness translation of 1961, unless otherwise specified.
2 This argument is reminiscent of Peirce's comparable distinction between type and token – cf. Misak 2016 on the relation between Wittgenstein and American pragmatism.
3 The same is true of other concepts such as the 'Laws of Inference', upon which Russell and Frege depended, which have to state what the truth tables merely show.
4 A version of this position is also sometimes referred to as the 'positivist' or 'neo-positivist' reading of the text adopted by some of the logical positivists, such as Rudolf Carnap, in the 1930s (e.g. 1932).
5 Though Das does make brief reference in a footnote to the debates I describe below (2018: 155).

6 Though Cora Diamond also claims Anscombe as an inspiration for the alternative reading I outline below (Diamond 2004).
7 There is a third, or middle way reading, espoused by Marie McGinn amongst others and based on the showing/saying distinction (e.g. McGinn 2001), which I lack the space to describe.
8 Though Conant and Diamond do point to some errors – or metaphysical commitments, which is what count for errors in this context – in the *Tractatus*, and do see some change, this change is argued to come not in the form of Wittgenstein abandoning consciously held to commitments (the realist metaphysics of the *Tractatus*, for example, or the remarks about solipsism) but rather of noticing commitments that had previously appeared innocent. Other resolute readings, which some call 'jacobin', as opposed to the 'girondin' form in which they appear in Conant and Diamond, deny even this (e.g. Read 2006), and insist that Wittgenstein was right all along, and always in the same way.
9 If the resolute reading is correct of course then these objections and others aimed at the body of the book may be dismissed, as the issues they concern are merely 'elucidatory nonsense'; but one suspects this will not encourage a great many further anthropologists to attempt to make sense of them. On the other hand, the resolute reading does allow us to imagine a connection between the author of the *Tractatus* and the author of the *Investigations*, whom anthropologists have certainly been very interested in, where Gellner makes it appear as if the two were almost entirely alien to one another, united only by their mutual imbrication in the wider context of the late Habsburg empire. The resolute reading achieves this by concentrating on what it takes to be the 'therapeutic', problem-dissolving, anti-philosophical elements of the *Tractatus*, elements very much also present in Wittgenstein's later work, and about which we'll learn more in later chapters.

Chapter 2

1 Perhaps part of the reason for its obscurity in comparison to *Argonauts* is that the fieldwork upon which it was based seems to have been more or less a failure, despite being modelled on Rivers's methodological injunctions. Radcliffe-Brown proved largely unable to learn local languages and experienced a great deal of difficulty with the 'genealogical method', and his self-declared interest when beginning his research was in pre-colonial social organization, thus rendering moot a lot of what he actually observed (Kuper 1973: 41–42; Tomas 1991: 95–97). Nonetheless, the book was hailed as 'revolutionary' upon its publication

thanks to its purported reliance on 'modern' methods, and to the analytical arguments it advanced (Temple 1922 in Fortes 1955; Tomas 1991).

2 Stocking, the foremost historian of anthropology, is sceptical (1995: 305), and beyond the fact that all three were at Trinity at the same time (though Russell was not usually physically present in this period), actual historical evidence for this claim is sparse.

3 Needham implies that Radcliffe-Brown plagiarized his form of notation from an 1883 paper by Alexander Macfarlane, a collaborator of Francis Galton, and notes that Alfred Kroeber made a similar case for logical notation in 1909 (1971: xxii–xxv).

4 Leach is rather scathing about James, depicting him as a vulgarizer of the more intellectually robust C. S. Peirce, and points to what he sees as analogous differences between Peircean and Jamesian pragmatism, on the one hand, and Durkheimian/Radcliffe-Brownian and Malinowskian functionalism on the other (1957: 122). He credits Malinowski's biological functionalism to the equally simplistic understanding of function he finds in James.

5 Though on at least one occasion Wittgenstein wrote to Russell that he found Mach's style 'horrid'. There remains ongoing dispute about the exact extent of this influence: on the one hand Gilbert Ryle insisted Wittgenstein got everything he needed from 'Frege and Russell, not Mach' (1951), though, again, Russell also read Mach (Banks 2014); on the other hand, Finnish Wittgensteinian Jaako Hintikka, among others, argued that a very great deal of the *Tractatus* was derived from Mach's philosophy, including aspects of its solipsism, and the view that the truths of logic are empty (2001) and one of Wittgenstein's biographers, Brian McGuinness, suggests Mach would have been an early influence (1988: 38–40). The later Wittgenstein's reliance on thought-experiments is also sometimes said to be a consequence of Mach's influence, given the extent to which Mach is associated with this method (Visser 2001; and see Heywood 2023b). Whatever the historical and biographical reality in the case of Wittgenstein, there is no doubt about Mach's major influence on positivist thinkers adjacent to Wittgenstein, such as Schlick (under whom Nadel studied) and Rudolf Carnap (Holton 1992). Interestingly, as Thornton describes, Mach himself also read and often referred to some of the anthropologists we have encountered so far in this chapter, including Tylor and Haddon (1985).

6 The idea that context is isomorphic with a sense of the specificity of a culture is of course though itself a modernist artefact.

7 One notes he does not even merit an entry in the index of the most scholarly recent account of comparison in anthropology (Candea 2018).

Notes to pages 91–98

8 See, for example, his posthumously published *A Scientific Theory of Culture and Other Essays* and a 1929 letter to Raymond Firth in which Malinowski urges firth to write a holistic monograph on the Tikopia (quoted in Kuper 1973: 24)

Chapter 3

1 Though as we have seen some would wish to deny Wittgenstein's thought ever underwent major transition (see e.g. Crary and Read 2000; Medina 2002). In describing this period ('transitional', 'middle' or whatever we wish to call it), my intention is not – as it is not at any point in this book – to adjudicate on debates about the philosophical interpretation of Wittgenstein's oeuvre. It is not in other words to assess the question of exactly how philosophically significant the differences are between the *Tractatus* and *Philosophical Investigations* (though it seems absurd to deny that there are some such differences). My interest instead is in how those differences – and other developments and changes in his thought – map onto and affect developments and changes in anthropology.
2 To add to the irony, only shortly after Wittgenstein wrote his first notes on Frazer, Frazer himself was in Cambridge giving the inaugural William Wyse lectures at Trinity (Palmié 2018: 4).
3 Drury himself thinks he remembers it as 1930 but Monk has it as 1931 (1991: 310), and since 1931 is clearly the year in which the 'Remarks' were written it is plausible to imagine Drury got the year wrong.
4 This absence of consideration for the context of Wittgenstein's own work is reflected in occasional confusion about dates: a recent commentator, for example, incorrectly asserts that the remarks were written 'between 1931 and 1936' (McGee 2023: 21); and for reasons that are unclear de Zengotita specifies that the 'Remarks' were written exactly one year before the episode of Sraffa's gesture we will meet later in this chapter (which he also narrates rather colourfully in a manner that departs from the orthodox version) despite the fact that the Sraffa story is undated and possibly entirely apocryphal (1989: 392). It is also reflected in the occasional comment to the effect that the 'Remarks' were contained in the typescript of the manuscript that would become the *Philosophical Investigations* (e.g. de Zengotita 1989: 390) – this is true in the broadest possible sense, in that from this period until the end of his life Wittgenstein was continually taking notes, dictating them into typescripts, and then revising the result, and that some of these revisions would result in the posthumous publication of the *Philosophical Investigations*. But it is certainly

not the case that there was 'a manuscript' in 1931 that then became the *Philosophical Investigations* two decades later – this is to vastly underplay the nature of the 'revisions' Wittgenstein engaged in over that period, and in fact the typescript in which the 'Remarks' were retained is so different from the *Philosophical Investigations* that it has been published separately as *The Big Typescript*, parts of which were also themselves separately published as *Philosophical Remarks* and *Philosophical Grammar*. None of the 'Remarks on Frazer' survive into the text of the *Philosophical Investigations*. Furthermore, no anthropological commentator to my knowledge has noted the fact that Wittgenstein's thinking in 1931 – when the first portion of the 'Remarks' was written – was different to his thinking 'after 1948', as Rhees has it, when the second portion was written, and that the two parts may therefore reflect some of these differences.

5 Here he found another, more 'ordinary', alternative to philosophy in the form of architecture. More specifically, he took on the task of helping to design his sister Gretl's new house (cf. Lambek 2022). It took two years to construct the house to Wittgenstein's exacting design specifications, during which time he caused an engineer to break down in tears and had the ceilings of one of the rooms raised by three centimetres just before it was time to complete the house. Though apparently appropriate to Gretl's personality, Wittgenstein's other sister Hermine described the finished product as 'more a dwelling for the gods than for a small mortal' (Monk 1991: 236–237).

6 On this distinction see Chapter 1.

7 Somewhat surprisingly given this uncharacteristic gratitude on Wittgenstein's part, Sraffa himself, according to Sen, claimed to be unable to remember the event in question (Sen 2003: 1242 – though elsewhere Sraffa noted his agreement with von Wright's version, see Engelmann 2013: 152). In Sen's recollections Sraffa viewed any such claim on his part, if made, as 'rather obvious'. Perhaps something of this attitude may be gleaned from the gesture itself, which can mean, among other things, 'I don't care.'

8 In fact, there is considerable debate over whether or not the *Tractatus* is committed to any kind of realism about the objects it describes (see e.g. McGinn 2009). Consider for example its critique of Russell's Theory of Types, which we met in Chapter 1 as an attempt to resolve Russell's eponymous paradox. Russell's theory functions by making claims about the reference of logical signs – it declares that they refer to different 'types' of entities. The point of Wittgenstein's critique of this purported resolution of the paradox is that reference to entities in the world is unnecessary and incoherent in logic; rather, that signs mean different things is given by the way in which they are logically

deployed, as in grammar, including on occasions on which we may use the same notation to mean two different things: if I say 'this fly cannot fly' then it is clear I mean two different things by 'fly' because of the way the words are used in relation to one another. We will have cause shortly to return to the question of grammar, and of internal relations.

9 It is also noteworthy that both Wittgenstein and Saussure used 'games' as an analogy for language.

10 This also explains the appearance of what is sometimes called a 'verificationist' phase in Wittgenstein's philosophy. Verificationism – the idea, roughly speaking, that for a proposition to be meaningful it must be verifiable – is usually associated with the positivist/empiricist philosophy of the Vienna Circle (and, relatedly, of Oxford philosopher A. J. Ayer), and was developing, partly in dialogue with Wittgenstein, in this period. In Wittgenstein's version, however – and even this version he was later to deny holding – the point of verification is not scientific or empirical, that is, it is not that we must be able to test a hypothesis for it to be 'good' science; rather, understanding how we would verify a proposition 'gives the grammar of the proposition', by showing its relation to other propositions: it shows 'what [a proposition] follows from and what follows from it.' (AWL: 19–20; and see Medina 2001) In other words, it shows the 'grammatical system' in which a proposition has sense in any given case. I verify that 'this is red' by going and checking which among the particular possibilities given by the colour system applies to 'this', showing me that the sense of 'this is red' is determined by that system of possibilities. What this also shows us is the existence of the grammatical rule that 'this' cannot be one colour and another at the same time. This rule is not itself verifiable, and therefore is a different sort of proposition to 'this is red'. Given the place of rules in Wittgenstein's conception of 'grammar' at this point, exactly how different is a crucial question, and leads partly on to the shift into his so-called 'anthropological perspective'.

11 Perhaps the most famous instance of this interpretation is that critiqued by Stanley Cavell in one of his first publications on Wittgenstein in 1962, in which he inveighs against David Pole's understanding of the *Philosophical Investigations* as arguing that rules 'determine' language (Cavell 1962; and see Chapter 5).

12 Cf. Candea's notion of 'ejection' – the idea that anthropologists analogize their own methods with what they observe (2018: 256–259)

13 This is also quite in accord with the affinities between Wittgenstein, Spengler, Ernst, and Frazer in terms of pessimism – that is, it is in accord with the view that there is nothing qualitatively different about 'savage' and 'civilised' myth/language (cf. Kwon 2018).

14 And see McGee (2023) who not only does not see the comparison with Wittgenstein but in fact compares Lévi-Strauss with Frazer by reading him as a naturalist. See Remotti (2015) by contrast for a brilliant discussion of Wittgenstein and Lévi-Strauss's commonalities.

Chapter 4

1 From what Matei Candea calls 'typology' to 'topology' (2018: 96).
2 Though see Gellner (1962) for the point that this is itself an uncharitable reading of Lévy-Bruhl's argument.
3 Another line of connection is through the historian R. G. Collingwood. Several scholars have noted the parallels between Collingwood and Wittgenstein on problems of understanding others (e.g. Sandis 2016), and though Collingwood and Evans-Pritchard never met, Collingwood cited the Azande work long before the rationality debates, and his influence on Evans-Pritchard's view of historiography is clear (as is his influence on Peter Winch, who cites him often).
4 Yet other commentators object to reading either Lévy-Bruhl or Wittgenstein in this way, noting – as indeed did anthropologists like John Beattie, often also taken to occupy this position (see e.g. 1964: 204) – that in actual practice the distinction between instrumental and affective action is blurred and hard to draw, and that Lévy-Bruhl and Wittgenstein were cognizant of this. Some have suggested that Lévy-Bruhl's point, rather than to distinguish sharply peoples or societies, was to distinguish ideal-typical modes of thought, and to suggest that the mystical was the 'affective fringe' of every human experience, rather than only those that take place in human societies (see de Lara 2000; Leenhardt 1975 [1949]).
5 Winch himself anticipates some objections that speak directly to our concern here:

One is inclined to think of the laws of logic as forming a *given* rigid structure to which men try, with greater or less (but never complete) success, to make what they say in their actual linguistic behaviour and social intercourse conform. One thinks of propositions as something ethereal, which just because of their ethereal, non-physical nature, can fit together more tightly than can be conceived in the case of anything so grossly material as flesh-and-blood men and their actions. In a sense, one is right in this; for to treat of logical relations in a formal systematic way is to think at a very high level of abstraction, at which all the anomalies, imperfections and crudities which characterize men's actual intercourse with each other in society have been removed... It may make one forget that it is only from their roots in this actual flesh-and-blood intercourse that those formal systems draw such life as they have; for the whole idea of a logical relation is only possible by virtue of the sort of agreement between men and their actions which is discussed by Wittgenstein in the *Philosophical Investigations*. (1958: 125–126; italics in original)

Both the reference to the *Philosophical Investigations* and the rejection of logical relations as consisting in a '*given* rigid structure' might lead us to imagine that we are dealing here with Wittgenstein's later 'anthropological perspective' on context rather than that of his transitional work. Yet the very idea of social life and context as made up of 'logical relations' has a strongly formalist flavour to it no matter Winch's protestations to the contrary, as indeed does the reliance on the notion of 'internal relations'.

6 Collingwood had quoted Evans-Pritchard as early as 1938: 8.
7 Macintyre assumes that Evans-Pritchard aims at confining himself to Zande contextual norms. Confusingly, Winch assumes the reverse.
8 He makes the accusation after quoting Evans-Pritchard on the subject of contradiction within Zande witchcraft beliefs, specifically around the question of 'witchcraft-substance', an 'oval blackish swelling or bag ... attached to the liver' of witches (1937: 22). The substance, and therefore status as a witch, is 'transmitted by unilinear descent from parent to child' (1937: 23). The potential contradiction involved in these ideas is 'if a man is proven a witch the whole of his clan are *ipso facto* witches, since the Zande clan is a group of persons related biologically to one another through the male line' (1937: 24), and consistent application of the rule about witchcraft substance transmission would presumably oblige the Azande to declare whole clans – and possibly the whole of Zande society by extension – either permanently tainted by witchcraft or permanently free of it.
9 Interestingly, Winch's position changes subtly once again later in life, perhaps as scholarly distinctions between different parts of Wittgenstein's oeuvre hardened and philosophers became more self-conscious about the relations between the parts they drew on. In a final return to these questions over thirty years later and shortly before his death, in a paper titled 'Can We Understand Ourselves?', this last vestige of transitional Wittgensteinianism seems to have all but disappeared from Winch's thinking (1997). As suggested by the paper's title, Winch's problem of 'understanding' has morphed from being one about whether 'we' can understand 'primitive societies' to one about 'understanding' (and misunderstanding) much more generally.
10 Gellner isn't the only commentator to accuse Wittgenstein of political conservatism (see e.g. Nyiri 1981). Equally, a large amount of ink has been spilled in

attempts to enlist Wittgenstein in the cause of critical and progressive politics (despite his avowed pessimism, and very overt misogyny). Such arguments seem often to say more about the way in which commentators have a tendency to project themselves into Wittgenstein than they do about Wittgenstein himself, who made his general lack of interest in political questions clear: '"Just improve yourself", Wittgenstein would later say to many of his friends, "that is all you can do to improve the world." Political questions, for him, would always be secondary to questions of personal integrity'. (Monk 1991: 17-18).

11 Gellner is also critical of what he calls the 'contrast' theory of meaning, by which he presumably has in mind ideas such as those of the middle period of Wittgenstein's thought (1959: 74-78).

12 That Gellner's point about the naturalistic fallacy has at least some substance to it is clear if we return to Winch's conceptions of 'rules' and 'contexts'. The idea that 'all specifically human behaviour ... is rule-governed' does suggest that the mere existence of a behaviour is evidence for its meaning in relation to a system of rules. And despite the qualifications we noted Winch is adding, the idea that 'criteria of intelligibility' are peculiar to specific modes of life and not portable across them makes such criteria and associated 'rules' appear impervious to either practical or conceptual alterations, as indeed is also suggested by Wittgenstein's transitional notion of the 'autonomy of grammar'. In other words, as is more broadly true of mid-century anthropological and other invocations of Wittgenstein, the validity of Gellner's point about the naturalistic fallacy depends on the conceptualization of context at issue, and this in turn depends on which Wittgenstein one credits: that of the transitional period we met in the last chapter, or that of the 'anthropological perspective' we will meet in more depth in the next chapter.

13 See Lambek (2021) for a particularly nuanced reading that draws directly on Wittgenstein.

Chapter 5

1 See Peters 2022, Hacking 1975, and Davidson & Gros 2011, for comparisons between Wittgenstein and Foucault as antifoundationalists.

2 One might well wish to have an argument about which came first, the antifoundationalism or the particularism – both in Wittgenstein's case and in that of anthropology.

3 For only a few recent examples, see, for example, Baker & Hacker 2009 [1985]; Das 2016, 2020; Gaffal 2011; Han & Das 2015; Laugier 2018b; Majetschak 2010; Moyal-Sharrock & Donatelli 2015; Padilla Gálvez 2011.

4 See Monk 1991: 336–337; on the relation between Wittgenstein and Oxford Ordinary Language Philosophy see also Harris & Unnsteinsson 2018; Krishnan 2023; Rowe 2023.
5 See Han & Das 2015, and also Clément 1996 for other anthropological surveys of usage of form of life in the *Investigations*.
6 It's also used once in *On Certainty* (OC 358) and a few times in other manuscripts – see Majetschak 2010: 76.
7 Or as minimal a grammar.
8 Goldfarb and others make a similar claim in denying the existence of a 'use-based theory of meaning' in Wittgenstein in the famous passage in §43. In that passage, Wittgenstein is not giving a general theory of use (one like Malinowski's, say), and 'given that invoking use by itself carries little information, [we should] take his remark in §43 to be, by and large, a denial of the possibility and appropriateness of theorizing about meaning' (1983: 279).
9 A still earlier version has 'facts of living' and 'forms of life' as slashed alternatives here – see MS 133, 28r.

Chapter 6

1 See the epigraph to Chapter 5 for the phrase in a fuller context.
2 Take, for example a part of the fragments later published as *Culture and Value* in which Wittgenstein sets out some of what he means by an 'anthropological point of view': 'What I am opposed to is the concept of some idea of exactitude given us *a priori*, as it were. At different times we have different ideals of exactitude; and none of them is supreme' (CV 37). This, of course, resembles an idea at least as old as Aristotle's Nicomachean Ethics, namely that the adequacy of exactness or precision of different kinds of knowledge depends in part on what it is knowledge of and for (Anagnostopoulos 1994).
3 See also Keesing (1974: 88) in direct critique of Geertz's Wittgensteinian contextualism: 'We will be poorly served if we weather the next revolutionary storms in philosophy poring over Husserly, Ryle, and Wittgenstein'.
4 After briefly summarizing Wittgenstein's career, the assessment of Pole's book begins as follows:

[t]he extent to which the ideas in [Wittgenstein's later work] are available, now seven years after the publication of the *Investigations*, is a matter of some question even after the appearance of the first book on the later philosophy, for none of its thought is to be found in David Pole's *The Later Philosophy of Wittgenstein*.

What I find most remarkable about this book is not the modesty of its understanding nor the pretentiousness and condescension of its criticism, but the pervasive absence of any worry that some remark of Wittgenstein's may not be utterly obvious in its meaning and implications. (1962: 68)

Conclusion

1 I am grateful to Michael Degani for drawing my attention to this particular passage.
2 Readers may have other iterations of this picture in mind that I have not described here. Candea, for example, points to the way in which anthropologists have wielded and generated a range of popular concepts as open-ended and even self-contradictory, as, for example, in invocations of neoliberalism that understand it to be capable of subsuming its own negations (2025; Heywood 2014; Muehlebach 2010).
3 Timothy Choy has made a somewhat similar argument in relation to environment forms (2021).
4 That said, there does seem to be an increasing appetite for more explicitly formalist approaches in anthropology: Candea identifies how antiformalism has become 'parasitic on what it claimed to reject' – even approaches focused on gaps and exceptions required an underlying conception of form to make sense, while simultaneously disavowing such form's possibility. As he notes, you can't attend to 'liminality, borders, migration, hybridity, and passing', as much brilliant contemporary anthropology does (2025), without some kind of social morphology. The very rejection of form requires form to reject. Candea's own program for a new comparativism (2018) exemplifies the ways in which formalism can be both immensely productive and lightly-worn. Similarly, Tanya Luhrmann's commitment to anthropology that generates 'findings' across diverse ethnographic contexts demonstrates how systematic and rigorous comparison can illuminate patterns without sacrificing complexity (e.g. 2023); Michael Degani's analysis of 'modes' illuminates how forms can be both structured and flexible (2022, 2025). Drawing on examples ranging from electrical infrastructure and postsocialist dance to paved road networks, he shows how anthropologists describe actors moving between different formalized patterns or styles – whether these are, for instance, bodily techniques, infrastructural systems, or ethical orientations. A Guinean dancer shifts between traditional and improvisational modes (Cohen 2016); a road system and dirt footpaths in New Guinea produce distinct forms of spiritual modality and gendered

Notes to pages 258-260

embodiment (Handman 2017); Urapmin Christians alternate between different ethical stances (Robbins 2004). Each mode has its constraints and affordances, but crucially, actors can often shift between them while maintaining their distinctiveness. Degani's own work on modal reasoning and electrical infrastructure in Tanzania is itself a testament to the productive potential of 'modality' as an anthropological form (2022; and see Kockelman 2020). Paul Kockelman's wider corpus stands as a testament to the broader potential of analytic and formalist approaches to core anthropological questions (e.g. 2013, 2017, 2022), as does that of Alberto Corsin-Jiménez (e.g. 2003, 2013); Michael Lempert's investigations of political discourse (2012) and communicative form (2024) are exemplary in the field of contemporary linguistic anthropology in showing how formal features of interaction can be analysed without sacrificing attention to historical contingency and social complexity. New approaches to regions like the Mediterranean showcase the ways in which formal devices such as scale may be artfully and self-consciously deployed in analysis (e.g. Ben-Yehoyada 2017); meanwhile beyond anthropology, as Nick Seaver points out, formal models of context are increasingly crucial to thinking creatively and critically about data and machine intelligence (2015).
5 Even though such approaches themselves can often take a rather abstract tone – see Heywood 2018b.
6 Suits himself seemed to have thought it distinctly possible that life really is a game (1967), but he also recognized, like the Grasshopper, that even if it were it would be in many ways unsustainable for people to believe it to be (cf. Lambek 2015).
7 Hadot was also one of the first significant Francophone commentators on Wittgenstein.
8 Robbins puts a similar point powerfully in a recent discussion of culture, specifically:

I would like to plant a stake in the ground to the effect that we have now reached the point where it makes good sense to call time on drive-by, argument-free dismissals of the idea of culture. It has been ages since anyone I know has held to an understanding of culture as a fully coherent system of meanings that is unchanging and shared in its entirety by every single person living in a well bounded population. As Rob Brightman (1995) pointed out long ago, the only anthropologists who have ever believed that culture was once considered something like this are critics of the culture concept, who oddly seem to evidence this kind of fixed, wholly shared understanding of how everyone once understood culture in precisely the way they claim no one else shares anything of the sort (2025: 106).

References

Abreu e Silva Neto, N. 2011. The Uses of 'Forms of Life' and the Meanings of Life. In J. Padilla Gálvez & M. Gaffal, eds. *Forms of Life and Language Games*. Frankfurt: Ontos Verlag. 75–106.

Ammerman, N. 2007. *Everyday Religion: Observing Modern Religious Lives*. Oxford: Oxford University Press.

Anagnostopoulos, G. 1994. *Aristotle on the Goals and Exactness of Ethics*. Berkeley: University of California Press.

Anand, N. 2017. *Hydraulic City: Water and the Infrastructures of Citizenship in Mumbai*. Durham: Duke University Press.

Anscombe, G. E. M. 1959. *An Introduction to Wittgenstein's Tractatus*. London: Hutchinson University Library.

Antze, P. & Lambek, M. 1996. *Tense Past: Cultural Essays in Trauma and Memory*. London: Routledge.

Appel, H. 2019. *The Licit Life of Capitalism: US Oil in Equatorial Guinea*. Durham: Duke University Press.

Ardener, E. 1971. The New Anthropology and Its Critics. *Man* 6 (3): 449–467.

Asad, T. 1986. The Concept of Cultural Translation in British Social Anthropology. In J. Clifford & G. E. Marcus, eds. *Writing Culture: The Poetics and Politics of Ethnography*. Berkeley: University of California Press. 141–165.

——— 1993. *Genealogies of Religion: Discipline and Reasons of Power in Christianity and Islam*. Baltimore: Johns Hopkins University Press.

——— 2020. Thinking about Religion through Wittgenstein. *Critical Times* 3 (3): 403–442.

Austin, J. L. 1961. *Philosophical Papers*. Oxford: Clarendon Press.

——— 1962. *How to Do Things with Words*. Oxford: Clarendon Press.

Baker, G. & Hacker, P. M. S. 1980. *An Analytical Commentary on Wittgenstein's Philosophical Investigations, Vol 1: Wittgenstein, Understanding, and Meaning*. Oxford: Blackwell.

References

2009 [1985]. *An Analytical Commentary on Wittgenstein's Philosophical Investigations, Vol 2: Wittgenstein, Rules, Grammar, and Necessity*. Oxford: Blackwell.

Banks, E. 2014. *The Realistic Empiricism of James, Mach, and Russell*. Cambridge: Cambridge University Press.

Bastianelli, M. 2013. Wittgenstein and the Mythology in the Forms of Language. In L. Perissinotto, ed. *The Darkness of His Time: Ethics, Politics, and Religion in Wittgenstein*. Mimesis: Milan. 87–115.

Beattie, J. 1964. *Other Cultures: Aims, Methods, and Achievements in Social Anthropology*. London: Routledge.

Ben-Yehoyada, N. 2017. *The Mediterranean Incarnate: Region Formation between Sicily and Tunisia since World War Two*. Chicago: University of Chicago Press.

Bessire, L. & Bond, D. 2014. Ontological Anthropology and the Deferral of Critique. *American Ethnologist* 41 (3): 440–456.

Bialecki, J. & Reed, A. 2018. Introduction: Anthropology and Character. *Social Anthropology* 26: 159–167.

Biehl, J. & Locke, P. 2010. Deleuze and the Anthropology of Becoming. *Current Anthropology* 51: 317–351.

Blank, A. 2007. Wittgenstein on Colors and Internal Relations, 1930–1932. In C. Kanzian & E. Runggaldier, eds. *Cultures: Conflict – Analysis – Dialogue: Proceedings of the 29th International Ludwig Wittgenstein Symposium*. Frankfurt: Ontos Verlag. 21–33.

2008. Wittgenstein on Colors and Logical Multiplicities, 1930–1932. *Dialogue: Canadian Philosophical Review* 47: 311–328.

2011. Wittgenstein on Verification and Seeing-As, 1930–1932. *Inquiry: An Interdisciplinary Journal of Philosophy* 54 (6): 614–632.

Boltanski, L. & Thévenot, L. 2006. *On Justification*. Princeton: Princeton University Press.

Boon, J. 1982. *Other Tribes, Other Scribes: Symbolic Anthropology in the Comparative Study of Cultures, Histories, Religions, and Texts*. Cambridge: Cambridge University Press.

1983. Functionalists write, too: Frazer/Malinowski and the semiotics of the monograph. *Semiotica* 46: 131–149.

Bourgois, P. 1998. The Moral Economies of Homeless Heroin Addicts: Confronting Ethnography, HIV Risk, and Everyday Violence in San Francisco Shooting Encampments. *Substance Use and Misuse* 33: 2323–2351.

Bouveresse, J. 1977. L'animal cérémoniel: Wittgenstein et l'anthropologie. *Actes de la recherche en sciences sociales* 16 (1): 43–54.

References

Boyer, P. & Yurchak, A. 2010. American Stiob: Or, What Late-Socialist Aesthetics of Parody Reveal about Contemporary Political Culture in the West. *Cultural Anthropology* 25: 179-221.

Boyte, H. 2004. *Everyday Politics: Reconnecting Citizens and Public Life*. Philadelphia: University of Pennsylvania Press.

Brightman, R. 1995. Forget Culture: Replacement, Transcendence, Relexification. *Cultural Anthropology* 10: 509-546.

Bronzo, S. 2012. The Resolute Reading and Its Critics: An Introduction to the Literature. *Wittgenstein-Studien* 3 (1): 45-80.

Burke, P. 2002. Context in Context. *Common Knowledge* 8 (1): 152-177.

Candea, M. 2018. *Comparison in Anthropology: The Impossible Method*. Cambridge: Cambridge University Press.

2022. On Visual Coherence and Visual Excess: Writing, Diagrams, and Anthropological Form. In L. Englemann, C. Humphrey, & C. Lynteris, eds. *Working with Diagrams*. Oxford: Berghahn. 63-89.

2025. A Return to Form. *Social Analysis* 69: 46-60.

Candea, M., Cook, J., Trundle, C., & Yarrow, T. 2022. Introduction: Reconsidering Detachment. In *Detachment: Essays on the Limits of Relational Thinking*. Manchester: Manchester University Press.

Candea, M., Heywood, P., Reed, A., & Yarrow, T. 2025. Ethnographies of Interest: Between Enthusiasm and the Instrumental. *Current Anthropology*.

Canfield, J. 2007. *Becoming Human: The Development of Language, Self, and Self-Consciousness*. Basingstoke: Macmillan.

Carnap, R. 1932. The Elimination of Metaphysics through Logical Analysis of Language. *Erkenntnis* 2 (1): 60-81.

Cavell, S. 1962. The Availability of Wittgenstein's Later Philosophy. *The Philosophical Review* 71 (1): 67-93.

1969. *Must We Mean What We Say: A Book of Essays*. Cambridge: Cambridge University Press.

1979. *The Claim of Reason: Wittgenstein, Skepticism, Morality, and Tragedy*. Oxford: Oxford University Press.

1987. Notes after Austin. *The Yale Review* 86 (3): 315-316.

1988. Declining Decline: Wittgenstein as a Philosopher of Culture. *Inquiry* 31 (3): 253-264.

1989. *This New Yet Unapproachable America*. Albuquerque: Living Batch Press.

2010. *Little Did I Know: Excerpts from Memory*. Stanford: Stanford University Press.

Chamberlain, L. 2021. *Street Life and Morals: German Philosophy in Hitler's Lifetime*. London: Reaktion Books.

References

Choy, T. 2021. Externality, Breathers, Conspiracy: Forms for Atmospheric Reckoning. In D. Papadopoulos, M. Puig de la Bellacasa, & N. Myers, eds. *Reactivating Elements: Chemistry, Ecology, Practice*. Durham: Duke University Press.

Clarke, M. 2014. Cough Sweets and Angels: The Ordinary Ethics of the Extraordinary in Sufi Practice in Lebanon. *Journal of the Royal Anthropological Institute* 20: 407–425.

2016. Comment on Robbins. *Journal of the Royal Anthropological Institute* 22: 797–799.

2018. *Islam and Law in Lebanon: Sharia within and without the State*. Cambridge: Cambridge University Press.

Clarke, M. & Corran, E., eds. 2021. *Rules and Ethics: Perspectives from Anthropology and History*. Oxford: Oxford University Press.

Clément, F. 1996. Une nouvelle 'forme de vie' pour les sciences sociales. *Revue européenne des sciences sociales* 34 (106): 155–168.

Clifford, J. 1997. *Routes: Travel and Translation in the Late Twentieth Century*. Cambridge: Harvard University Press.

Cohen, A. 2016. Inalienable Performances, Mutable Heirlooms: Dance, Cultural Inheritance, and Political Transformation in the Republic of Guinea. *American Ethnologist* 43: 650–662.

Collingwood, R. G. 1938. *Principles of Art*. Oxford: Clarendon Press.

Conant, J. 1989. Must We Show What We Cannot Say? In R. Fleming & M. Payne, eds. *The Senses of Stanley Cavell*. Lewisburg: Bucknell University Press. 242–283.

Conant, J. & Diamond, C. 2004. On Reading the Tractatus Resolutely: Reply to Meredith Williams and Peter Sullivan. In M. Kölbel & B. Weiss, eds. *Wittgenstein's Lasting Significance*. London: Routledge. 42–97.

Cook, J. 2010. *Meditation in Modern Buddhism: Renunciation and Change in Thai Monastic Life*. Cambridge: Cambridge University Press.

2016. Ethnography: Translation. Correspondences, *Fieldsights*, May 11. https://culanth.org/fieldsights/ethnography-translation.

2023. *Making a Mindful Nation: Mental Health and Governance in the Twenty-First Century*. Princeton: Princeton University Press.

Cook, J. W. 1983. Magic, Science, and Religion. *Philosophical Investigations* 6 (10): 2–36.

Cooper, D. 2014. *Everyday Utopias: The Conceptual Life of Promising Spaces*. Durham: Duke University Press.

Corsin-Jimenez, A. 2003. The Form of the Relation, or Anthropology's Enchantment with the Algebraic Imagination. Unpublished manuscript.

References

2013. *An anthropological trompe l'oeil for a common world.* Oxford: Berghahn.
Crapanzano, V. 1986. Hermes's Dilemma: the Masking of Subversion in Ethnographic Description. In J. Clifford & G. E. Marcus, eds. *Writing Culture: The Poetics and Politics of Ethnography.* Berkeley: University of California Press. 51–77.
Crary, A. & Read, R. 2000. *The New Wittgenstein.* London: Routledge.
Csordas, T. 1994. *Embodiment and Experience.* Cambridge: Cambridge University Press.
Da Col, G. & Palmié, S., eds. 2018. *The Mythology in Our Language: Remarks on Frazer's Golden Bough.* Chicago: HAU Books.
Danford, J. W. 1978. *Wittgenstein and Political Philosophy: A Re-examination of the Foundations of Social Science.* Chicago: University of Chicago Press.
Daniel, E. V. 1996. Crushed Glass, or, Is There a Counterpoint to Culture? In E. V. Daniel & J. Peck, eds. *Culture/Contexture: Explorations in Anthropology and Literary Studies.* Berkeley: University of California Press. 357–375.
Daniel, E. V. & Peck, J. 1996. Culture/Contexture: An Introduction. In E. V. Daniel & J. Peck, eds. *Culture/Contexture: Explorations in Anthropology and Literary Studies.* Berkeley: University of California Press. 1–34.
Das, V. 1995. *Critical Events: An Anthropological Perspective on Contemporary India.* Oxford: Oxford University Press.
1997. Wittgenstein and Anthropology. *Annual Review of Anthropology* 27: 171–195.
2007. *Life and Words: Violence and the Descent into the Ordinary.* Berkeley: University of California Press.
2016. The Boundaries of the 'We': Cruelty, Responsibility and Forms of Life. *Critical Horizons* 17: 168–185.
2018. Of Mistakes, Errors, and Superstitions. In G. Da Col & S. Palmié, eds. *The Mythology in Our Language: Remarks on Frazer's Golden Bough.* Chicago: HAU Books. 155–181.
2020. *Textures of the Ordinary: Doing Anthropology after Wittgenstein.* New York: Fordham University Press.
2023. *Slum Acts.* Oxford: Blackwell.
Davidson, A. 2004. *The Emergence of Sexuality.* Cambridge: Harvard University Press.
Davidson, A. & F. Gros. 2011. *Foucault, Wittgenstein: de possibles rencontres.* Paris: KIME.
De Lara, P. 2000. Wittgenstein and Evans-Pritchard on Ritual: Twenty-Two Reasons to Think that Wittgenstein Was an Anthropologist. *Journal of the Anthropological Society of Oxford* 31 (20): 119–132.

References

Degani, M. 2022. *The City Electric: Infrastructure and Ingenuity in Postsocialist Tanzania.* Durham: Duke University Press.
2025. Towards a Modal Anthropology. *Social Analysis* 68: 60–84.
Deleuze, G. 1997. *Essays Critical and Clinical.* Minneapolis: University of Minnesota Press.
Descola, P. 2005. *Beyond Nature and Culture.* Chicago: University of Chicago Press.
Diamond, C. 1988. Throwing Away the Ladder: How to Read the *Tractatus* Resolutely. *Philosophy* 63 (243): 5–27.
2004. Saying and Showing: An Example from Anscombe. In B. Stocker, ed. *Post-Analytic Tractatus.* Aldershot: Ashgate. 151–167.
Dilley, R. 1999. *The Problem of Context.* Oxford: Berghahn Books.
Douglas, M. 1978. Judgements on James Frazer. *Daedalus* 107 (4): 151–164.
1980. *Evans-Pritchard.* London: Fontana.
Dresch, P. & Scheele, J. 2015. *Legalism: rules and categories.* Oxford: Oxford University Press.
Duranti, A. & Goodwin, C. 1992. *Rethinking Context: Language as an Interactive Phenomenon.* Cambridge: Cambridge University Press.
Edmonds, D. & Eldinow, J. 2001. *Wittgenstein's Poker.* London: Faber & Faber.
Engelmann, M. 2013. *Wittgenstein's Philosophical Development: Phenomenology, Grammar, Method, and the Anthropological View.* Basingstoke: Macmillan.
Evans-Pritchard, E. 1934. Lévy-Bruhl's Theory of Primitive Mentality. *Bulletin of the Faculty of Arts, King Fuad 1st University* 2 (2): 1–26.
1937. *Witchcraft, Oracles and Magic among the Azande.* Oxford: Clarendon Press.
1950. Social Anthropology: Past and Present. *Man* 50: 118–124.
1965. *Theories of Primitive Religion.* Oxford: Clarendon Press.
Fadil, N. & Fernando, M. 2015. Rediscovering the Everyday Muslim. Notes on an Anthropological Divide. *HAU: Journal of Ethnographic Theory* 5: 59–88.
Fassin, D. & Rechtman, R. 2009. *The Empire of Trauma: An Enquiry into the Condition of Victimhood.* Princeton: Princeton University Press.
Faubion, J. 2001. Towards an Anthropology of Ethics: Foucault, and the Pedagogies of Autopoesis. *Representations* 74: 83–104.
Firth, R. 1957. Introduction: Malinowski as Scientist and Man. In R. Firth, ed. *Man and Culture: An Evaluation of the Work of Bronislaw Malinowski.* London: Routledge. 1–15.
Foks, F. 2024. Finding Modernity in England's Past: Social Anthropology and the Remaking of Social History in Britain, 1959–1977. *History of the Human Sciences* 37 (3–4): 106–129.

References

Fortes, M. 1955. Alfred Reginald Radcliffe-Brown, F.B.A., 1881-1955: A Memoir. *Man* 56: 149-153.

Gaffal, M. 2011. Forms of Life as Social Techniques. In J. Padilla Gálvez & M. Gaffal, eds. *Forms of Life and Language Games*. Frankfurt: Ontos Verlag. 57-74.

Garver, N. 1994. *This Complicated Form of Life: Essays on Wittgenstein*. Chicago: Open Court.

Geach, P. 1976. Saying and Showing in Frege and Wittgenstein. *Acta Philosophica Fennica* 28: 54-70

Gebauer, G. 2017. *Wittgenstein's Anthropological Philosophy*. Basingstoke: Macmillan.

Geertz, C. 1971. Introduction. In C. Geertz, ed. *Myth, Symbol, and Culture*. New York: Norton. ix-xi.

1973. *The Interpretation of Cultures*. New York: Basic Books.

1984. Anti Anti-Relativism. *American Anthropologist* 86 (2): 263-278.

1988. *Works and Lives: The Anthropologist as Author*. Stanford: Stanford University Press.

2000. *Available Light: Anthropological Reflections on Philosophical Topics*. Princeton: Princeton University Press.

Geertz, C., Geertz, H., & Rosen, L. 1979. *Meaning and Order in Moroccan Society: Three Essays in Cultural Analysis*. Cambridge: Cambridge University Press.

Gell, A. 1998. *Art and Agency: An Anthropological Theory*. Oxford: Oxford University Press.

Gellner, E. 1959. *Words and Things*. London: Routledge & Kegan Paul.

1962. Concepts and Society. *Transactions of the Fifth World Congress of Sociology* 1: 153-183.

1992. *Postmodernism, Reason, and Religion*. London: Psychology Press.

1998. *Language and Solitude: Wittgenstein, Malinowski, and the Habsburg Dilemma*. Cambridge: Cambridge University Press.

Geoghegan, B. 2020. Textocracy, or the Cybernetic Logic of French Theory. *History of the Human Sciences* 33 (1): 52-79.

2022. *Code: From Information Theory to French Theory*. Durham: Duke University Press.

Goldfarb, W. 1983. I Want You to Bring Me a Slab: Remarks on the Opening Sections of the 'Philosophical Investigations'. *Synthese* 56 (3): 265-282.

Graeber, D. 2001. *Toward an Anthropological Theory of Value: The False Coin of Our Own Dreams*. Basingstoke: Palgrave.

2015. Radical Alterity Is Just Another Way of Saying 'Reality'. *HAU: Journal of Ethnographic Theory* 5 (2): 1-41.

References

Grant Watson, E. L. 1946. *But to What Purpose: The Autobiography of a Contemporary*. London: Cresset Press.

Green, S. 2014. Anthropological Knots: Conditions of Possibilities and Interventions. *HAU: Journal of Ethnographic Theory* 4: 1–21.

2024. Mathematical Moments. *Social Analysis* 68: 101–105.

Guter, E. 2020. *Wittgenstein on Music*. Cambridge: Cambridge University Press.

Hacker, P. M. S. 1972. *Insight and Illusion*. Oxford: Oxford University Press.

1992. Developmental Hypotheses and Perspicuous Representations: Wittgenstein on Frazer's 'Golden Bough'. *Iyyun: The Jerusalem Philosophical Quarterly* 41: 277–299.

2013. Wittgenstein's Anthropological and Ethnographical Approach. In P. M. S. Hacker, ed. *Wittgenstein: Comparisons and Context*. Oxford: Oxford University Press. 111–127.

2015. Forms of Life. *Nordic Wittgenstein Review* 4: 1–20.

Hacker, P. M. S. & Schulte, J. 2009. *The Text of the Philosophische Untersuchungen*. Oxford: Blackwell.

Hacking, I. 1975. *Why Does Language Matter to Philosophy?* Cambridge: Cambridge University Press.

Hadot, P. 1995. *Philosophy as a Way of Life*. Oxford; Blackwell.

Haller, R. 1988. *Questions on Wittgenstein*. London: Routledge.

Han, C. & Das, V. 2015. Introduction: A Concept Note. In V. Das & C. Han, eds. *Living and Dying in the Contemporary World: A Compendium*. Berkeley: University of California Press. 1–39.

Handler, R. 2009. The Uses of Incommensurability in Anthropology. *New Literary History* 40 (3): 627–647.

Handman, C. 2017. Walking like a Christian: Roads, Translation, and Gendered Bodies as Religious Infrastructure in Papua New Guinea. *American Ethnologist* 44: 315–327.

Hanfling, O. 1989. *Wittgenstein's Later Philosophy*. New York: State University of New York Press.

Harris, D. & Unnsteinsson, E. 2017. Wittgenstein's Influence on Austin's Philosophy of Language. *British Journal for the History of Philosophy* 26 (2): 371–395.

Harris, R. 1988. *Language, Saussure and Wittgenstein: How to Play Games with Words*. London: Routledge.

2010. Wittgenstein on 'Primitive' Languages. In V. Munz, K. Puhl, & J. Wang, eds. *Essays on the Philosophy of Wittgenstein: Language and the World, Part One*. Frankfurt: Ontos Verlag. 243–265.

Haynes, N. 2017. *Moved by the Spirit. Pentecostal Life on the Zambian Copperbelt*. Berkeley: University of California Press.

References

Helmreich, S. & Roosth, S. 2010. Life Forms: A Keyword Entry. *Representations* 112 (1): 27–53.

Hénaff, M. & Doran, R. 2013. Living with Others: Reciprocity and Alterity in Lévi-Strauss. *Yale French Studies* 123: 63–82.

Henare, A., Holbraad, M., & Wastell, S. 2007. *Thinking through Things: Theorising Artefacts Ethnographically*. London: Routledge.

Henson, H. 1974. *British Social Anthropologists and Language: A History of Separate Development*. Oxford: Clarendon Press.

Heywood, P. 2012. Anthropology and What There Is: Reflections on 'Ontology'. *The Cambridge Journal of Anthropology* 30 (1): 143–151.

——— 2014. Neoliberal Nation? *Journal of the Royal Anthropological Institute* 20: 151–153.

——— 2018a. *After Difference: Queer Activism and Anthropological Theory*. Oxford: Berghahn.

——— 2018b. Making Difference: Queer Activism and Anthropological Theory. *Current Anthropology* 59: 314–331.

——— 2020. 'All the Difference in the World': The Nature of Difference and Different Natures. *Philosophy of the Social Sciences* 50 (6): 543–564.

——— 2022. Ordinary Exemplars: Cultivating 'the Everyday' in the Birthplace of Fascism. *Comparative Studies in Society and History* 64 (1): 91–121.

——— 2023a. Are There Anthropological Problems?. In P. Heywood & M. Candea, eds. *Beyond Description: Anthropologies of Explanation*. Cornell: Cornell University Press. 25–44.

——— 2023b. A Thought Experiment in the wild. *Social Analysis* 67 (3): 118–124.

——— 2023c. Out of the Ordinary: Everyday Life and the 'Carnival of Mussolini'. *American Anthropologist* 125: 493–504.

——— 2024. *Burying Mussolini: Ordinary Life in the Shadows of Fascism*. Cornell: Cornell University Press.

Heywood, P. & Candea, M. 2023. *Beyond Description: Anthropologies of Explanation*. Cornell: Cornell University Press.

Hintikka, J. 2001. Ernst Mach at the Crossroads of Twentieth-Century Philosophy. In J. Floyd & S. Shieh, eds. *Future Pasts: The Analytic Tradition in Twentieth Century Philosophy*. Oxford: Oxford University Press. 81–100.

Holbraad, M. 2012. *Truth in Motion: The Recursive Anthropology of Cuban Divination*. Chicago: University of Chicago Press.

——— 2017. The Contingency of Concepts: Transcendental Deduction and Ethnographic Expression in Anthropological Thinking. In P. Charbonnier, G. Salmon, & P. Skafish, eds. *Comparative Metaphysics: Ontology after Anthropology*. London: Rowman & Littlefield. 133–158.

References

Holbraad, M. & Pedersen, M. 2018. *The Ontological Turn: An Anthropological Exposition*. Cambridge: Cambridge University Press.

Holton, G. 1992. Ernst Mach and the Fortunes of Positivism in America. *Isis* 83 (1): 27–60.

Holy, L. 1999. Contextualization and Paradigm Shifts. In R. Dilley, ed. *The Problem of Context*. Oxford: Berghahn. 47–61.

Horton, R. 1967. African Traditional Thought and Western Science. *Africa* 37 (1–2): 50–71.

Humphrey, C. 2008. Reassembling Individual Subjects: Events and Decisions in Troubled Times. *Anthropological Theory* 8: 357–380.

Hyman, S. 1959. *The Tangled Bank: Darwin, Marx, Frazer and Freud as Imaginative Writers*. New York: Atheneum.

Inglis, F. 2000. *Clifford Geertz: Culture, Custom, and Ethics*. Cambridge: Polity Press.

Ingold, T. 2010. The Textility of Making. *Cambridge Journal of Economics* 34: 91–102.

2014. That's Enough about Ethnography! *HAU: Journal of Ethnographic Theory* 4 (1): 383–395.

2021. *Imagining for Real: Essays on Creation, Attention, and Correspondence*. London: Routledge.

James, W. 2003. *The Ceremonial Animal: A New Portrait of Anthropology*. Oxford: Oxford University Press.

2007. 'A Feeling for Form and Pattern, and a Touch of Genius': E-P's Vision and the Institute 1946-1970. In P. Rivière, ed. *A History of Oxford Anthropology*. Oxford: Berghahn. 98–118.

Janik, A. & Toulmin, S. 1973. *Wittgenstein's Vienna*. New York: Simon & Schuster.

Jansen, S. 2019. Anthropological (In)fidelities to Alain Badiou. *Anthropological Theory* 19: 238–258.

Jean-Klein, I. & Riles, A. 2005. Anthropology and Human Rights Administrations: Expert Observation and Representation after the Fact. *Polar* 28 (2): 173–202.

Keane, W. 2018. *Ethical Life: Its Natural and Social Histories*. Princeton: Princeton University Press.

Keesing, R. 1974. Theories of Culture. *Annual Review of Anthropology* 3: 73–97.

Kockelman, P. 2013. *Agent, Person, Subject, Self*. Oxford: Oxford University Press.

2017. *The Art of Interpretation in the Age of Computation*. Oxford: Oxford University Press.

2020. *Kinds of Value: An Experiment in Modal Anthropology*. Chicahgo: University of Chicago Press.

2022. *The Anthropology of Intensity*. Cambridge: Cambridge University Press.

Koethe, J. 2003. On the 'Resolute' Reading of the *Tractatus*. *Philosophical Investigations* 26 (3): 187–204.

References

Krishnan, N. 2023. *A Terribly Serious Adventure: Philosophy at Oxford 1900-1960*. London: Profile Books.
Kuper, A. 1973 [1983]. *Anthropologists and Anthropology: The Modern British School*. London: Routledge.
Kuusela, O., Ometita, M., & Uçan, T. 2018. *Wittgenstein and Phenomenology*. London: Routledge.
Kwon, H. 2018. Wittgenstein's Spirit, Frazer's Ghost. In G. Da Col & S. Palmié, eds. *The Mythology in Our Language: Remarks on Frazer's Golden Bough*. Chicago: HAU Books. 87-97.
Laidlaw, J. 2002. For an Anthropology of Ethics and Freedom. *Journal of the Royal Anthropological Institute* 8: 311-332.
— 2012. Ontologically Challenged. *Anthropology of this Century* 4.
— 2013. *The Subject of Virtue: An Anthropology of Ethics and Freedom*. Cambridge: Cambridge University Press.
— 2018. Interpretive Cultural Anthropology: Geertz and His 'Writing Culture' Critics. In M. Candea, ed. *Schools and Styles of Anthropological Theory*. London: Routledge. 148-158.
Laidlaw, J. & Heywood, P. 2013. One More Turn and You're There. *Anthropology of This Century* 7. http://aotcpress.com/articles/turn/
Lambek, M. 2010. *Ordinary Ethics: Anthropology, Language, and Action*. New York: Fordham University Press.
— 2015. Living As If It Mattered. In M. Lambek, V. Das, D. Fassin, & W. Keane, eds. *Four Lectures on Ethics*. Chicago: HAU Books. 5-53.
— 2018. Remarks on Wittgenstein's 'Remarks on Frazer's Golden Bough': Ritual in the Practice of Life. In G. Da Col & S. Palmié, eds. *The Mythology in Our Language: Remarks on Frazer's Golden Bough*. Chicago: HAU Books. 181-199.
— 2021. *Concepts and Persons*. Toronto: University of Toronto Press.
— 2022. *Behind the Glass: The Villa Tugendhat and Its Family*. Toronto: University of Toronto Press.
— 2023. The Wrong Question? *Philosophies* 8 (2): 38.
Langham, I. 1981. *The Building of British Social Anthropology: W. H. R. Rivers and His Cambridge Disciples in the Development of Kinship Studies, 1898-1931*. Dordrecht: D. Reidel.
Larkin, B. 2013. The Politics and Poetics of Infrastructure. *Annual Review of Anthropology* 42: 327-343.
— 2017. Promising Forms: The Political Aesthetics of Infrastructure. In N. Anand, A. Gupta, & H. Appel, eds. *The Promise of Infrastructure*. Durham: Duke University Press. 175-202.

References

Latour, B. 2005. *Reassembling the Social: An Introduction to Actor Network Theory.* Oxford: Oxford University Press.
Latronico, V. 2025. *Perfection.* London: Fitzcarraldo.
Laugier, S. 2017. Concepts of the Ordinary. Paper presented at Panel on Concepts, Experience and the Claims to the Real. American Anthropological Association, Washington, DC, November 30, 2017.
2018a. On an Anthropological Tone in Philosophy. In G. Da Col & S. Palmié, eds. *The Mythology in Our Language: Remarks on Frazer's Golden Bough.* Chicago: HAU Books. 207–227.
2018b. This Is Us: Wittgenstein and the Social. *Philosophical Investigations* 41 (2): 204–222.
Le Roux, R. 2009. Lévi-Strauss, une reception paradoxale de la cybernétique. *L'Homme* 189: 165–190.
Leach, E. 1957. The Epistemological Background to Malinowski's Empiricism. In R. Firth, ed. *Man and Culture: An Evaluation of the Work of Bronislaw Malinowski.* London: Routledge. 119–139.
1961. *Rethinking Anthropology.* London: Athlone Press.
1966. Frazer and Malinowski: A CA Discussion. *Current Anthropology* 7 (5): 560–576.
1968. Nonsense and Sensibility. *The New York Review.* May 23rd Issue.
1970. Telstar and the Aborigines or La pensée sauvage. In D. Emmet & A. MacIntyre, eds. *Sociological Theory and Philosophical Analysis.* Basingstoke: Macmillan. 183–203.
1971. Kimil: A Category of Andamanese Thought. In P. Miranda & E. K. Maranda, eds. *Structural Analysis of Oral Tradition.* Philadelphia: University of Pennsylvania Press. 22–49.
1976. Social Anthropology: A Natural Science of Society? *Proceedings of the British Academy* 62: 157–180.
1984. Glimpses of the Unmentionable in the History of British Social Anthropology. *Annual Review of Anthropology* 13: 1–24.
Leenhardt, M. 1975 [1949]. *Preface to Lévy-Bruhl's Notebooks on Primitve Mentality.* Oxford: Blackwell.
Lempert, M. 2012. *Discipline and Debate: The Language of Violence in a Tibetan Buddhist Monastery.* Berkeley: University of California Press.
2013. No Ordinary Ethics. *Anthropological Theory* 13: 370–393.
2024. *From Small Talk to Microaggression: A History of Scale.* Chicago: University of Chicago Press.
Lévi-Strauss, C. 1963. *Totemism.* London: Merlin Press.
Lévi-Strauss, C. & Eribon, D. 1988. *De près et de loin.* Paris: Editions Edile Jacob.

References

Lévy-Bruhl, L. 1926. *How Natives Think*. London: Allen & Unwin.

——— 1936. *Primitives and the Supernatural*. London: Allen and Unwin.

Lienhardt, G. 1954. Modes of Thought. In E. Evans-Pritchard, ed. *The Institutions of Primitive Society*. Oxford: Blackwell. 95–107.

——— 1974. E-P: A Personal View. Sir Edward Evans-Pritchard, 1902–1973. *Man* 9 (2): 299–304.

Lockwood, P. 2025. There is no such thing as an African value of dependence. *Social Analysis* 69: 82-98.

Low, S. 1994. Embodied Metaphors: Nerves as Lived Experience. In T. Csordas, ed. *Embodiment and Experience*. Cambridge: Cambridge University Press. 139–162.

Luhrmann, T. 2013. Response. *Spiritus: A Journal of Christian Spirituality* 13 (1): 138–140.

——— 2023. On Anthropological Findings. In P. Heywood & Candea, M., eds. *Beyond Description: Anthropologies of Explanation*. Cornell: Cornell University Press. 45–62.

MacIntyre, A. 1964. Is Understanding Religion Compatible with Believing? In J. Hick, ed. *Faith and the Philosophers*. Basingstoke: Macmillan. 115–133.

Mahmood, S. 2004. *The Politics of Piety: The Islamic Revival and the Feminist Subject*. Princeton: Princeton University Press.

Majetschak, S. 2010. Forms and Patterns of Life: A Reassessment of a So-Called Basic Concept in the Late Philosophy of Wittgenstein. In A. Marques & N. Venturinha, eds. *Wittgenstein on Form(s) of Life and the Nature of Experience*. Berlin: Lang. 75–96.

Malcolm, N. 1958. *Ludwig Wittgenstein: A Memoir*. Oxford: Oxford University Press.

Malinowski, B. 1922. *Argonauts of the Western Pacific*. London: Routledge.

——— 1923. The Problem of Meaning in Primitive Languages. In C. K. Ogden & I. A. Richards, eds. *The Meaning of Meaning*. London: Routledge. 296–336.

——— 1948. *Magic, Science and Religion and Other Essays*. Boston: Beacon Press.

——— 1967. *A Diary in the Strict Sense of the Term*. London: Athlone Press.

Martin, E. 1994. *Flexible Bodies: Thinking Immunity in American Culture from the Days of Polio to the Age of AIDS*. Boston: Beacon Press.

McDonald, M. 2018. From 'the Body' to 'Embodiment', with Help from Phenomenology. In M. Candea, ed. *Schools and Styles of Anthropological Theory*. London: Routledge. 185–194.

McGee, M. 2023. The Logic of Magic: Reading Wittgenstein's Remarks on Frazer's The Golden Bough. *HAU: Journal of Ethnographic Theory* 13 (1): 21–38.

McGinn, M. 2001. Saying and Showing and the Continuity of Wittgenstein's Thought. *The Harvard Review of Philosophy* 11: 24–36.

References

2009. Wittgenstein and Internal Relations. *European Journal of Philosophy* 18 (4): 495–509.
McGuinness, B. 1988. *Wittgenstein: A Life.* Berkeley: University of California Press.
Medina, J. 2001. Verificationism and Inferentialism in Wittgenstein's Philosophy. *Philosophical Investigations* 24 (4): 304–313.
—— 2002. *The Unity of Wittgenstein's Philosophy: Necessity, Intelligibility, and Normativity.* New York: SUNY Press.
—— 2003. Anthropologism, Naturalism, and the Pragmatic Study of Language. *Journal of Pragmatics* 36: 549–573.
Mehta, V. 1962. *Fly and the Fly-Bottle: Encounters with British Intellectuals.* London: Penguin.
Misak, C. 2016. *Cambridge Pragmatism: From Peirce and James to Ramsey and Wittgenstein.* Oxford: Oxford University Press.
—— 2020. *Frank Ramsey: A Sheer Excess of Powers.* Oxford: Oxford University Press.
Miyazaki, H. 2004. *The Method of Hope: Anthropology, Philosophy, and Fijian Knowledge.* Stanford: Stanford University Press.
Monk, R. 1991. *Ludwig Wittgenstein: The Duty of Genius.* London: Vintage.
Mosse, D. 2005. *Cultivating Development: An Ethnography of Aid Policy and Practice.* London: Pluto Press.
—— 2013. The Anthropology of International Development. *Annual Review of Anthropology* 42: 227–246.
Moyal-Sharrock, D. 2015. Wittgenstein on Forms of Life, Patterns of Life, and Ways of Living. *Nordic Wittgenstein Review* 4: 21–42.
Moyal-Sharrock, D. & Donatelli, P. 2015. *Wittgenstein and Forms of Life. Special Issue of Nordic Wittgenstein Review* 4.
Moyn, S. 2010. *The Last Utopia: Human Rights in History.* Cambridge, MA: Harvard University Press.
Muehlebach, A. 2010. *The Moral Neoliberal: Welfare and Citizenship in Italy.* Chicago: University of Chicago Press.
Munz, V. 2017. Philosophy from an 'Anthropological' Point of View: Wittgenstein and Sraffa. *Conceptus* 42: 101–102.
Myhre, K. 2006. The Truth of Anthropology: Epistemology, Meaning, and Residual Positivism. *Anthropology Today* 22 (6): 16–19.
—— 2007. Family Resemblances, Practical Interrelations and Material Extensions: Understanding Sexual Prohibitions, Production and Consumption in Kilimanjaro. *Africa* 77 (3): 307–330.
—— 2018 a. *Returning Life: Language, Life Force and History in Kilimanjaro.* Oxford: Berghahn.

References

2018b. Deep Pragmatism. In G. Da Col & S. Palmié, eds. *The Mythology in Our Language: Remarks on Frazer's Golden Bough*. Chicago: HAU Books. 97–117.

Nadel, S. 1957. *The Theory of Social Structure*. London: Routledge.

Navaro, Y. 2009. Affective Spaces, Melancholic Objects: Ruination and the Production of Anthropological Knowledge. *Journal of the Royal Anthropological Institute* 15: 1–18.

Needham, R. 1971. *Rethinking Kinship and Marriage*. London: Tavistock.

1972. *Belief, Language and Experience*. Oxford: Blackwell.

1975. Polythetic Classification: Convergence and Consequences. *Man* 10 (3): 349–369.

1985. *Exemplars*. Berkeley: University of California Press.

North, M. 1999. *Reading 1922: A Return to the Scene of the Modern*. Oxford: Oxford University Press.

Nyíri, J. C. 1981. Wittgenstein's Later Work in Relation to Conservatism. In A. Kenny & B. McGuinness, eds. *Wittgenstein and His Times*. Chicago: University of Chicago Press. 44–69.

Ogden, C. K. & Richards, I. A. 1923. *The Meaning of Meaning*. London: Routledge.

Ong, A. & Collier, S. 2005. *Global Assemblages: Technology, Politics, and Ethics as Anthropological Problems*. Oxford: Blackwell.

Padilla Gálvez, J. 2011. Language as Forms of Life. In J. Padilla Gálvez & M. Gaffal, eds. *Forms of Life and Language Games*. Frankfurt: Ontos Verlag. 37–56.

Palmié, S. 2018. Translation Is Not Explanation: Remarks on the Intellectual History and Context of Wittgenstein's Remarks on Frazer. In G. Da Col & S. Palmié, eds. *The Mythology in our Language: Remarks on Frazer's Golden Bough*. Chicago: HAU Books. 1–29.

2022. Unhinged: On Ethnographic Games of Doubt and Certainty. *Social Anthropology* 30 (1): 74–90.

Perloff, M. 2022. *Ludwig Wittgenstein: Private Notebooks: 1914–1916*. New York: Norton & Co.

Peters, M. 2022. Wittgenstein/Foucault/Antiphilosophy: Contingency, Community, and the Ethics of Self-Cultivation. *Educational Philosophy and Theory* 54 (10): 1495–1500.

Petitot, J. 2009. Morphology and Structural Aesthetics: From Goethe to Lévi-Strauss. In B. Wiseman, ed. *The Cambridge Companion to Lévi-Strauss*. Cambridge: Cambridge University Press. 275–295.

Pettit, P. 1972. Wittgenstein and Case for Structuralism. *Journal of the British Society for Phenomenology* 3 (1): 46–57.

References

Pichler, A. 2018. Wittgenstein on Understanding: Language, Calculus, and Practice. In D. G. Stern, ed. *Wittgenstein in the 1930s*. Cambridge: Cambridge University Press. 45–60.

Pitkin, H. 1972. *Wittgenstein and Justice*. Berkeley: University of California Press.

Pole, D. 1958. *The Later Philosophy of Wittgenstein*. London: Athlone Press.

Probyn, E. 2004. Everyday Shame. *Cultural Studies* 18: 328–349.

Rabinow, P. 1986. Representations Are Social Facts: Modernity and Post-Modernity in Anthropology. In J. Clifford & G. E. Marcus, eds. *Writing Culture: The Poetics and Politics of Ethnography*. Berkeley: University of California Press. 234–262.

Radcliffe-Brown, A. R. 1930. A System of Notation for Relationships. *Man* 30 (93): 212–122.

——— 1940. On Social Structure. *Journal of the Royal Anthropological Institute* 70 (1): 1–12.

——— 1941. The Study of Kinship Systems. *Journal of the Royal Anthropological Institute* 71 (1/2): 1–18.

——— 1951. The Comparative Method in Social Anthropology. *Journal of the Royal Anthropological Institute* 81 (1/2): 15–22.

——— 1952. *Structure and Function in Primitive Society*. Glencoe: The Free Press.

——— 1957. *A Natural Science of Society*. Glencoe: The Free Press.

——— 1964 [1922]. *The Andaman Islanders*. New York: The Free Press of Glencoe.

Ramsey, F. 1923. Review of *Tractatus Logico-Philosophicus*. *Mind* 32 (128): 465–478.

Read, R. 2006. A No-Theory? Against Hutto on Wittgenstein. *Philosophical Investigations* 29 (1): 73–81.

Remotti, F. 2015. From Lévi-Strauss to Wittgenstein: The Idea of 'Imperfectionism' in Anthropology. *Diogenes* 60 (2): 40–52.

Rhees, R. 1960. Wittgenstein's Builders. *Proceedings of the Aristotelian Society* 60 (1): 171–186.

——— 1984. *Recollections of Wittgenstein*. Oxford: Oxford University Press.

Riles, A. 2000. *The Network Inside Out*. Ann Arbor: University of Michigan Press.

——— 2006. *Documents: Artifacts of Modern Knowledge*. Ann Arbor: University of Michigan Press.

Rivers, W. H. R. 1923. *Conflict and Dream*. London: Routledge.

Robbins, J. 2004. *Becoming Sinners: Christianity and Moral Torment in a Papua Guinea Society*. Berkeley: University of California Press.

——— 2007. Between Reproduction and Freedom: Morality, Value, and Radical Cultural Change. *Ethnos* 72: 293–314.

——— 2013. Beyond the Suffering Slot: Toward an Anthropology of the Good. *Journal of the Royal Anthropological Institute* 19 (3): 447–462.

References

2014. Sad Stories of the Lives of Things. A Comment on Chris Gregory's 'On Religiosity and Commercial Life.' *HAU: Journal of Ethnographic Theory* 4: 69–72.

2024. Anthropology Bright and Dark: Relativism, Value Pluralism, and the Comparative Study of the Good. *Social Analysis* 67 (4): 43-100.

2025. What is the matter with values? *Social Analysis* 69: 99-108.

Robbins, J. & Sommerschuh, J. 2016. Values. In F. Stein, ed. *The Open Encyclopedia of Anthropology*. http://doi.org/10.29164/16values.

Robinson, C. 2009. *Wittgenstein and Political Theory: A View from Somewhere*. Edinburgh: Edinburgh University Press.

Rowe, M. 2023. *J.L. Austin: A Biography*. Oxford: Oxford University Press.

Russell, B. 1922. Introduction to Wittgenstein's *Tractatus*. London: Kegan Paul.

1959. *My Philosophical Development*. London: Routledge.

1971 [1919]. *An Introduction to Mathematical Philosophy*. New York: Simon & Schuster.

Ryle, G. 1949. *The Concept of Mind*. London: Hutchinson.

1951. Ludwig Wittgenstein. *Analysis* 12 (1): 1–9.

Salgues, C. 2008. Un nouveau Wittgenstein encore inapprochable. Le rôle et la place du philosophe dans l'anthropologie. *L'Homme* 187 (188): 201-222.

Salmon, G. 2013. *Les structures de l'esprit: Lévi-Strauss e les mythes*. Paris: Presses Universitaires de France.

Sandis, C. 2016. Period and Place: Collingwood and Wittgenstein on Understanding Others. *Collingwood and British Idealism Studies* 22 (1): 167-193.

Scharfstein, B-A. 1989. *The Dilemma of Context*. New York: NYU Press.

Schieffelin, B. & Doucet, R. 1994. The 'Real' Haitian Creole: Ideology, Metalinguistics, and Orthographic Choice. *American Ethnologist* 21 (3): 176-200.

Schielke, S. 2009. Being Good in Ramadan: Ambivalence, Fragmentation, and the Moral Self in the Lives of Young Egyptians. *Journal of the Royal Anthropological Institute* 15: 24–40.

Scott, J. 1985. *Weapons of the Weak: Everyday Forms of Peasant Resistance*. New Haven: Yale University Press.

Seaver, N. 2015. The Nice Thing about Context Is That Everyone Has It. *Media, Culture, and Society* 37: 1101-1109.

Sen, A. 2003. Sraffa, Wittgenstein, and Gramsci. *Journal of Economic Literature* 41 (4): 1240–1255.

Severi, C. 2018. On Wittgenstein's Remarks on Frazer's Golden Bough. In G. Da Col & S. Palmié, eds. *The Mythology in our Language: Remarks on Frazer's Golden Bough*. Chicago: HAU Books. 77-87.

References

Shah, A. 2024. When Decolonization Is Hijacked. *American Anthropologist* 126 (4): 553–566.

Shankman, P. 1984. The Thick and the Thin: On the Interpretative Theoretical Program of Clifford Geertz. *Current Anthropology* 25: 261–281.

Sheringham, M. 2006. *Everyday Life: Theories and Practices from Surrealism to the Present*. Oxford: Oxford University Press.

Shryock, A. & Lord Smail, D. 2017. On Containers: A Forum. Introduction. *History and Anthropology* 29: 1–6.

Shryock, A. & Scheele, J. 2019. *The Scandal of Continuity in Middle East Anthropology: Form, Duration, Difference*. Bloomington: Indiana University Press.

Shweder, R. 2007. The Resolute Irresolution of Clifford Geertz. *Common Knowledge* 13 (2–3): 191–205.

Singer, M. 1984. A Neglected Source of Structuralism: Radcliffe-Brown, Russell, and Whitehead. *Semiotica* 48 (1/2): 11–96.

Singh, B. 2018. *Foreword to the Second Edition of Critical Events*. Oxford: Oxford University Press.

Skorupski, J. 1983. *Symbol and Theory*. Cambridge: Cambridge University Press.

Spengler, O. 1965 [1918]. *The Decline of the West*. New York: Modern Library.

Staley, R. 2023. The Economic Explanation. In P. Heywood & M. Candea, eds. *Beyond Description: Anthropologies of Explanation*. Cornell: Cornell University Press. 125–145.

Stern, D. 2018. Wittgenstein and Moore on Grammar. In D. G. Stern, ed. *Wittgenstein in the 1930s*. Cambridge: Cambridge University Press. 27–44.

Stewart, K. 2007. *Ordinary Affects*. Durham: Duke University Press.

Stocking, G. W., 1983. *Observers Observed: Essays on Ethnographic Fieldwork*. Madison: University of Wisconsin Press.

1995. *After Tylor: British Social Anthropology, 1888–1951*. Madison: University of Wisconsin Press.

Strathern, M. 1987a. Out of Context: The Persuasive Fictions of Anthropology. *Current Anthropology* 28 (3): 251–281.

1987b. An Awkward Relationship: The Case of Feminism and Anthropology. *Signs* 12 (2): 276–292.

1988. *The Gender of the Gift: Problems with Women and Problems with Society in Melanesia*. Berkeley: University of California Press.

1991. *Partial Connections*. Lanham, MD: Rowman & Littlefield.

1992. *After Nature: English Kinship in the Late Twentieth Century*. Cambridge: Cambridge University Press.

1995. *Shifting Contexts: Transformations in Anthropological Knowledge*. London: Routledge.

References

Suits, B. 1967. Is Life a Game We Are Playing? *Ethics* 77: 209-213.
　1978. *The Grasshopper: Games, Life, and Utopia*. Toronto: University of Toronto Press.
Tambiah, S. 1990. *Magic, Science, Religion, and the Scope of Rationality*. Cambridge: Cambridge University Press.
Tanney, J. 2009. *Rethinking Ryle: A Critical Discussion of The Concept of Mind*. London: Routledge.
Taussig, M. 1992. *The Nervous System*. London: Routledge.
　1993. *Mimesis and Alterity: A Particular History of the Senses*. London: Routledge.
Tejedor, C. 2015. Tractarian Form as the Precursor to Forms of Life. *Nordic Wittgenstein Review* 4: 83-109.
Temelini, M. 2015. *Wittgenstein and the Study of Politics*. Toronto: University of Toronto Press.
Temple, R. 1922. A Revolutionary Theory of Social Anthropology. *Man* 22: 121-127.
Thompson, D. W. 1917. *On Growth and Form*. Cambridge: Cambridge University Press.
Thornton, R. 1985. 'Imagine Yourself Set Down...': Mach, Frazer, Conrad, Malinowski and the Role of the Imagination in Ethnography. *Anthropology Today* 1 (5): 7-14.
Tomas, D. 1991. Tools of the Trade: The Production of Ethnographic Knowledge on the Andaman Islands, 1858-1922. In G. Stocking, ed. *Colonial Situations: Essays on the Contextualisation of Ethnographic Knowledge*. Madison: University of Wisconsin Press. 75-109.
Toren, C. 2012. Imagining the World That Warrants Our Imagination: The Revelation of Ontogeny. *Cambridge Anthropology* 30: 64-79.
Tsing, A. 2015. *The Mushroom at the End of the World: On the Possibility of Life in Capitalist Ruins*. Princeton: Princeton University Press.
Ulin, R. 1988. *Understanding Cultures: Perspectives in Anthropology and Social Theory*. Austin: University of Texas Press.
Urry, J. 1972. Notes and Queries on Anthropology and the Development of Field Methods in British Anthropology 1870-1920. *Proceedings of the Royal Anthropological Institute of Great Britain and Ireland* 1972: 45-57.
Venkatesan, S. 2025. *Decolonizing Anthropology: An Introduction*. Oxford: Wiley.
Venkatesan, S., Carrithers, M., Candea, M., Sykes, K., & Holbraad, M. 2010. Ontology Is Just Another Word for Culture. *Critique of Anthropology* 30: 152-200.
Venkatesan, S., Das, V., Al-Mohammad, H., Robbins, J., Stafford, C., & Mair, J. 2015. There Is No Such Thing as the Good. *Critique of Anthropology* 35: 430-480.

References

Venturinha, N. 2013. *The Textual Genesis of Wittgenstein's Philosophical Investigations.* London: Routledge.

Vigh, H. & Sausdal, D. 2014. From Essence Back to Existence: Anthropology beyond the Ontological Turn. *Anthropological Theory* 14 (1): 49-73.

Vinten R. 2020. *Wittgenstein and the Social Sciences: Action, Ideology, and Justice.* London: Athlone Press.

Visser, H. 2001. Wittgenstein's Machist Sources. In J. Blackmore, R. Itagaki, & S. Tanaka, eds. *Ernst Mach's Vienna 1895-1930.* London: Kluwer. 139-158.

Viveiros de Castro, E. 1998. Cosmological Deixis and Amerindian Perspectivism. *Journal of the Royal Anthropological Institute* 4 (3): 469-488.

2004. Perspectival Anthropology and the Method of Controlled Equivocation. *Tipití: Journal of the Society for the Anthropology of Lowland South America* 2 (1): 2-20.

Wagner R. 1975. *The Invention of Culture.* Chicago: University of Chicago Press.

Waismann, F. 1965. Notes on Talks with Wittgenstein. *The Philosophical Review* 74 (1): 12-16.

Ware, B. 2011. Williams and Wittgenstein. *Key Words: A Journal of Cultural Materialism* 9: 41-57.

Warnock, M. 2000. *A Memoir: People and Places.* London: Duckworth.

Weiss, E. 2024. Comment on Robbins. *Social Analysis* 67 (4): 69-73.

Williams, R. 1989 [1958]. Culture Is Ordinary. In *Resources of Hope: Culture, Democracy, Socialism.* London: Verso. 3-19.

Wilson, A. 2018. Visual Kinship. *History of Anthropology Newsletter* 42.

Wilson R. A. 2004. The Trouble with Truth: Anthropology's Epistemological Hypochondria. *Anthropology Today* 20 (5): 14-17.

2006. Words, Things and the Hippopotamus in the Room. *Anthropology Today* 22 (6): 23-24.

Winch, P. 1958. *The Idea of a Social Science.* London: Routledge.

1964. Understanding a Primitive Society. *American Philosophical Quarterly* 1 (4): 307-324.

1997. Can We Understand Ourselves? *Philosophical Investigations* 20 (3): 193-204.

Wittgenstein, L. 1929. Some Remarks on Logical Form. *Proceedings of the Aristotelian Society* 9: 162-171.

Yarrow, T. 2011. *Development Beyond Politics: Aid, Activism, and NGOs in Ghana.* Basingstoke: Palgrave Macmillan.

2019. *Architects: Portrait of a Practice.* Cornell: Cornell University Press.

Young, M. 2004. *Malinowski: Odyssey of an Anthropologist.* New Haven: Yale University Press.

References

Zambito, P. 2019. *'Logic Is a Geometry of Thinking': Space and Spatial Frameworks in Wittgenstein's Writings.* Thesis submitted to the University of Cambridge, August 2019.

Zeitlyn, D. n.d. On Anthropological Trading Zones and Thin Description.

Zengotita, de T. 1989. On Wittgenstein's Remarks on Frazer's Golden Bough. *Cultural Anthropology* 4 (4): 390–398.

Index

Actor Network Theory, 251–252
Affective turn, the, 253
Analytic philosophy, 41
Andaman Islanders, The, 34, 69–72
Animism, 257
Anscombe, G. E. M. (Elizabeth), 19, 55, 58, 178, 229
Anthropology
    affective turn in, 253
    the armchair variety, 65, 86
    crisis of representation in, 209
    of ethics, 255
    of everyday life or the ordinary, 3, 28, 166, 197–200, 209, 217, 237–242
    the linguistic turn, 224
    the material turn, 212, 249
    new anthropology, 132
    the ontological turn, 4, 133, 162, 164–166, 252–254
    its relation to philosophy, 28–29, 131
    as translation of cultures, 131–132, 163
    turn to infrastructure, 253
Antiformalism, 17, 91–92, 140–141, 153–154, 173, 189, 209–214
    in Cavell's interpretation of the *Investigations*, 230–231
    and ethnography, 236–237
    in Geertz, 218–219
    and suffering, 226–227, 235–236
    in *Writing Culture*, 222–223
    its paradoxical rigidity, 243
Antifoundationalism, 53, 60, 169–171
Ardener, Edwin, 132
Argonauts of the Western Pacific, 81, 86–92
Asad, Talal, 131, 163–164, 222
Assemblage, 254
Atomic facts, 48, 54, 60
Augustine, 177–179, 181
Austin, J. L., 9, 83, 131, 145, 215, 228–230
Australia, 82
Azande, 141, 146, 151, 156

Badiou, Alain, 249
Baker, Gordon, 195
Barthes, Roland, 253
Bastianelli, Marco, 125
Bateson, Gregory, 91
Belief, 78, 136
Bell, Julian, 18
Berlin, Isaiah, 145
Big Typescript, The, 176
Biology and the natural sciences, 193–194
Bloomsbury Group, 38
Blue and Brown Books, 176–177, 196, 232

295

Index

Boltanski, Luc, 249
Bourdieu, Pierre, 247, 254
Boyer, Dominic, 256
British Empire, 80
Burke, Kenneth, 90, 215
Burke, Peter, 6–8, 95

Cambridge, 44, 58, 131, 173
  the Cambridge Union, 97
  establishment of anthropology at, 66
  Moral Sciences Club, the, 67
  Moral Sciences Tripos, 65, 69
  Trinity College, 21, 38, 42, 64, 69, 104
Cambridge School, The, 64–69, 134
Candea, Matei, 73, 76, 80, 134, 136, 211, 237, 247
Carnap, Rudolf, 74, 102
Category mistake, 133, 154–157, 165
Cavell, Stanley, 18, 58, 197–201
Certainty in mathematics, 191–192
Clarke, Morgan, 240, 256–257
Clifford, James, 222
Collier, Stephen, 254
Collingwood, R. G., 7
Colour, 108–109, 111, 181
Comparison in anthropology, 10–11, 90, 134–135
Conant, James, 56
Concepts, blurred, 169, 245, 258
Concrete processualism, 249–254
Contextualism, 3–4, 23, 29
  in *The Andaman Islanders*, 70–72
  and antiformalism, 211–212
  anthropology's central role in, 8
  in *Argonauts of the Western Pacific*, 87
  closed and open contexts, 146–149, 158
  context as God, 71
  context of contextualism, 125
  contingency of, 5–6
  decontextualization, 85–86
  and description, 122–124

and the ethnographic monograph, 70
  in ethnographic fieldwork, 65, 67–68, 81, 87
  historical emergence of, 6–8
  and language, 109, 111–112, 181, 245
  Malinowski on, 85
  in Malinowski's work, 63, 81–92
  ordinary life as a model for, 174
  and post-structural anthropology, 223
  of the postmodern, 212
  and pragmatism, 83
  the problem of boundaries, 80–81, 119–120, 134, 140, 152, 160–166, 182–184, 195–196
  and social evolutionism, 65–66
  and social structure, 73–76
  in structural-functionalism, 142–143
  and the suffering slot, 13, 225–228
  of the *Tractatus*, 44–45, 47–53, 60–61, 106–107
  in Winch, 156–157
  Wittgenstein's central role in, 9
Contradiction, 155–156
Conway, Gertrud, 201
Cook, Joanna, 255–256
Coral Gardens, 91
Csordas, Thomas, 250
Custom, 91, 178, 187, 204–205
Cybernetics, 111

Darwin, Charles, 66
Das, Veena, 35, 55, 198–201, 233–239
de Zengotita, Thomas, 97–98, 128
Degani, Michael, 212
Deleuze, Gilles, 248–249, 254
Descola, Philippe, 255, 257
Description, 114–116, 122–124
Diamond, Cora, 56–58
Dilley, Roy, 4

296

Index

Divination, 165
Douglas, Mary, 97, 144
Drury, Maurice, 96, 173
Duranti, Alessandro, 4
Durkheim, Émile, 70, 75, 85

Eggan, Fred, 74
Embodiment, 250–251
Emmet, Dorothy, 74
Empiricism, 84–85
Epistemology, 221–222
Ernst, Paul, 125
Ethics, 53
Ethnographic fieldwork, 68, 81, 87–88
  genealogical method, 67, 87
Evans-Pritchard, E. E. (Edward), 98, 131, 141, 152, 156–157, 164–165
  influence of Wittgenstein on, 144–145
Explanation, 122–124

Family resemblance concepts, 120, 171, 176
Faubion, James, 255
Firth, Raymond, 159
Form of life, 121, 129, 164, 171–175
  as the common behaviour of mankind, 196–197, 201
  as isomorphic with a society, 194–197
  in *Philosophical Investigations*, 178–193
  as the union of the cultural and the biological, 197–199, 202–203
Formalism, 147, 213
  condemned as hubris, 257
  in contemporary anthropology, and the ontological turn, 166, 254–258
  in structural functionalism, 74–75, 125, 138
  in Wittgenstein, 115–116, 203–204
  of Winch, 149–151

Foucault, Michel, 248, 254
Frazer, James George, 7, 66, 86–87, 122–129
  influence on Malinowski, 85–86
Frege, Gottlob, 37, 60
Functionalism, 78, 91

Game theory, 111
Games, 25, 170
Geach, Peter, 55, 58
Geertz, Clifford, 85, 149, 209–210, 214–221, 242, 261
Gellner, Ernest, 60, 82–83, 159–163, 221–222
  on the *Tractatus*, 35–36, 44
  Words and things, 20
Gluckman, Max, 74
Goethe, Johann Wolfgang von, 124
Golden Bough, The, 84, 87
  Wittgenstein's reading of, 96
Goodwin, Charles, 4
Graeber, David, 162
Grammar, 111–112, 115–118, 172, 176, 201, 230
Green, Sarah, 29, 256

Hacker, P. M. S. (Peter), 55, 125, 194–196
Haddon, Alfred, 65–66, 84, 86
Hadot, Pierre, 259
Handler, Richard, 80
Hanfling, Oswald, 177
Harvard, 228
Haynes, Naomi, 256
Holism, 67, 84, 90, 177
Holy, Ladislav, 211
Homologies, 79
How to Do Things with Words, 229
Hyman, Stanley, 90

Imponderabilia, 70, 87–88
Ineffability, 55, 57, 206–207
Inglis, Fred, 215

Index

Ingold, Tim, 251
Intellectualism, Frazerian, 78, 157

James, Wendy, 133
James, William, 83, 86, 104

Keynes, John Maynard, 42, 104
Kinship, 67, 76, 138
Kockelman, Paul, 244
Kuper, Adam, 81–82, 91
Kwon, Heonik, 128

Laidlaw, James, 219, 255
Lambek, Michael, 144, 146, 255
Language, 52–53, 106, 111–115, 230–233
  according to Malinowski, 63
  of animals, 190–191
  builders' language, 179–183
  calculus of, 111, 113, 122, 154–157, 176–177
  of gesture, 119
  language learning, 178–179
  limits of, 55, 61
  as a model for culture, 131–132, 158, 163
  mythology deposited in, 125–126
  as open-ended series of language games, 182
  philosophy as saying, 175
  primitive language, 118–122
  translation, 67, 164
Language games, 118–122, 153, 176
Larkin, Brian, 255–256
Latour, Bruno, 251–252, 254, 257
Laugier, Sandra, 198
Leach, Edmund, 73, 77–78, 83, 89, 111, 132, 137–138, 140, 145
Leavis, F. R., 131
Lévi-Strauss, Claude, 73, 75, 127, 132, 139
  influence on Wittgenstein, 111
Lévy-Bruhl, Lucien, 142–143, 147

Lienhardt, Godfrey, 131
Linguistic turn, the, 224
Lived experience, 248
Logic, 41–42, 54–56, 91, 108
  and social structure, 73–78
  as context, 46–49, 72, 138
  doesn't govern form of life, 184–186
Logical atomism, 7, 54, 107–110
Logical empiricism, 228
Logical form, 107
Logical notation in anthropology, 71–72, 76–78, 135, 138
Logical positivism, 35, 54, 102
Logical space, 17, 109, 147, 181
London School of Economics, The, 82, 85, 159
Low, Setha, 250

Mach, Ernst, 83, 85
MacIntyre, Alasdair, 151
Magic, 127–129, 143–144, 152
Mahieddin, Emir, 246
Malcolm, Norman, 105
Malinowski, Bronislaw, 10, 62, 67–69, 76, 81–92
  1925 Frazer Lecture, 84
  biographical context, 81–82
  as charter myth for social anthropology, 82
  diaries of, 85
  as founder of fieldwork method, 87
Manchester, 74
Mannheim, Karl, 7
Marett, R. R., 68
Martin, Emily, 250
Material turn, the, 249
Materiality, 212
McDonald, Maryon, 250
Meaning is use, doctrine of, 55, 73, 105, 121, 160
Meaning of Meaning, The, 38, 62–63, 110

Index

Metaphysics, 47, 53–54, 60, 107, 115, 157–166, 172–173, 201, 243
  anthropologists' rejection of, 3, 22–24, 27–29
  of magic, 127–129
  rejection of in Wittgenstein's late work, 169–172
Misak, Cheryl, 83, 111
Monk, Ray, 39, 43, 174
Moore, G. E., 38, 42, 44, 116–117, 120, 187
Moyal-Sharrock, Danièle, 201, 204–205
Music, 65, 75
Myers, Charles S., 65–66, 75, 98, 260

Nadel, Siegfried, 76, 135
Nature, 79
  and life form, 193–207
Needham, Rodney, 26–27, 97, 111, 132, 136–140
Nietzsche, 234
Nonsense, 56–57, 72, 113–114, 154–156
North, Michael, 70–71
Notes and Queries on Anthropology, 65–66, 68
Nuer, The, 141, 151

Ogden, C. K., 38–39, 110, 114
Ong, Aihwa, 254
Ontological turn, the, 4, 134, 162, 164–166, 252–254
Orders, following of, 188
Ordinary language philosophy, 83, 145, 154, 159, 215
  anthropologists' reading of, 131
Ordinary life as the opposite of philosophy, 192–193
Ordinary life, philosophy of, 185, 228–232
Oxford, 74, 131, 145, 154, 159, 176

Pain and suffering, 233–239
Palmié, Stephan, 124, 127, 133

Parsons, Talcott, 219
Particularism, 170
Peirce, C. S. (Charles), 83, 103
Perfect language, 49
Performative contradiction, 128, 169, 172, 235, 245
Philosophical Grammar, 176
Philosophical Investigations, writing of, 177–178
Picture theory of language, 46, 51, 55, 75, 79, 169, 181, 206
Pictures, captivity of, 1–3, 186
Pinsent, David, 40, 43, 62, 65
Pole, David, 230
Polythetic categories, 136–137
Post-structuralism, 212–213
Power, 163
Practice, 78, 178
Pragmatism, 83–84, 103–104, 215
Private language, 215–216
Propositions, 45–46, 53, 55, 107–110, 182–183
Psychology, 65, 75

Radcliffe-Brown, A. R., 67–84, 90, 134
Radical alterity, 164
Ramsey, Frank, 39, 83, 102–104, 108–109, 111
Rationality debates, 133–134, 140–141, 147, 149–154, 160–162
  expressivism, 148
  as question of formalism, 133, 141–144
Reflexivity, 80–81, 85, 223
Relativism, 216, 221
Religion, 68, 151
  as a context, 150
Remarks on Frazer's 'Golden Bough', 50, 78, 96–100, 122–129
  anthropologists' readings of, 133
  context of writing, 99–100
Rhees, Rush, 97, 123, 127, 178
Riles, Annelise, 256

Index

Ritual, 67
Rivers, W. H. R., 38, 65, 85
   contextualism, 67
Robbins, Joel, 12, 27, 225–228, 233, 246, 256–257
Romanticism, 215
Rules, 113–114, 151, 184, 256–257
   finitude of, 186–187
   impossibility of private rules, 187
   of grammar, 117
Russell, Bertrand, 7, 37, 60, 114
   influence on anthropologists, 72, 74
   influence on the *Tractatus*, 41–42
   interpretation of the *Tractatus*, 49–50, 52, 54
   on the 'late' Wittgenstein, 170
   relationship with Wittgenstein, 44
   Theory of Types, 46–47, 109
Ryle, Gilbert, 150, 154, 215

Salmon, Gildas, 139
Saussure, Ferdinand de, 110, 127
Scharfstein, Ben-Ami, 223
Schlick, Moritz, 76, 101
Schopenhauer, Arthur, 51
Science, 150, 156
Self, nature of the, 51
Seligman, C. G., 65, 84
Set theory, 46–47
Severi, Carlo, 35, 128
Shweder, Richard, 214
Shyrock, Andrew, 256
Singer, Milton, 74, 80
Skjolden, 44
Smail, Daniel Lord, 256
Smith, W. Robertson (William), 86
Social evolutionism, 65–66, 85, 87, 98
Social structure, 64
   its relation to formal logic, 73–78
Socrates, 176
Solipsism, 52–53, 60, 81, 223, 234
sort, 273
Spengler, Oswald, 125, 194, 198

Spranger, Eduard, 194
Sraffa, Piero, 104–106, 116, 118, 176
Srinivas, M. N., 74
Stewart, Kathleen, 253
Stocking, George, 66, 68, 73
Strathern, Marilyn, 4, 205, 212, 223–224, 260
   on contextualism, 113–114, 152
   on Frazer, 89–90
Structural functionalism, 72–79, 141
Structuralism, 73, 126
   and formalism, 133
   British, 136
   influence on Wittgenstein, 110–111
Suffering slot, 12–13, 225, 233
Suits, Bernard, 25

Tambiah, Stanley, 97, 127
Taussig, Michael, 222
Tejedor, Chon, 206–207
Thévenot, Laurent, 249
Thick description, 215, 220
Time, 177
Toren, Christina, 250
Torres Straits Expedition, 65–67, 260
Totemism, 73
Tractatus Logico-Philosophicus, 45, 75
   anthropologists' reading of, 35, 56
   anticulturalism of, 60
   circumstances of its writing, 36–37
   origin of the title, 38
   origins in notes dictated to Russell and Moore, 44
   psychological or therapeutic effects of, 58
   publication of, 189
   resolute reading of, 56–59, 61, 231–232
   traditional or ineffabilistic reading of, 55–56, 70–71
Truth tables, 47–49, 108
Tsing, Anna, 254
Turn to infrastructure, 253

Index

Tylor, Edward Burnett, 65, 86
Type-token distinction, 104
Typology, 136–138

Valentine, Daniel E., 224–225, 234, 236
Vienna, 40–41
Vienna Circle, 76, 101, 109
Viveiros de Castro, Eduardo, 164, 206
von Neumann, John, 111
von Wright, G. H., 105

Wagner, Roy, 206
Warnock, Mary, 19
Weschler, Alfred, 194
Whitehead, Alfred North, 72, 74
Wilson, Richard A., 222
Winch, Peter, 149–154
Witchcraft, 156
Witchcraft, Oracles and Magic, 143, 146
Wittgenstein, Ludwig
  anthropological perspective of, 24–26, 68, 92, 106–107, 118, 121, 147, 155, 170–171, 176, 189, 259
  the cult of, 18–19
  biographical context, 36–37, 40–41, 61–62, 100–106, 173–174
  encounters with anthropologists, 64–65, 68–69, 82
  as his own context, 59–60
  'exile' in Norway, 43–44
  his unhappiness, 39–40, 51, 62
  Jewish background, 40–41
  military experience, 37, 39–40, 51–52
  and the 'ordinary', 100–101
  periodization of his work, 54–56, 59, 83, 96, 146, 156
  PhD viva, 103
  sexuality, 39–40
Words and Things, 159
Writing Culture, 209, 221, 249

Yarrow, Thomas, 256
Yurchak, Alexei, 256

Zambito, Pascal, 147

For EU product safety concerns, contact us at Calle de José Abascal, 56–1°,
28003 Madrid, Spain or eugpsr@cambridge.org.

www.ingramcontent.com/pod-product-compliance
Ingram Content Group UK Ltd.
Pitfield, Milton Keynes, MK11 3LW, UK
UKHW020821180326
469097UK00018B/1340